Ulrich Becher

American University Studies

Series I
Germanic Languages and Literatures

Vol. 7

PETER LANG
Berne · Francfort on the Main · New York

Nancy Anne McClure Zeller

Ulrich Becher

A Computer-Assisted Case Study
of the Reception of an Exile

PETER LANG
Berne · Francfort on the Main · New York

Library of Congress Catalog Card Number:
82-84614
ISBN 0-8204-0006-8

Printed by Lang Druck Ltd., Liebefeld/Berne (Switzerland)

For the most patient of husbands.

ACKNOWLEDGMENTS

The research of this dissertation was made possible by a Travel Grant from The University of Texas Graduate School and by a Short-term Study Grant from the Deutscher Akademischer Austausch-Dienst (DAAD) which enabled me to spend the Fall semester of 1978 examining the exile collections of the Institut für Zeitgeschichte in Munich and the Deutsche Bibliothek in Frankfurt. I am indebted to these institutions for permission to peruse and employ the materials pertaining to Ulrich Becher. In addition, I should like to express my gratitude to Rowohlt Verlag, Benziger Verlag, Sessler Verlag, and to Ulrich Becher himself for providing me with the critical material in their archives. A final word of thanks must go to my adviser, Hans-Bernhard Moeller, and especially to my husband, Dennis E. Zeller, for sustained encouragement, advice, and hours of manual labor on my behalf.

TABLE OF CONTENTS

Chapter I: Introduction

Ulrich Becher's name has been unknown to all
but a few scholars of contemporary German literature.
His works have not been canonized by inclusion in the
surveys and anthologies of post-World War II German
literature taught in schools. Yet his publishing career
has spanned fifty years, a longevity attained by few
others of his generation, a generation for whom mere
survival was often considered a mark of distinction.
Becher has survived the vicissitudes of the twentieth
century, and with the renewal of interest in the Hitler
era in general and exile literature in particular, is
now enjoying a revival of interest in his works as
well.

Becher's works have amassed an impressive
spectrum of criticism by recognized critics. Männer
machen Fehler (1931) and Die Eroberer (1936), his
earliest prose works, were praised by Klaus Mann, Lion
Feuchtwanger, and F.C. Weiskopf in the exile journals,
Das Neue Tagebuch and Das Wort.[1] Evaluations of his
early works by Paul Hühnerfeld, Jürgen Rühle, Friedrich
Heer, and Valentin Herzog, representing the main-line

critical tradition of both German states, Austria, and

Switzerland respectively, were glowing.[2] The famous

critic, Herbert Ihering, placed Becher's dramas along-

side those of Brecht as an alternative form of quality

drama: "Brecht und Ulrich Becher--das deutsche Theater

ist nicht so arm an Werken, wie diejenigen, die sie nicht

spielen wollen, angeben."[3]

Yet Becher's works have also provoked their

share of critical rejection. Influential negative

critiques on his giant novel, Murmeljagd (1969), ap-

peared in such important newspapers as Die Zeit and

Frankfurter Allgemeine Zeitung, newspapers which are

influential in establishing the public's view of an

author.[4] The critical jury is still out on Ulrich

Becher, and this dissertation examines the critical

literature of five decades, in part to determine why

Becher's reception has been marked by such a lack of

consensus.

In addition, as the subtitle of this dis-

sertation indicates, the investigation of Ulrich

Becher's reception serves as a case study for the

reception of exile literature in general, using the

evaluative tool of reception aesthetics.

In discussing the works of Ulrich Becher,

I apply the theories developed by Hans Robert Jauß in the early 1970s, theories known collectively as reception aesthetics to show how Becher's reception is dependent on the prevailing ways of thinking in the time and place in which the works are received.

In applying reception aesthetics to Ulrich Becher as an example of exile literature, the assumption here is that the special focus of reception aesthetics will contribute greatly to the understanding of the special problems of exile literature. It is indeed reception--loss of audience upon going into exile, acquisition of experiences unshared by the audience, reestablishment in the post-exile period-- that is an inescapable negative fact of life for most exiles. Reception aesthetics centers its attention precisely on the most important factor of exile literature, the influence of the audience, and thus it allows a critical stance from which it becomes possible to evaluate the products of exile authors more appropriately.

Reception aesthetics will provide a more objectively verifiable analysis of the exile author precisely because it is impossible to determine why an exile author who has returned to his home country may be judged differently than his non-exile contemporaries if one does not investigate the impact of the audience in the literary process. Without an audience, an author is left to develop in a vacuum. Often, in this circumstance, development is retarded or even halted completely, as in the case of Ulrich Becher; or an author develops along different lines than his former audience to which the exile author then returns. Even well-known exiles, such as Thomas Mann or Bertolt Brecht, whose international stature and fame prior to exile guaranteed them an audience during exile, recorded the changes in their audience in each successive work. The shock of stepping back into the literary process was even greater for lesser known exiles, such as Becher. Reception aesthetics illuminates these formative factors, and this is Jauß' major contribution to the study of authors who are outside the literary canon, such as exile authors.

Moreover, if not for the questions asked by reception aesthetics and its focus on the concretization of an author and his works in the critical views, little could be discovered about Ulrich Becher from traditional sources, such as literary histories, anthologies, etc. The newspaper critiques collected on

4

Becher represent almost all the printed evidence of his reception. Such a situation allows not only an investigation of the author and his works, but also of 1) exile literature reception in general, 2) reception aesthetics, and 3) the literary norms of the post-war period in Central Europe. Becher's reception is perfectly suited to such a multi-purpose task.

The process of practical implementation of reception aesthetics involves grounding in the theory and in the discussion surrounding it. Established forms of German literary criticism, e.g., the work-centered approach of werkimmanent criticism as well as the society-oriented concerns of Marxist criticism, have been in a state of crisis since the 1960s. It was then that younger writers began to challenge the "ivory tower" attitudes that the German literary establishment had held since 1945. Since 1968 at the latest, when literature was proclaimed dead in the pages of Kursbuch, there has been a lack of consensus in the accepted methodology and this has led to the lack of legitimation for any one school of literary criticism.

One expression of this crisis was Peter Handke's infamous chastisement of the "Gruppe 47"

critics at their 1966 Princeton meeting. Another is
the work of the "Konstanzer Schule," in particular
Jauß' systematic theory set forth in a series of
publications beginning in 1967 with his manifesto
of reception aesthetics, "Literaturgeschichte als
Provokation der Literaturwissenschaft."[5] Jauß declares that a new paradigm for literary criticism
is necessary in the face of increasing disdain for
existing approaches, and that this new paradigm will
produce a new literary history. A paradigm is the
thought construct available in any given historical
period. The idea of a paradigm change was borrowed
by Jauß from Thomas Kuhn's understanding of systematic
methodological changes in the natural sciences, e.g.,
the change from the Ptolemaic to Copernican System.[6]
The first literary paradigm Jauß considers (the clas-
sical-humanist approach) looked to Greece as example
and norm. The second paradigm (the historical-positi-
vist approach) arose in the nationally-oriented historicity of Romanticism; it was this paradigm which resulted in the existing national literary histories.
Finally, Jauß sees in stylistics and work-oriented
aestheticism the third paradigm (the aesthetic-formal-
istic approach). While Jauß does not expect his

6

reception aesthetics to be the next paradigm which
will replace the werkimmanent method, he does expect,
in conjunction with the efforts of others, to contribute to the building of a new paradigm. Where werkimmanent criticism considered only the work and Marxist
criticism only the social impact, Jauß' reception aesthetics would include the reader in the literary process in an effort to bridge the gap between the two
extremes. Because the reader is the only significant
dimension of the literary process not included in the
previous paradigms, Jauß in his early works feels that
the new paradigm must proceed in that direction.

If he is to unite such disparate lines of
thought, Jauß must accomplish two tasks:

1) he must define the "aesthetic," and

2) he must show how a literary work can
have an effect on society, i.e., he must define his
variation of the Marxist term "gesellschaftsbildend."

Jauß puts his program in the form of seven
theses. The first of these calls for a reworking of
literary history to include an aesthetic based on
reception and effect. The literary history would then
become more than a mere collection of historical facts;
it would become the description of a process of inter-

actions among the reader, the reflective critic and the producing author. The inclusion of the readership in this scheme incorporates the extraliterary, social factors hitherto exclusively the domain of Marxist criticism.

Thesis two explains how the inclusion of the reader can be more than a psychological investigation of individual readers.[7] Jauß claims that the literary experience of the reader is a time-limited consensus based on an objectifiable and historically locatable system of expectations that exists at the moment of a work's publication. Jauß terms this the "Erwartungshorizont" of a work. The "Erwartungshorizont" can be described by:

a) the recognized norms of the literary genre to which the work belongs, as established in the literary canon,

b) the implicit relationship to known works of the time, and

c) the opposition between fiction and reality as expressed in the poetic versus the practical functions of language.

Jauß does not specify further the basis for judging between fiction and reality; indeed this lack of specificity is a major drawback to Jauß' early work.

The "Erwartungshorizont" helps Jauß measure the aesthetic value of a work, as he describes in the third thesis. The distance between the "Erwartungshorizont" and a new work is called the aesthetic distance. Great literature will create a "Horizontwandel," i.e., will lead to new expectations on the part of the reading public. Thus, the aesthetic distance between a masterpiece and its "Erwartungshorizont" will be greater than the aesthetic distance between a work of popular fiction (Unterhaltungskunst) and its "Erwartungshorizont." Jauß' first three theses fulfill the first part of his task, in that they offer his definition of aesthetic quality as based on reception.

Jauß' fourth thesis begins the discussion of the effect of literature on society, literature as "gesellschaftsbildend." This task is essentially one of developing a new literary history, the basis of which is an understanding of a work of literature as having potential meaning, rather than a single, timeless meaning. The work of art is not merely the end-product of an author's labor. It is rather the result of the reader's interaction with that end-product. The author's product simply sets limits as to how the meaning can be plausibly defined, but without the reader, the work itself has only potential meaning. In this way, literature answers different questions for its different readers in different time periods. Thus, in this thesis Jauß ties the meaning of a work to social change. This allows the philologist to ask more legitimate questions of a work and makes one more aware that one's own viewpoint is influenced and limited by one's own experiences.

Having established the foundation for his reception-based literary history in thesis four, Jauß sets out in theses five through seven the three requirements which account for the historicity of literature. Thesis five calls for the diachronic categorization of literary works by examining each work's relationship to prior and later works. In other words, Jauß views literature as a process in which each work leads to the production of new works which answer problems left unresolved by the earlier works. This is the diachronic categorization of literature. Jauß' literary history would differ from the traditional positivist literary history in that it would group works together which represent direct relationships, rather than by arbitrary time periods or national literatures.

10

Under Jauß' scheme there would, for example, be no
Goethezeit or Middle High German literature, but
rather the novel of letters, Bildungsroman, or courtly
epic, regardless of date or place or language.

Thesis six calls for a synchronic investigation in conjunction with the diachronic. The synchronic analysis is concerned with one time slice, i.e.,
the duration of an "Erwartungshorizont." Within this
period there exist side by side works of unequal aesthetic nature. The task of synchronic analysis is to
arrange these various works into a hierarchy in which
some works will be closer to the existing "Erwartungshorizont" and some will be leading the way towards a
"Horizontwandel." When the synchronic approach is
combined with the diachronic, one obtains a virtually
complete literary history.

Without explicitly saying so, Jauß applies
Kuhn's notion of paradigm change not only to literature
but to literary theory as well. The "Erwartungshorizont" is the equivalent of Kuhn's paradigm notion
in that it identifies the features of a fundamental
historical consensus about literary norms. Jauß
argues that this consensus notion of literary norms
provides the only method for determining when and why

those norms change.

It is in thesis seven that Jauß explains
how literature affects society, rather than serving
merely as a mirror of society. The experience of literature is just one type of experience which helps
the reader shape his understanding of the world. A
literary history, in Jauß' view, must examine this function of literature in order to fully explain what
literature is.

With his seven theses Jauß has provoked
much criticism of his theories of reception aesthetics.[8]
This criticism is leveled by Western Germanists who dis-
agree that Jauß has established a viable aesthetic and
Marxists who do not believe Jauß has properly defined
the social role of literature. Typical of the former
is the study by Manfred Durzak of the variances of
the reception of Grass' örtlich betäubt in the Federal
Republic of Germany as compared with the United States.
Durzak concludes that the differences in the reception
of örtlich betäubt cannot lead to conclusions about the
aesthetic nature of the work, but only about other
factors influencing opinions, such as political, economic, national, religious, and societal factors.

> Rezeptionsästhetik . . . erweitert sich also
> zu einer Reflexion der Bedingungen der Mög-

12

lichkeit von kritischer Urteilsfindung. Aber
diese Bedingungen haben weniger mit der Rein-
heit bestimmter Kriterien und ihrem Konse-
quenten Gebrauch zu tun als mit dem politischen
und soziologischen Bewußtseinsfeld, innerhalb dessen sich kritische Urteilsfindung
vollzieht.[9]

The implication of Durzak's criticism is that Jauß has

not adequately fulfilled the first part of his task,

because he has not explained how the aesthetic, as such,

can exist, apart from these other factors.

On the other hand, Jauß has focused too much

on the aesthetic for the Marxist critic Manfred Naumann.

Naumann complains Jauß has misrepresented Marxist aes-

thetics by his improper understanding of how the "gesell-

schaftsbildend" function of literature operates, and

this is an indication of Jauß' allegiance to the aes-

thetic canon.

Jauß' Theorie habe im Grunde nur eine
(systemkritische) Berechtigung im Rahmen
der spätbürgerlichen Gesellschaft, da sie
nur das Einverständniss der bürgerlichen
Bildungselite mit ihrer Tradition kritisiere.
[Die Rezeptionsästhetik stellt] nur eine
methodologische Ergänzung der immanenten
Literaturbetrachtung durch eine immanent
aufgefaßte Rezeptionsgeschichte dar.[10]

From the standpoint of Naumann's ideology, which puts

social practice in the foreground and understands

13

literature as produced by and influencing society,
Jauß's theories uniting literature and readership
with indefinite literary and social goals must appear
as formalism, as a specific product of a capitalist
society which sees itself as the standard giver.

What both the formalist and Marxist criti-
cisms have in common is that their reasons for reject-
ing Jauß' theses are founded in understandings of
society and literature which are inherently contrary
to Jauß' model. Jauß did not bridge the gap between
formalist and Marxist literary criticism, however discussion of his proposals has succeeded in stimulating
recent Marxist reevaluations of aesthetics and in
creating yet another group equally as dedicated to
reception aesthetics.[11]

Aside from theoretical considerations, easily
discounted by noting the incompatibility of the assumptions made by the proponents on either side, the practical difficulties involved in implementing reception
aesthetics are numerous. Later works by Jauß recognize
and elaborate on some of these difficulties. By and
large the only individual readers who record their
reception of a work are professional critics, and there
is real doubt that their expectations can be considered

typical. Indirect evidence of reception by readers
other than professional critics is obtained from sales
figures, numbers of editions, works by others that
mention or copy the work in question, inclusion in
anthologies, accounts in literary histories or other
indications of canonization. Karl Robert Mandelkow
even suggests that more than one "Erwartungshorizont"
must be reconstructed.[12] Mandelkow differentiates
between three different types of expectations: the
expectations of the epoch, the work expectations, and
the author expectations. The first approximates a
strict interpretation of Jauß' "Erwartungshorizont."
The second occur when the public expects an author
to continue in the vein of one particular work, for
example, Werther as a measure of the rest of Goethe's
work. The author expectations are stereotyped views
of the author which may hinder him from experimentation. It is probable, however, that Jauß intends his
"Erwartungshorizont" to take all these factors into
consideration.

A further difficulty of reception aesthetics
lies for Mandelkow in the feedback effect of the process of literary criticism. There is never a single
understanding of a work, but rather a multitude of

conceptions which continually modify one another.
There seems to be no way of arriving at one gener-
alized "Erwartungshorizont" without resorting to the
empirical, demographic methods of the social sciences.
Such methods would only be applicable to more recent
literature and would disqualify reception aesthetics
as a viable method for the study of older works. However, even for recent works, construction of a general
"Erwartungshorizont" for any given moment in the literary process would be extraordinarily difficult. The
coexistence of varying literary norms and the plethora
of sociological and demographic data which contribute
to any "Erwartungshorizont" would require a time-consuming processing effort, disproportionate to the utility
of the results.

Perhaps this is the reason why in a later
explication of his theories, Jauß switches his emphasis
from the "Erwartungshorizont" to the structuralist-in-
spired notion of concretization.[13] The concretization
of a work is the public and accepted view of an author
or a work, presumably reflecting the interaction of the
work with an existing implied "Erwartungshorizont."
What this shift of emphasis does is enable Jauß to
bypass the most difficult requirement, in terms of

16

practicability, of reception aesthetics, namely the
systematic construction of an "Erwartungshorizont"
for each individual work. Instead, the critical reactions to the text coupled with indications about the
scope of its audience provide a reasonably accurate
basis for assuming the parameters of an "Erwartungshorizont."

Jauß' shift justifies a reliance on published
literary criticism as the primary factor influencing
the concretization of a work or an author. Literary
criticism alone would be insufficient in establishing
an "Erwartungshorizont," but in determining the publically accepted view of works and authors, it is para-
mount. As noted earlier, Jauß has genuine doubts about
whether expectations of critics are the same as those
of the general reader. It is, after all, entirely
plausible to suggest that the public and accepted view
of a work is actually created by professional critics.
The effect of emphasizing concretization is, thus,
to make the use of reception aesthetics more practical
by permitting reliance principally on critical reactions.

In this sense, this dissertation sidesteps
Jauß' main program, as delineated in his early works,

i.e., the rewriting of literary history, by focusing on concretization to gain insights into a work and an author. Indeed, Jauß' new literary history might only be accomplished by means of multitudes of concretization studies like this one, which together would provide the necessary information to infer an "Erwartungshorizont."

In applying reception aesthetics to an investigation of the reception of Ulrich Becher, I have tried to take into account any information which impinges on the public and accepted view of the author or his works. In addition to considerations from the primary and secondary literature, an author's reception includes evaluations of publishing criteria, historical-social-political events, literary trends, the author's place in the literary canon, as well as the critical stance of the researcher. Furthermore, if the concretization has changed over time, this change must be recorded. These data constitute the essence of Jauß' second thesis discussed above, and analysis of this material will provide the substance for conclusions about Becher's reception.

A general presentation of Ulrich Becher's times and works, in Chapter II sketches his life and works up to the beginning of his exile in New York. It is a period marked by very limited reception, because Becher's debut as a writer coincided with the Nazi rise to power, and Becher's literary activity in his first years of exile in Vienna and Brazil was almost non-existent. The information in this early chapter was assembled with the expectation that it would provide explanations for much of Becher's later literary development.

Chapter III begins with a similar discussion of Becher's New York years and proceeds to Becher's literary production after his return to Europe in 1948. Some evidence of reception, such as sales figures, is included here. However, the emphasis is on Becher's literary development, and thus each work is considered chronologically rather than thematically to highlight any stylistic or thematic changes in Becher's work.

Chapter IV is a preliminary analysis of over 400 newspaper critiques of Becher's works. These critiques were obtained from the files of Becher's publishers, Rowohlt, Sessler, and Benziger; from major German newspapers such as the Frankfurter Allgemeine Zeitung and the Frankfurter Rundschau; from libraries

such as the Deutsche Bibliothek, the Stadtbibliothek
Basel, and the Institut für Zeitgeschichte in Munich;
from Becher himself; and from producers of Becher's
theatrical works such as Zweites Deutsches Fernsehen
and the Nationaltheater Mannheim. They represent probably 80-90% of all post-1955 critiques on Becher's
works. Because Rowohlt's archives were destroyed by
fire in 1955, critiques prior to that date were obtained primarily through time-consuming research in
libraries. It is therefore difficult to ascertain
the exact percentage of pre-1955 critiques utilized
by this study. Even if two critiques were obviously
the same (i.e., same author, same text), they were
counted as individual publications if they appeared
in different papers, because it was assumed that they
reached two different audiences.

Thus, available recorded sources have been
examined in order to ascertain the concretization of
Becher's work. In addition, the critiques are examined
chronologically work by work to detect shifts in that
concretization over time. This examination results
in specific theses about Becher's reception at given
points in time and in different geographical locations,
illustrated by representative prominent quotes from the

critiques. These theses are evaluated statistically in the final chapter.

In order to solve the practical problem of processing so much information in a reasonable amount of time as well as to minimize the subjective values of the researcher, this dissertation takes the additional step of computer statistical analysis of the newspaper critiques. Chapter V introduces content analysis, the methodology used to quantify the data for processing by the computer. Content analysis is a method designed specifically to quantify communication content. Quantitative analysis is not used here to replace narrative analysis, because too much valuable information would be lost. Rather this study employs both methods to provide the most complete picture possible of Becher's reception. In addition, the formal statement of hypotheses is included at the end of chapter V.

The results of the statistical operations performed by the computer software package SPSS are given in Chapter VI, and finally the results of both the quantitative and narrative analyses will be summarized.

FOOTNOTES

[1]Klaus Mann, "Ulrich Becher," Das Neue Tage-
buch, 5 (1937), No. 30, 719; Lion Feuchtwanger, "Ulrich
Becher," Das Wort, No. 8 (August 1937), 90-92; F.C.
Weiskopf, "Neue deutsche Novellen," Das Wort, No. 4-5
(April-May 1937), 117-120.

[2]Paul Hühnerfeld, "Auf der Suche nach dem
alten Europa: Die Wege und Irrwege des Schriftstellers
Ulrich Becher," Die Zeit, No. 21 (23 May 1957), 6;
Friedrich Heer, "Tragödie der Zwischenwelt," Die Furche
(Vienna), 20 March 1954, n.p.; Jürgen Rühle, "Karneval
der Heimatlosen," Sonntag (Berlin-Ost), 9, No. 17 (25
April 1954), 4; Valentin Herzog, "Schicksalsnächte in
New York und Basel," National Zeitung (Basel), 20
November 1974, n.p.

[3]Herbert Ihering, "Episches und dramatisches
Theater," Sonntag (Berlin-Ost), 11, No. 3 (15 January
1956), 11.

[4]Martin Gregor-Dellin, "Jeder Satz exotisch,"
Die Zeit, 29 August 1969, n.p.; Lothar Romain, "Akrobatik ohne Abgrund," FAZ, 21 June 1969, n.p.

[5]Hans Robert Jauß, Literaturgeschichte als

22

Provokation der Literaturwissenschaft (Constance:
Konstanzer Universitätsverlag, 1967 and 1969), revised in Literaturgeschichte als Provokation (Frankfurt
on Main: Suhrkamp, 1970), pp. 144-207; ed., Die nicht
mehr schönen Künste. Grenzphänomene des Ästhetischen
(Munich: W. Fink Verlag, 1968); "Provokation des Lesers
im modernen Roman," in Die nicht mehr schönen Künste;
"Paradigmawechsel in der Literaturwissenschaft," Linguistische Berichte, 3 (1969), 44-56; Kleine Apologie
der ästhetischen Erfahrung (Constance: Universitätsverlag, 1972); "Racines und Goethes Iphigenie. Mit
einem Nachwort über die Partialität der rezeptionsästhetischen Methode," neue hefte für philosophie, 4
(1973), 1-46.

[6]Thomas S. Kuhn, Die Struktur Wissenschaft-
licher Revolutionen (Frankfurt on Main: Suhrkamp,
1967);

[7]This thesis is in answer to René Wellek's
objection that an aesthetic based on the effect of the
work of art can never achieve anything but a sociology
of public taste, René Wellek, "Zur methodischen Aporie
einer Rezeptionsgeschichte," in: Geschichte; Ereignis
und Erzählung. Ed. Reinhart Koselleck and Wolf-Dieter
Stempel (Munich: W. Fink Verlag, 1973), p. 515.

[8]Gunter Grimm, "Einführung in die Rezeptions-forschung," in: Literatur und Leser: Theorien und Modelle zur Rezeption literarische Werke. Ed. Gunter Grimm (Stuttgart: Reclam, 1975), p. 34-51. Grimm assesses the criticism of Western critics Max Wehrli, Karl Robert Mandelkow, Hinrich C. Seeba, Dietrich Harth, Gerhard Kaiser, Hartmut Eggert, Werner Braun, Wolfram Mauser, Susanne Müller-Hanpft, Norbert Groeben, Peter Rusterholz, Urs Jaeggi, Horst Albert Glaser and René Wellek, as well as of the Marxist critics Robert Weimann, Manfred Naumann, Michael Nerlich, Claus Träger and Bernd Jürgen Warneken. My choice of Durzak, Naumann and Mandelkow represents the main themes in the criticism of reception aesthetics.

[9]Manfred Durzak, "Rezeptionsästhetik als Literaturkritik," in: Kritik der Literaturkritik, ed. Olaf Schwencke, (Stuttgart: Kohlhammer, 1973), p. 69.

[10]Gesellschaft, Literatur, Lesen: Literatur-rezeption in theoretischer Sicht, ed. Manfred Naumann et al. (Berlin: Aufbau Verlag, 1973), p. 139, 143.

[11]Grimm, p. 51.

[12]Karl Robert Mandelkow, "Probleme der Wirkungsgeschichte," Jahrbuch für Internationale Germanistik, 2 (1970), No. 1, 73.

[13]Jauß, "Racines und Goethes Iphigenie," p. 3. Here Jauß writes: "Den Begriff 'Konkretisation' verwende ich nicht im engeren Sinne von R. Ingarden als Ergänzung der Lücken und imaginative Auffüllung von Unbestimmtheitsstellen in der schematischen Werkstruktur, sondern bezeichne damit im Einklang mit der ästhetischen Theorie des Prager Strukturalismus den immer neuen Charakter, den das Werk in seiner ganzen Struktur unter veränderten, geschichtlich-gesellschaftlichen Rezeptionsbedingungen erhalten kann."

Chapter II:

Pre-1944 Biography and Reception

The literary histories that list him at all
sketch only a brief biographical outline of Ulrich
Becher (born 1910).[1] Among the particulars we find
the influences which contributed to political attitudes typical of his fellow German exiles who rejected National Socialism. His family was solidly bourgeois, his father a prominent lawyer, his mother a
gifted Swiss pianist and art connoisseur. Becher's
earliest memory was his feeling of loss as he watched
his father march off to participate in World War I,
and in his autobiographical writings Becher cites this
incident as the beginning of his anti-militarism.

The absence of his father during the war
years allowed his maternal grandfather, Martin Ulrich,
to exert the primary influence on the young boy. And
a powerful influence it was, for Martin Ulrich is described by Becher as a free-thinker, a socialist and
an ardent anti-militarist and anti-imperialist, who
was later a charter member of the Berliner Arbeiter-
und Soldatenrat or Workers- and Soldiers-Council.[2]

Martin Ulrich was widely traveled and Ulrich Becher's
mother worked to finance her father's Wanderlust. He
had lived in Russia for a time and even tried the United
States, where one branch of Becher's family remained.
These travels provided the source both for many interesting stories that the grandfather told his grand-
son and of Martin Ulrich's personal convictions on the
"unheilfrohen Mächten des Goldes und des Eisens."[3] In
Switzerland the grandfather was a tenant farmer for
Rütli, a giant corporation that still controls the
food supply in that country.

Aside from his grandfather, Becher seems to
have been most impressed by people he met as a teenager
in Berlin. Some of the clients of his father's law
firm in the 1920s in Berlin were Max Planck, the
physicist, and the poet Klabund, as well as officials
of the Czechoslovakian embassy. Becher, who describes
this Berlin period as the "turbulent 1920s," seems to
have absorbed much of its flavor and adopted many of
the prevailing ideas.

The cultural climate of this period has been
the subject of numerous investigations in recent years.[4]
For the purposes of this study only those characteristics
which relate to Ulrich Becher will be discussed. It

is clearly the artistic developments of the 1920s
which affected Becher most strongly. It was a time
of revolution in all the arts. The basic experimentation and resultant destruction of old traditions and
conventions had already been accomplished in the
graphic arts prior to World War I by Expressionism and
the various constructivist tendencies (e.g., cubism).
Thus, artists of the 1920s were free to use or reject any of the plurality of forms available. This
was, however, not an artistic revolution in the normal sense, because its motivation was outside the
world of art. This motivation was a new feeling on
the part of artists that their work could influence
the political and social problems of their time. This
was expressed either in a rejection of the existing
order, as in the case of Dada, or in the attempt to
change the contours of the modern world (e.g., Bauhaus).
The center for all this revolutionary activity in the
world of art was Berlin, which drew to its cafes and
salons not only leading artists from the German-speaking world, but from all of Europe as well. The van-
guard of experimentation in art, architecture, music,
theater, and literature could be found in Berlin.
This was the cultural climate in which Ulrich Becher

spent his impressionable teenage years.

Aside from adopting the political engagement
of 1920s Berlin, Becher was receptive to the formal
experimentation of the time. The popular idea of
simultaneity, originating in the philosophy of Berg-
son, conveyed the hectic pace of life in Berlin. Authors such as Proust, Joyce, and Döblin were attempt-
ing to express this idea of simultaneity through the
use of cinematic techniques in their prose works. Film
and other technological advancements in the realm of
entertainment, such as radio or the stylized poses of
the models or machine-like movements of the precision
tap dancers in Broadway revues, were generally touted
as stylistic progressiveness. The music world especially felt the impact of this technological approach
as well as a corresponding influence from the negro
rhythms of jazz. The source of these innovations
was America, land of the future and unlimited opportunity. America had become in the 1920s a symbol of
a vital life style, a standard against which one could
compare and critique an enervated Europe. All of
these elements are reflected in Ulrich Becher's later
works.

Perhaps because of his predisposition to

dissidence and nonconformism by the influence of his
grandfather, Becher seems to have absorbed much of the
Geniezeit of Berlin. Episodes in his youth reflect
this inclination. At twelve, Becher was leader of
a jazz band and delighted in singing negro songs. It
was also at this tender age that Becher first collided
with a group of Nazis. Becher describes this confrontation in a letter:

> als 12-jähriger Quartaner des Berliner
> Werner-Siemens-Gymnasiums griff er bei
> Regenwetter zwei Schüler eines andern Gym-
> nasiums, die Hakenkreuzflugblätter verteil-
> ten . . . mit seinem Schlagring an, worauf
> er verhaftet wurde und auf dem Berlin-Wilmers-
> dorfer Polizeirevier am Prager Platz landete.[5]

Becher finished his pre-University studies in a prep-
school in Thuringia, where one of his teachers introduced him to George Grosz's bitterly aggressive sketches
from Das Gesicht der herrschenden Klasse. Shortly
thereafter, Becher began painting his own burlesque
watercolors in Grosz's style, some of which were ex-
hibited in Locarno in 1925.

Before settling down to study law in Berlin,
Becher spent his Wanderjahre tramping through Europe,
especially enjoying England. He also takes pride in
noting that he trained for long-distance running with

30

Dr. Otto Pelzer, who was the trainer for the Norwegian
Olympic champion, Umi.

In 1927 at the age of 17, Becher began his
study of law in Berlin and Geneva. It was in Berlin
that several formative relationships for Ulrich Becher
began, perhaps the foremost being his life-long friendship with "der traurigste Mensch in Europa," George
Grosz, to whom he was referred by a drawing instructor.
Becher describes his first meeting with Grosz in "Der
große Grosz und eine große Zeit."[6] Here Becher credits Grosz, whom he calls "der Kronzeuge der tollen
20er Jahre," and Grosz's work with a major influence
on his own writing, an influence on both his style
and his thought.

Becher was accepted as the Benjamin of the
Grosz circle, a fact which speaks for his precocious-
ness or the length to which he identified with the
members of an older generation. This group included
such established names as Erwin Piscator, Max Herrmann-
Neisse, Wieland Herzfelde, John Heartfield, and Ernst
Rowohlt.

In addition to frequent contact with this
circle, Becher visited Das Romanische Café and came under
the influence of a completely different set of elders.

The satirist Alexander Roda Roda, as well as the artist
Max Slevogt, Emil Orlich, and "der rasende Reporter"
Egon Erwin Kisch, who were members of this group,
represent the more literary, Austrian brand of social
satire. Roda Roda's satire was entertaining, much
less biting than Grosz's.

These two men--Grosz and Roda Roda--represent
the two styles of social criticism which influenced
Becher's works. On the one extreme there was Grosz's
focus on the grotesque hypocrisy of bourgeoise capitalists caught in obscene acts. His drawings represent
the Marxist conviction of the inevitable self-destruc-
tion of capitalism. In contrast, Roda Roda's was a
gentle satire, the objective of which was edification
and reform through laughter. Even in Berlin, Roda
Roda remained an Austrian of the old school full of
anecdotes and Jewish stories. Although Roda Roda's
influence became more evident in Becher's later works,
Becher's initial venture as a playwright reflects the
influence of Grosz and the Berlin years almost exclusively.

In 1928, Becher was allowed as a law student
to observe the trial brought against Grosz and Malik
Verlag for blasphemy. Becher writes that this trial

and Grosz's backdrop pictures from Piscator's Schwejk production, especially Christus mit Gasmaske, gave him the impulse to try to become a playwright.[7] The result was Niemand, written in 1931, but not produced until 1936 at the Stadttheater in Berne, because, according to Becher, the Berlin Volksbühne premiere was effectively canceled by the Nazi's ascension to power. (Volksbühne producer Alfred Ibach, who had accepted Becher's play, had gone into exile.) Niemand clearly shows the influence of Grosz. In this play, Christ returns to earth and is again rejected by those in authority, the military and the capitalists, for his pacifism and solidarity with the working class.

This play brought Ulrich Becher the distinction of becoming at 23 the youngest author to have his books burned.[8] Just two years earlier, his first collection of short stories, Männer machen Fehler, had earned him the position of youngest Pen-Club member. Ironically, Ulrich Becher points with pride to his age; he sees himself in terms of his being the youngest in so many respects. But his youth created a lifelong problem, the search for his own literary style, a task made more difficult by exile. The talented novice was surrounded by artists who had established themselves a decade before, expressionists, dadaists, politically and socially engaged artists. Association with them confirmed Becher's own tendencies, but also locked him into the role of eternal disciple or historian to the masters of artistic movements whose glory was already fading when Becher was old enough to join the inner circle.

During the Berlin years Becher was primarily under the influence of Grosz. However, later, as Roda Roda's son-in-law, Becher was increasingly influenced by Roda Roda's humanist interpretation of political events. These were Becher's teachers. One of Becher's continuing problems was his uncomfortable synthesis of the Marxist caricature of Grosz with the Austrian satire of Roda Roda.

Becher's earliest prose work, Männer machen Fehler, some of whose stories even preceded Niemand, is a potpourri of styles and themes that testifies to the impact that 1920s experimental art had on the adolescent Ulrich Becher, as the following discussion of the individual stories shows. "Joshua war kein Feldherr," which describes the beating to death of an old zither player, can be read almost as an allegory of the brutality of capitalism. Joshua, whose delicate

34

zither music only lovers seem to understand, is the
victim of Hans Moritzpeter, an innkeeper who uses
his wife and Joshua, as well as the other employees
of the inn, to attract customers. Joshua's role in
the enterprise is to play his zither when the regular
guitar player is tired and to allow anyone who so de-
sires to hit him on the head. Joshua is the artist-
clown-outcast whom we see in so much of Expressionist
literature and his milieu is the night-life of the bar
with its brutality and sexual innuendos, a world
where the bourgeoisie lets its hair down and reveals
its true character. Joshua, with his child-like in-
nocence and half-crazed mannerisms, provides a contrast
to the upstanding citizens of the community, and Becher
glorifies this lowly and most insignificant artist
until he almost assumes the role of a saint.

The same themes are found in "Ein toller
Hund," the story of a strange, dirty, tattered tramp,
another social outcast, who is shot to death by the
forester Mattus. Mattus represents the hated face of
bourgeois authority, a bureaucrat who uses his position to rid the world of someone who challenges authority. Even more than in "Joshua," Becher parodies the
Christ legend with the outcast motif, as is most evi-

dent in the scene in the prison in which three prison
guards mock him and crown him. The setting of this
story is a small city and, in a further connection to
Expressionism, this city with its cold gray buildings
and technology becomes a testimony to man's inhumanity
to man, a place where money is more important than human kindness.

The inhuman world of technology is again a
theme in "Junger Mann kommt zum Vater zurück." Here,
too, the setting is a city with its factories and
bars, its gaslit streets alive with partygoers, night-
shift workers, and bohemian types. We see the city
through the eyes of the young man of the title as he
moves like a camera from scene to scene, first arguing
with his father, then attending a party, then walking
home through the night streets, and finally returning
to his father. The party is supposed to be an orgy
thrown by a wealthy factory owner in his factory and
this provides Becher with the opportunity to make some
Expressionistic comments on the world of work, comments
that show his sympathy for the working class and disdain for the rich idle youth. The orgy mood is destroyed by the smell of oil and sweat in the factory,
which Becher says has consecrated the factory as in-

36

cense consecrates a church. This elevates the milieu
of the worker to the higher plane of religion. The
problems of a young man from a good family who has
completed his schooling and does not quite know how
to develop himself is another theme predominant in
Expressionism and one that is generally found in
connection with the generation conflict and its almost
psychoanalytic (Oedipal) interpretation. This is the
case in Becher's story, "Junger Mann," as well.

A similar constellation of Expressionist
themes can be found in "Zwei im Frack," which could
as well bear the title "Kleider machen Leute." The
unnamed brothers from the upper reaches of society
who have seen better times are able to gain admittance
to bourgeois celebrations by virtue of their tuxedoes
and top-hats, the only clothing they still possess.
They are mistaken for pallbearers, for rich American
uncles at a christening, for waiters, and for wedding
guests, where they are fed and take part in the fes-
tivities and afterwards even dream they can be elected
to high office because of their tuxedoes. As in Gott-
fried Keller's story, the characters become symbols,
used to satirize bourgeois convention and its super-
ficiality. Implicitly the reader is asked to identify

with the conartists and to note that their crime is far less ugly than the crime committed against poor people by capitalist society.

"Schrecken in einer Pension" deals with the generation conflict, too, but differently than "Junger Mann." In this hotel live only old people who are waiting to die, the "ich-Leichen" of Expressionism. Their daily life consists of eating, watering the flowers in the garden, and arguing about who will be the first to die. Into this world of the living dead comes a pregnant girl, and her cries in labor shake the old people into the realization that their own lives are about to end. Frightened by this confrontation with life they forget to eat and to water their gardens. The old people of the story represent the complacent bourgeoisie that wants to maintain the status quo at all costs. The confrontation of generations is another typical Expressionist theme used here by Becher. The birth of the baby can be compared to the same effect that the birth of Expressionism, Dadaism, or the impact of youth would have on society, a general shaking up for the better.

Expressionist theories of art are most clearly brought out in "Der Maler," the story which can be

38

seen as Becher's earliest commemoration of his friend
George Grosz. A visitor to the artist's studio discovers everything but the painter himself: piles of
dirty laundry, a nude model, an old girlfriend of the
painter. Just when he is about to leave, the visitor
hears a cry from above and discovers the painter hang-
ing from a trapeze. From this vantage point the painter
has been surveying his work, a gigantic painting of
Madonna and child which covers the entire floor of
the studio and in the middle of which the visitor is
standing. In his effort to reach the edge of the
picture, the visitor almost destroys the painting,
a conscious attempt by Becher to distort any religious
value the painting might have. After the painter
himself falls into the middle of the painting, he
entertains the visitor with his views of the role of
the artist in modern society. These views read like
a manifesto of Expressionism or Dadaism. There is
the theme of art as a weapon, not art for art's sake,
performed by the great genius, the Faustian outsider.
For this man, art has become an escape from the world
of technology as well as nature. By being between
the two worlds, he is not really a part of either.
The painter has a lust for life and that includes sex

and drink, which he perceives as life's most worth-
while components. At the same time, the painter rejects the world. He must criticize it, and yet he
is drawn to life and the world in which he lives. This
ambivalence is expressed in his painting. On the one
hand he creates paintings which show infinity, a cosmic feeling, and on the other hand he has drawings
that show the pain of being forced to exist in this
incomprehensible world.

In keeping with the Expressionist view of
the artist as a politician, the opinions of the painter are written in a loud and vehement proclamatory
style, which shows its emotional quality in run-on
sentences. There are exclamation points and itali-
cized words and repetition for effect, many super-
latives and many active verbs. This all gives the
impression of loud speech-making. The exaggerated
prose style of "Der Maler" is not typical of Männer
machen Fehler as a whole; there is another style to be
found in "Junger Mann" and "Zwei im Frack": very
short, simple sentences, free of adjectives and articles. Both these styles can be found in Expressionist
writings. Yet another style can be discovered in
"Joshua": a more descriptive, realistic prose with

a 19th century flavor, evidence of Roda Roda's influence. And there are also non-derivative elements in this book, elements that are specific to Becher's work rather than of a specific movement or mentor. In almost every story there is a connection to the English-speaking world. For example, the innkeeper in "Joshua" had lived and worked for five years in England and delighted in speaking English with his guests whenever he perceived them to be foreigners. The brothers in "Zwei im Frack" are mistaken for American uncles at a christening and are able to answer questions with their meager English. The young pregnant girl in "Schrecken" is taken to be English since she speaks a language that no one understands. In addition to the English language fragments that dot his works, Becher's settings very often are bars or hotels. Music in some form is always present throughout his stories, but especially negro music or that music which was considered to originate with the negro at the time--jazz.

Although there are some innovative elements in Becher's first work, it is fair to say that while Männer machen Fehler reflects the influence of Dada and Expressionism, this work does not match other

Expressionist models in intensity. Works by Georg
Heym, Gustav Sack and Albert Ehrenstein make more
radical "Expressionist" statements about sex and
society than do these stories by Becher.

Why, then, was it necessary for Ulrich
Becher to flee Germany when the Nazis came to power
in 1933? To be sure his writings expressed an anti-
militarism and anti-authoritarianism, to be sure they
are pro-leftist and pro-union, but at most they provided corroborating evidence for the main charge
against him, namely guilt by association with known
radicals. He was associated with the group of artists
around Grosz, and these were men at the top of the
Nazi list of undesirables. Niemand had been accepted by famous directors, Ibach in Berlin and Lustig-
Prean in Berne, both of whom abruptly left their
posts after the Nazi ascension to power.[9] Becher's
second volume of short stories, Die Eroberer, was published by Oprecht Verlag in Zurich. It is this later
volume of short stories published in 1936, after
Becher had gone into exile, that was finally included on the Nazi "Liste des schädlichen und unerwünsch-
ten Schrifttums" of December 31, 1938. A note on
the first page of the 1938 blacklist collectively

42

forbids all Oprecht publications. While the anti-
militarist, anti-capitalist content of Becher's
early stories and Niemand was sufficient to recommend
his exile should they have come to the attention of
the Nazis, they probably were not included on the
earlier lists due to Becher's lack of fame in 1933.
Thus it is possible to infer that the 1938 blacklist-
ing is due more to Becher's association with Oprecht
than to the fact that the Nazis had read and were
afraid of having Becher's works distributed. In addition Becher had provoked a fight with Nazi youths in
1932, which he later described with pride.[10] Because
Becher was younger and thus not yet sufficiently well-
known as an author to have his democratic cultural-
political orientation arouse the wrath of the Nazis,
it was connection with Oprecht and the Grosz circle,
as well as his public hostility to the Nazis, in addition to the evidence provided by his writings, that
caused his exile. Becher also mentions a Jewish
ancestor.[11] Apparently, however, his Jewish ancestry
was not known to the Nazis, at least not at that time.

At first, Ulrich Becher wanted to stay in
Germany to protest the new government, but Roda Roda
convinced him to try Austria after 1933. His friend

George Grosz and the circle around the Malik Verlag immigrated in 1933 to New York and Ulrich Becher came under the influence of a new mentor, his future father-in-law, Roda Roda.

A writer's career depends on his native tongue. Like the majority of other exiled writers, Becher consequently chose to remain in a German-speaking country so long as his life was not in immediate danger. He became a citizen of Austria, the "'Christlicher Ständestaat' der Dollfuß and Schuschnigg"[12] and married Roda Roda's daughter, Dana, in Vienna. Niemand was published in 1934 in Mährisch-Ostrau by J. Kittls Nachfolger. He was able to contribute a few essays to antifascist newspapers in Switzerland (Volksstimme) and Paris (Das Neue Tage-Buch). One essay, "Einigt euch um Gottes willen" (Europa, No. 13, 28 March 1936), in which Becher calls for unity between Christians, Socialists, Democrats, and friends of peace in the fight against fascism, was reprinted in Heinrich Mann's Mitteilungen der Deutschen Freiheitsbibliothek and in the Deutsche Volkszeitung (Prag-Paris-Basel), both socialist publications.[13]

More important than anything Becher wrote while in Austria, is the atmosphere he absorbed. It would manifest itself in the post-war period of Becher's publication. His Viennese acquaintances, Joseph Roth, Roda Roda, Ödön von Horvath, introduced him to the darker side of the broken Hapsburg empire. He has remarked: "Ohne diese bizarre Wiener Schule, absolviert während der kümmerlichen Herrschaft der Austrofaschisten, hätte ich 45/46 nicht . . . den Bockerer . . . Ebensowenig den Roman Kurz nach 4 schreiben können."[14]

On the day of Hitler's invasion of Austria, March, 1938, at the urging of his father-in-law, Becher took the last unsearched train to Switzerland, where his play Niemand and his second volume of stories Eroberer, had both appeared in 1936. From Switzerland it was still possible (until 1939) to publish for the European market, although many authors resorted to what was known as "Negerarbeit," publishing under the name of Swiss authors due to the difficulty of obtaining police permits.[15] Becher first described the difficult situation of exiles in Switzerland in 1943 in his series of essays for Das andere Deutschland "In der Alpenkatakombe," and later in his novel Murmeljagd.

It was during his three-year Swiss exile

that Becher began work on his first novel, Der Hampel-
mann, based on the life of his socialist grandfather,
Martin Ulrich. The manuscript was lost as a result
of his hasty departure from Switzerland in March,
1941, when, after the fall of France, Swiss authorities informed him they could no longer grant him im-
munity in spite of his mother's Swiss citizenship.[16]

After waiting for an American "Emergency
Visa" for more than six months, Becher managed, with
the help of his father's connections at the Czech
Embassy, to acquire a forged passport identifying him
as a Czech engineer travelling with an industrial
advisory group to Brazil.[17] Becher made his way
from Geneva over Vichy France and Franco Spain to
Lisbon, where he sailed to Rio de Janeiro on the
Cabo de Hornos. From mid-1941 to mid-1944 Becher
lived in Rio de Janeiro or on its outskirts on what
he called his "Urwaldfarm."

With his arrival in South America, Becher
found himself in the professional straits he had tried
so long to avoid. For almost any writer the exile
experience brings the significance of reception into
relief. Cut off from publishers, critics, and readers,
the author is robbed of his livelihood and even of

46

the stimulation provided by reactions to his work.
In Becher's case the isolation was magnified by the
cultural diaspora in South America, as well as by
his youth--no one of his generation had had the
time to establish a reputation comparable to that
of a Stefan Zweig and capable of guaranteeing continued attention for himself.

Within this general framework the types of
things Becher did--and did not--publish during the
1940s acquire a more adequate perspective. In this
very restrictive environment and competing with others
in similar circumstances, he established new contacts
where they were available and drew on continental
acquaintances in an attempt to create some degree
of reception for his works, no matter how slight.

Herbert Baldus, Director of the Museo
Paulisto in São Paulo, who had had some connections
with the Malik Verlag in the 1920s, managed to find
Becher a position as cultural-political reporter for
Brazil's largest daily, Estado de São Paulo. "In
Brasil wurde damals einer, der sich auf Paris berufen
konnte, französisch parlieren und als Sendbote der
europäischen Culture (sic) und des Widerstands gegen
die sogenannte Barbarei auftreten konnte, relativ

herzlich aufgenommen."[18]   Becher also wrote some

articles for Hoje, a small Rio paper, Freies Deutsch-

land/Alemania Libre (Mexico City), and both Femina

and Das andere Deutschland/La Otra Alemania of Buenos

Aires.

Becher's association with August Siemsen's

Das andere Deutschland (DAD) began with the publica-

tion of "Mahn-Sonette" in the September, 1942 issue.

It was through Hans Siemsen, brother of August and

friend of Grosz, and more directly through Willy Kel-

ler, an old friend of Becher's who represented DAD in

Brazil, that Becher made such immediate contact with

an exile publication.[19]   In the September, 1942 issue

Siemsen introduced Becher to the readership of DAD

as "einen Dichter . . . der, wie wenige andere, un-

serem Zeitgeschehen den ihm angemessenen Ausdruck zu

geben vermag."[20]

The essays and poems Becher published in

DAD up to 1944, when he moved to New York, demonstrate

the development of seminal themes in his later fiction.

The "Mahn-Sonette" lay the blame for Hitler and the

outbreak of war at the door of capitalist society,

which "im Jagen nach dem Bestgeschäfte" traded its

ideals for gold, in rejection of the socialist alter-

native.[21] "Drohlied der Erschlagenen"[22] expresses
Becher's solidarity with the downtrodden and perse-
cuted of the world. He rejects the inevitability
of war in "Die sieben stummen Fragen."[23] "Verhör
eines Passlosen"[24] is a parable about a vagrant who
has no papers to show the police, no money, who says
his father is Heaven, his mother Earth, his brother
in Spain, Muerte. This vagrant who knows no national
identity is a clear personification of war.

Becher also took his message to non-literary
sectors, a task that was not too difficult given the
political nature of the message and the tenor of the
times. In "Zehn Jahre,"[25] written to be read at the
First Congress of German Anti-Fascists in Montevideo,
the themes of Niemand and Männer machen Fehler find
renewed expression. There, Becher proclaims the future
victory of anti-fascists over Hitler, der Moloch (a
Semite god who demanded continual human sacrifice).
"In der Alpenkatakombe"[26] describes the shoddy treatment of exiles by Swiss authorities, especially by
the police department of Berne, which Becher claims
was full of fascist sympathizers. Becher details
the deliberate and systematic negation of the Swiss
democratic tradition, as well as of the position of

neutrality by pro-Nazi officials, and their success
in forcing the socialists out of government. He argues
that the suppression of people like Leonard Ragaz
(Neue Wege), J.B. Rusch (Republikanische Blätter),
Eduard Behrens (Demokratie im Angriff), and of journals
and newspapers such as Volksrecht, Volksstimme, and
Tagwacht in effect forced the true Swiss spirit of
freedom and democracy underground into the catacombs
of the Alps.

These two essays, while demonstrating
Becher's pro-socialist stance, also contain the germs
of later works in Becher's attempts to define fascism.
Here is the comparison of fascism to cancer, which
becomes the central metaphor in New Yorker Novellen
and Feuerwasser: "die allgemeine Erkrankung des
abendländischen Körpers . . . die Alterskrankheit . . .
an der dies Leben zugrunde geht . . . der bei lebendigem Leibe Verwesende . . ." The basis for Mademoiselle Löwenzorn can also be found in Becher's comparison of Nazism to the grotesque carnival masks that
hid an amorphous, chaotic identity. These same images
of cancer and carnival are repeated in other essays
from DAD. "Gefallene Kameraden der Freiheit"[27] re-
counts the world-wide presence of evil that led to the

deaths of so many literary men in the decade since
the Nazi book burnings: "Keiner der nicht an der
Leukämie des Hasses and Ekels erstickte." In describing George Grosz's art in "Der große Grosz und
eine große Zeit"[28] Becher compares Grosz to Shake-
speare, Brueghel, and Balzac, who all portray "den
gespenstischbunte, von Todes- und Teufelslarven be-
völkerten Karneval: dieses Leben."

The poems Becher published in DAD echo the
themes of his essays. "Ostersegen"[29] begins as a
nature poem celebrating the return of life to an early
spring landscape, but the second part of the poem
transforms this landscape into one of death and destruction, the scenery of war in 1943. "Krieg der
Mirakel"[30] describes some of the unbelievable events
in the course of World War II: the speed with which
France fell, Hitler's delay in attacking England,
the German-Russian Non-Aggression Pact, the parcel-
ing out of Czechoslovakia ("bei lebendigem Leib zer-
stückten . . ."). "Abendländisches Gelübde"[31] is a
plea for the unification of Europe after the war.

In order to understand why Becher, a dramatist and much later a novelist, wrote almost nothing
but essays and poems during his tenure in South Amer-

ica, it is necessary to look at the outlets he had
available. Those outlets were restricted in their
influence. Das andere Deutschland was the most influential of the exile journals in South America.
Still, it did not represent the same kind of unified
leftist movement or organization to be found in the
Freies Deutschland movement in Mexico. Siemsen was
hoping to unite South American anti-Nazis under his
leadership when he called the Congress in Montevideo
in 1943.[32] According to Dr. Hans Lehmann, one of
DAD's chief contributors, circulation of the journal
never amounted to more than 2,000 copies, but Ilse
Grönewald, who typed and mailed DAD, estimated the
circulation between 4,000 and 5,000.[33]

But it was not merely the lack of readership that restricted Becher's activities, it was
also the nature of the journal itself. Because DAD
was conceived as a political fighting journal, its
literary-cultural contributions were downplayed.
". . .hin und wieder eine Buchrezension oder ein
Gedicht, welches jedoch nicht so sehr durch seine
lyrische Qualität, sondern vielmehr durch seinen
kämpferischen Inhalt beeindruckte."[34] Seven of Ulrich Becher's twelve contributions to DAD during

World War II were poems, and none of the poems can be considered lyrical, but fit quite well with the goals of the journal and with the tone of Becher's essays.

Becher's sole publication of anything approaching a book-length work during his Brazilian years was again dependent on his connections to antifascist groups. This time the significant person was Wilhelm Keller, who had immigrated to Brazil in 1935 and was an associate of Friedrich Kniestedt writing for Aktion under the pseudonym J. J. Sansombre.[35] At the end of 1942 Becher and Keller started the Notbücherei deutscher Anti-Faschisten "um die zu neunzig Prozent hitlerisierten großen deutschen Sprachinseln in Rio Grande do Sul and Parana zu beeinflussen."[36] The first and only publication of the Notbücherei was Becher's "Märchen vom Räuber der Schutzmann wurde," a pamphlet-like poem condemning Hitler, which appeared in a numbered, signed edition of 200 copies in December, 1943. It is characteristic of the isolation of exiles in South American that Keller saw himself as a one-man organization fighting against the general lack of organization among German exiles in Brazil. "In Brasilien gab es überhaupt keine Organisation. Wenn Kniestedt und ich in Porto Alegre und Rio nichts gemacht hätten, wäre überhaupt nichts geschehen."[37] Keller's view of his own position among exiled literary men is important, because Becher seems to have adopted or identified with Keller's stance. As Keller states in an interview: "Ich selbst würde mich . . . links von der kommunistischen Partei einordnen. Alles Funktionärswesen ist mir ein Greuel. Ich könnte auch nie einer politischen Partei angehören, weil die letztlich doch von ihren Funktionären getragen wird. Ich bin ein Outsider, aber ein disziplinierter Outsider."[38] Keller describes those who sympathized with his views, and this would include Becher, as liberals whose opinions were formed in the years 1918-1923, from the fall of Germany to the inflation, readers of Marx, Dostojevsky, Kafka, Hesse, people who practiced a humanist way of thinking.[39]

Keller provides the best available description of the way of life for German anti-fascist exiles in Brazil, and because of Becher's close working relationship with him, Keller's situation creates an even more suitable backdrop against which one can view Becher's life and work in those years. Keller's thoughts are found in an unpublished interview which

54

deserves extended attention here because of its relevance to Becher and his environment.

Keller reports that among the exiles themselves there was a degree of cooperation because conservative and liberal elements were united in their
common fight against foreign and local fascism.[40]
The German nationalist emigration had settled for the
most part in out-of-the-way regions of Brazil instead
of in the major cities and rarely confronted the anti-
fascist emigrants directly.[41] German nationalist
centers were, however, hotbeds of fifth column activity, the targets of the German propaganda effort called "Sonderauftrag Südamerika" to claim Brazil as a
Germany ally.[42] Until the mid-1940s there was much
admiration for German militarism and for Nazis in
particular in the armies and police forces of Latin
America, where fascism was viewed as the only salva-
tion for deformed South American economies and from
the threatening economic power of the United States.
Thus, German propaganda efforts helped pave the way
for the right-wing dictatorships of Peron and Vargas.
The Germans were especially interested in exploiting
what they perceived as their most favorable position
in Brazil because it contained 90% of the German

population in South America.[43] The German plan of
action was slowly to assume control of German clubs,
churches, banks, offices, and schools. Nazi sympathizers had direct or indirect control, through the
practice of payoffs, of over 40 radio stations in
Latin America, including the fifth largest transmit-
tor, Radio Ipanema.[44] Keller reports "Die Haltung der
Behörden war gegenüber den anti-faschistischen Deutschen
in Brasilien absolut feindlich, erstens weil sie den
Nationalsozialismus als Vorbild für eine brauchbare
Regierung bewunderten, zweitens, weil sie unter dem
massiven Druck der Auslandsvertretung der NSDAP stand-
en, bis Brasilien an der Seite der Allierten in den
Krieg eintrat."[45] Keller and Kniestedt were visited
often as four times a week by the police and harried
by bureaucratic paperwork in Puerto Alegre. Each time
a copy of Aktion appeared, it was immediately suppress-
ed by the local police and the printer was forbidden
to publish Aktion in the future. At Kniestedt's bi-
weekly public meetings there were never more than 40-
50 participants for fear of spies.[46] Similarly, in
Buenos Aires, August Siemsen was forced to move DAD
to Montevideo for a short time during a police crackdown in 1944.

56

If, as Keller indicates, the anti-fascists had problems in publishing their work due to official harassment, the more literary exiles, such as Becher, found even greater obstacles in their paths. Except for Stefan Zweig, most German literary exiles found it impossible to continue publishing in Brazil, due primarily to the language barrier, the Brazilian preference for French culture, and the lack of a market among the earlier German immigrant population, which still clung to the classics of the Wilhelmenian Germany they had left.[47] Few German exiles were capable of translating their own works into Portuguese, Keller being one notable exception, and were thus dependent on the services of mostly inferior translators.[48] Becher complains of distortions in his cultural-political articles for Estado de São Paulo and Hoje, which had been translated by "eine ausgerechnet ANTHROPOSOPHISCH eingestellte Übersetzerin."[49]

Becher had little contact with German literary exiles while in Brazil, in contrast to his later years in New York. He preferred entertaining his friends at home (a boarding house named Hotel Praia Leme or his later boarding house in Teresô-polis).[50] A great deal of his time was spent in a

favorite bar, the Spaniard, or Café Amarelinho, in
contact with Spanish emigrants such as Juan Alberti
or just observing the locals over their fifteenth
espresso.[51]

Towards the end of his Brazilian years,
Becher wrote two works of lyrical verse that gave expression to his exile in that country and reflected
the influence of the Spanish ballad form. It was,
however, typical of his exile experience that Reise
zum blauen Tag and Brasilianischer Romanzero, both
written in 1944, were not published until his return
to Germany, 1946 and 1950, respectively. Even the
lack of an audience did not completely stifle his
literary efforts. While Becher supported himself
financially by his cultural and political articles,
he was developing his basically Expressionist literary
style in his verse works. His writing is characterized by the inclusion of the colorful, luxuriant sur-
roundings of the Brazilian jungle, and his language
took on new depths of expression, described by Becher
and critics alike as "Urwaldbarock."[52]

Becher uses countless images, drastic or
fantastic word inventions, exotic local color, and
agglomeration to capture in words the Latin American

58

experience, the strange and dangerous beauty of the
landscape, the impoverished social conditions of its
poorer residents.

> Überall hausen die erdfarbnen Hunde,
> rostrot die Erde und rostrot die Hunde,
> flußlängs suchen die flußfarbnen Hunde,
> lehmgelb die Flüsse und lehmgelb die Hunde,
> urwaldein pirschen die waldfarbnen Hunde,
> blaugrüner Urwald und blaugrüne Hunde,
> dürftige magre verhutzelte Meute,
> hetzen ein Wild, sei es Stunde, Tag, Woche,
> wagen verrudelt sich gar an ein schwarzes
> ob seines Jähzorns gefürchtetes Waldschwein,
> schanzen sich hinter Agaven zum Schlafe,
> sechs oder zwölf, stellen Nachtwachen aus,
> welche die einsam, schwank, steil unter der
> im Zenit hängenden Wiege des Halbmonds
> vorüberreitenden pingabezechten
> Tabakbauern unflätig bekläffen.[53]

In general, Becher's Brazilian experience helped to
intensify some Expressionist elements already in his
work as well as to provide him with new, exotic images.

It is indicative of the type of European
reception accorded to exile works that Becher felt it
necessary to append ten pages of notes to the 1962
edition of Brasilianischer Romanzero explaining the
poems' more obscure references to the Brazilian leg-
ends of Makumba and Lampion, and to Brazilian customs,
and places. For even after he had managed, in spite of
the obstacles presented by exile, to continue his literary development after his return, the environment

that stimulated him was one that was completely unknown to the audience to which he had returned.

It was mid-1944 when Becher was called to
New York City to care for Alexander Roda Roda, his
father-in-law, who was dying of leukemia. Thus,
Becher's first impressions of the United States were
inevitably connected with the final tortured year of
the life and death of the "Mark Twain der Donau."[54]
Becher was no less shocked by the torture than by the
anonymity of this death; it seemed inconceivable that
a man whose red vest had been a symbol almost as well-
known in Austria as Chaplin's oversized shoes should
spend his last years unnoticed by the world. As if to
heighten the drama of this human tragedy, Roda Roda
and World War II came to an end on the same day in
August, 1945, a coincidence often noted by the dramatist Becher.[55] Many of Becher's negative impressions
of the United States appear to be identified in the
author's mind with this event.

But this alone cannot explain why his originally positive image of America, formed in America-
crazy Berlin, changed so drastically. Becher's ties
to the United States included two maternal uncles in
Detroit and Albany, both financially successful mem-

bers of the middle class.[56] His grandfather's stories,
as well as the early influence of Grosz, who saw in
the United States the democratic tradition lacking
in Germany, instilled in Becher a feeling of kinship,
so that, in spite of his criticism of the United
States in his works, he described himself as an
"Euroamerikaner."[57] Part of his disappointment in
the United States must have originated with the
bureaucratic confusion that had delayed his permission to enter the country in 1940.[58] Becher's four
years in Latin America and his association with Keller
had shown him the dark side of American economics:
the support of corrupt, repressive and often fascist
Latin American dictatorships by the power of the
dollar.[59]

When Becher finally did arrive in New York,
he came as an outsider, although many faces must have
been familiar from his Berlin years. As Cazden docu-
ments, New York was a kind of "Berlin Redivivus,"[60]
a wholesale transplantation of German intellectual
life from the Weimar Republic. The most promising
of Becher's connections was through Grosz and Wieland
Herzfelde to the group of prominent and/or radical
authors in the Aurora Verlag, a reincarnation of the

61

Malik Verlag.[61] These connections proved beneficial
to Becher only in 1949, when "Die Frau und der Tod"
was published in the Aurora-Reihe of the Aufbau Verlag,[62] but by then Becher had already returned to
Europe. Most of these authors, if they knew Becher's
name at all, probably knew him better as Grosz's
friend or Roda Roda's son-in-law than as the author
of Niemand or Männer machen Fehler. To make matters
worse, Becher was not recognized as a member of any
established exile group. His association with the
Malik-Aurora group, while not significant enough to
provide him with work, was enough to brand him as
a leftist.[63] Becher's independence in New York, en-
forced by what he perceived as an unspoken ostracism,
was later a source of pride, although at the time it
only heightened Becher's unfavorable evaluation of
his fellow emigrants. "Innerhalb der Emigration be-
gann der kalte Krieg früher als anderwärts," according to Becher in an article in 1964.[64] Becher implies
his inability to find work in New York was due to his
being denounced in some arch-conservative circles.

       Becher's New York address was a "Penthouse-
Kämmerlein" on West 88th Street near Riverside Drive
not far from Harlem. A son, Martin, was born shortly

after the Bechers arrived in the United States. Since
there was no regular job to occupy his days, Becher
spent most of his four years in New York taking notes
or writing the stories and plays that were only published and produced after his return to Europe.[65]
With the exception of an occasional cocktail or dinner party, Becher spent his nights, after the evening's
collaboration with Peter Preses on Der Bockerer, in
the Lucky Horse Shoe Inn on Columbus Avenue. The
barkeeper of this seedy bar, Charlie Brown, kept a
tab for Becher for over three years because Becher
rarely had cash.[66] Shortly before Becher's return to
Germany, Charlie Brown died of lung cancer in a welfare
hospital, thus connecting Becher's first and last impressions of America with death by cancer. Charlie's
bar provided the perfect setting for the study of
"Ober- und Unterwelt, republikanische Politiker, Boxer,
kleine Ganoven wie Joe Glick (Feuerwasser), mit denen
Ulrich Becher sich unterhielt, nicht indes mit großen
Gangstern, die er haßte und haßt."[67]

Becher was fascinated with "dirty dear old
New York City, was berühmte Kollegen wie Zuckmayer
night begreifen konnte [sic]."[68] Part of this fas-
cination must have resulted from the double life he

63

led, as a low-income resident of New York's West Side,
dependent on friends and relatives for his pocket
money, and as a guest at chic East Side cocktail
parties "wo sich Hollywood Stars tummelten sowie
amerikanische und europäische Maler, so Marc Chagall
. . ."[69] At these parties Becher heard stories about
New York celebrities, some of whom were acquaintances
of Grosz: John Dos Passos, Edmund Wilson, Ben Hecht,
Henry Miller, and Sinclair Lewis. The works of Dos
Passos, Lewis, and Upton Sinclair were widely known
in socialist literary circles due to wide distribution
by the Büchergilde Gutenberg,[70] and Becher was already
acquainted with their works from his student days.

Almost every weekend Becher was invited to
the Long Island home of George Grosz. This hospitality
helped Becher survive on the meagre allowance from his
parents in Switzerland and provided him with anecdotes
that he would later turn into prose in Profil, New Yorker Novellen and "Happy End."[71]

Becher also lived briefly in Vermont with
Carl Zuckmayer, who had written a letter to Hermann
Kesten in 1940 on Becher's behalf,[72] in New York with
Dorothy Thompson,[73] and in New Foundland, New Jersey,
with Hubertus Prinz zu Löwenstein. Löwenstein's wife,

Helga, had been a classmate of Becher's, and New Yorker Novellen was actually started at Prince Löwenstein's
summer house in 1945.[74] During the week, Becher rose
late, spent the daylight hours in bars or on the
streets absorbing local color, and worked by night
on his plays and prose. Becher's wife, Dana, and
their son, Martin, lived with her parents several
blocks from Becher's flat.

During his years in New York, Becher published little to add to his literary reputation. One
poem and two essays appeared in Freies Deutschland,
helped into print by Becher's acquaintance with Egon
Erwin Kisch dating from a Roda Roda party in Berlin
in 1932.[75] "Die Seine fließt nicht mehr durch Paris.
Porträt eines literarischen Kriegsverbrechers" is a
strident indictment of Ernst Glaeser's shift from de-
tractor to ardent supporter of the Nazis.[76] A twenty-
three line poem "Ahnung und Versprechen (Am 29. August
1939 an Max Herrmann-Neisse)" copies the exile sentiments of longing and fidelity for a lost country in-
trinsic to Herrmann-Neisse's poetry.[77] One of Becher's
tributes to Roda Roda can be found in the third of
these publications, "Väterchen." None of these short
works deals with Becher's New York exile, except per-

haps "Väterchen," which conveys indirectly his indignation at the anonymity of Roda Roda's death.

Only twice did Becher publish in that most
famous American German exile newspaper, Aufbau. "Das
arme Licht" is a love poem, the candle a symbol of
the love that continues to burn amid the storms of
life.[78] The second publication "Ein 'innerer Emigrant'
Der Typ Frank Thiess" is a polemic against the man
who claimed to have invented the term "inner emigration."[79] The essay portrays Thiess, who chose to remain in Germany, as a narcissist and coward who was
only concerned with saving his middle-class lifestyle.
Although Becher's stand on the issue of inner emigration expressed in this essay could have been controversial and thus an influence on his reception in post-war
Germany, the fact that the essay appeared in Aufbau
helped limit its readership primarily to the American
Jewish exile community. That readership could only
have been sympathetic to Becher's anti-Thiess dia-
tribe, especially since Becher traces the racist elements in Thiess' work to prove that Thiess' true beliefs were in line with Nazi preaching and his later
protestations of inner emigration merely a convenient
loophole.

66

Aside from these few publications in _Freies Deutschland_ and _Aufbau_ plus a two-week engagement in 1947 as stage manager at the Ogunquit Summer Playhouse in Maine, Becher was without earned income during the war years in New York.

Becher remained in New York until 1948. He continued his association with _Das andere Deutschland_ in the immediate post-war years, but also began re-establishing himself in Europe. In 1946 Becher published his condemnation of the Nuremberg trials in DAD.[80] The two-part essay proposes that a tribunal of concentration camp inmates would have been quicker, more thorough, and more just in dealing with the Nazis after the war. Becher has harsh words for the United States' insistence on the semblance of impartiality and their failure to see the connection between Hitler's backers, the capitalists, and Hitler's henchmen, whom they put on trial. He concludes that the evil that Hitler represented was not destroyed by these trials; it lives on in the society that now supports the building of atomic bombs, and just as surely as the lowly of the world were the first to feel Hitler's impact, they will be the first victims of the cosmic bomb.

In a paeon to the works of his friend
Grosz entitled "George Grosz' 'Dreißigjähriger Krieg
gegen den Krieg,'"[81] Becher discusses the unifying
theme of Grosz's works: the portrayal of man's inhumanity to man as an integral part of capitalist
society. "Der Rosenkavalier"[82] is a chapter from
a work identified as "Die unsichtbaren Hügel" but
which we recognize as part of the novella "Der schwarze
Hut," the portrait of the rose-loving commandant of
Dachau.

In 1946 <u>Reise zum blauen Tag</u> was published,
with a line drawing by Grosz, by the Verlag Buchdruckerei Volksstimme in St. Gallen, Switzerland, a socialist publisher. The 80-page poetry volume was dedicated to Becher's mother and contained poems first published in the exile journals, the shorter Brasilian
romances and a few new poems.

After trying for four years to gain a foot-
hold in New York and seeing that his works were being
accepted in Austria and Switzerland, Becher decided
in 1948 to return to the country that had been his
first station of exile. His passport still identified
him as a citizen of Austria, but it remained to be
seen whether this world citizen would find a home
there.

68

FOOTNOTES

[1]Ernst Alker, Profile und Gestalten der
deutschen Literature nach 1914. Ed. Eugen Thurnher
(Stuttgart: Alfred Kröner, 1977), p. 229-230; Handbuch der deutschen Gegenwartsliteratur, Bd. I: A-K.
Ed. Hermann Kunisch (Munich: Nymphenburger Verlagshandlung, 1969), p. 92-93; Internationale Bibliographie
zur Geschichte der deutschen Literature, Teil II, 2
(Munich-Pullach and Berlin: Verlag Dokumentation,
1972), p. 108; Lexikon deutschsprachiger Schriftsteller, Bd. I. Ed. G. Albrecht et al. (Kronberg:
Scriptor Verlag, 1974), p. 55-56.

[2]Ulrich Becher, SIFF: Selektive Identifizierung von Freund und Feind (Zurich: Benziger,
1978), p. 141. Most of the biographical information
on Becher comes from this source.

[3]SIFF, p. 141.

[4]Tendenzen der Zwanziger Jahre, 15. Europäische Kunstausstellung Berlin 1977 (Berlin: Dietrich
Reimer Verlag, 1977).

Wolf von Eckardt and Sander L. Gilman, Ber-

tolt Brecht´s Berlin: A Scrapbook of the Twenties
(Garden City, N.Y.: Anchor Press, 1975).

John Willett, Art and Politics in the Weimar
Republic: The New Sobriety, 1917-1933 (New York:
Pantheon, 1978).

Kurt Sontheimer, "Weimar--ein deutsches
Kaleidoskop," in: Die deutsche Literatur in der
Weimarer Republik. Ed. Wolfgang Rothe (Stuttgart:
Reclam, 1974); Peter Gay, Weimar Culture: The Out-
sider as Insider (New York: Harper & Row, 1968);
Die sogenannten Zwanziger Jahre. Ed. Reinhold Grimm
and Jost Hermand (Bad Homburg: Gehlen, 1970); Bruno
E. Werner, "Literatur und Theater in den Zwanziger
Jahren," in: Die Zeit ohne Eigenschaften: Eine
Bilanz der zwanziger Jahre. Ed. Leonhard Reinisch
(Stuttgart: Kohlhammer, 1961).

[5]Ulrich Becher, Letter to Prof. H.-B.
Moeller, Austin, Texas, 24 March 1977, p. 4.

[6]Ulrich Becher, Der große Grosz und eine
große Zeit (Reinbek bei Hamburg: Rowohlt Taschenbuch-
handlung, 1962), 24 pp.

[7]Ulrich Becher, "Aus der Spielmacher-Schule
geplaudert," Spiele der Zeit II (Berlin (Ost): Aufbau Verlag, 1968), p. 312-313. Henceforth cited as

"Spielmacher-Schule."

[8]Becher claims in SIFF p. 85 personally to have seen classmates throw copies of Männer machen Fehler and Niemand on the 1933 fires, although these works were never officially blacklisted by the Nazis.

[9]Ibach went directly into exile; Lustig-Prean became the director of the Volksoper in Vienna. Becher does imply that both men were the victims of Nazi cultural policy (Becher, "Spielmacher-Schule," p. 312).

Although Switzerland was officially neutral, some police officials sympathetic to the Nazi cause exerted pressure on socialists like Lustig-Prean to maintain silence or leave as quickly as possible.

[10]Becher, "Spielmacher-Schule," pp. 314-315. A reference to an earlier fight is found in his letter to Prof. Moeller, 24 March 1977, p. 4.

[11]"Nach Nazibegriffen entsprach sein Rassen-status dem von Zuckmayer, John Heartfield oder Johann Strauß dem Älteren." Becher, SIFF, p. 143.

[12]Becher, "Spielmacher-Schule," p. 316.

[13]Ulrich Becher, "Einigt Euch um Gottes Wil-len," Europa, 13, (24 March 1936), n.p. and Das freie Deutschland: Mitteilungen der deutschen Freiheits-

bibliothek (Paris) 1936, No. 12, n.p. and Deutsche

Volkszeitung I, No. 4.

[14]Becher, "Spielmacher-Schule," p. 316.

[15]Robert E. Cazden, German Exile Literature

in America 1933-1950 A History of the Free German

Press and Book Trade (Chicago: American Library

Association, 1970), p. 16, see footnote 32.

[16]SIFF, p. 41.

[17]Becher, SIFF, p. 144. Letters on behalf of

Becher´s emergency visa from Dr. Felix Pinner, former

editor of the Berliner Tageblatt, Princess Helga v.

Löwenstein, and Alexander Roda Roda can be found in

the Ulrich Becher Mappe in the Deutsche Bibliothek

Frankfurt. A further letter from Roda Roda to Princess

v. Löwenstein is contained in Nachlaß Prinz z. Löwen-

stein, No. 11/1, 13 March 1941, Institut für Zeit-

geschichte, Munich. I am indebted to IfZ for permis-

sion to peruse these materials.

[18]Ulrich Becher, Letter to Prof. H.-B. Moeller

Austin, Texas, 19 October 1976, p. 2.

[19]Ulrich Becher, Letter to Prof. H.-B.

Moeller, Austin, Texas, 19 October 1976, p. 2.

[20]Das andere Deutschland, 5, No. 54 (Sep-

tember 1942), 14.

72

[21]War as an imperialist capitalist plot is a typical leftist view, not the consensus of political scientists. See Joachim Radkau, Die deutsche Emigration in den USA (Dusseldorf: Bertelsmann, 1971), pp. 102-103.

[22]Ulrich Becher, "Drohlied der Erschlagenen," Das andere Deutschland, 5, No. 56 (November 1942), 21.

[23]Ulrich Becher, "Die sieben stummen Fragen," Das andere Deutschland, 5, No. 57 (December 1942), 19-20.

[24]Ulrich Becher, "Verhör eines Passlosen," Das andere Deutschland (Montevideo), 1, No. 1-2 (15 February 1944), 25-26.

[25]Ulrich Becher, "Zehn Jahre," Das andere Deutschland, 6, No. 60 (1 April 1943), 20-21.

[26]Ulrich Becher, "In der Alpenkatakombe," Das andere Deutschland, 6, No. 62 (1 April 1943), 6-9.

[27]Ulrich Becher, "Gefallene Kameraden der Freiheit," Das andere Deutschland, 6, No. 66 (1 June 1943), 1-6.

[28]Ulrich Becher, "Der große Grosz und eine große Zeit," Das andere Deutschland, 8, No. 83 (June 1944), 21-23; No. 84 (July 1944), 16-19; No. 85 (August 1944), 21-23; No. 86 (September 1944), 14-17.

[29]Ulrich Becher, "Ostersegen," Das andere Deutschland, 6, No. 63 (15 April 1943), 16.

[30]Ulrich Becher, "Krieg der Mirakel," Das andere Deutschland, 6, No. 69 (15 July 1943), 5-7.

[31]Ulrich Becher, "Abendländisches Gelübde," Das andere Deutschland, 7, No. 80-81 (April 1944), 12.

[32]Institut für Zeitgeschichte, Unpublished interview with Willy Keller of 5 October 1971, 5. I am indebted to the Insitut for permission to peruse these materials.

[33]Winfried Seelisch, "Das andere Deutschland. Eine politische Vereinigung deutscher Emigranten in Südamerika." Unpublished Diplomarbeit Otto-Suhr-Institut, p. 27. Henceforth cited as Seelisch.

[34]Seelisch, p. 37.

[35]Keller Interview, p. 1.

[36]"Spielmacher-Schule," p. 324.

[37]Keller Interview, pp. 4-5.

[38]Keller Interview, p. 6.

[39]Keller Interview, p. 7.

[40]Keller Interview, p. 8.

[41]Keller Interview, p. 8.

[42]M. Kossok, "Sonderauftrag Südamerika," in Lateinamerika zwischen Emanzipation und Imperial-

ismus ed. W. Markow (Berlin: Akademie Verlag, 1961),
p. 235.

[43]Seelisch, pp. 11-12. See also: Hugo
Fernández Artucio, The Nazi Underground in South
America (New York: Farrar & Rinehart, 1942), p. 51.

[44]Seelisch, pp. 18-19.

[45]Keller Interview, p. 10.

[46]Keller Interview, pp. 3-4.

[47]Susan Eisenberg-Bach, "French and German
Writers in Exile in Brazil: Reception and Translations," to be published in A Comparative View of European Exiles and Latin America ed. H.-B. Moeller, pp.
462-467.

[48]Eisenberg-Bach, pp. 471-472.

[49]Ulrich Becher, Letter to Prof. H.-B.
Moeller, Austin, Texas, 19 October 1976, p. 4.

[50]Ulrich Becher, Letter to Prof. H.-B.
Moeller, Austin, Texas, 19 October 1976, p. 2.

[51]Ulrich Becher, Letter to Prof. H.-B.
Moeller, Austin, Texas, 19 October 1976, p. 2.

[52]Karl Krowlow, "Dichtung im Banne der
Exotik" Saarbrücker Zeitung, 8/9 September 1962,
n.p. and Harry Neumann, "Wer im Dschungel singt:
Die Romanzen des Dramatikers Ulrich Becher" Saar-

brücker Zeitung, 16 June 1962, n.p.

[53]Ulrich Becher, Brasilianischer Romanzero (Hamburg: Rowohlt Verlag, 1962), p. 10-11.

[54]Ulrich Becher, "Väterchen," Freies/Neues Deutschland, 4, No. 12 (November/December 1945), 55.

[55]Ulrich Becher, Letter to Prof. H.-B. Moeller, Austin, Texas, 23 August 1976, p. 2 and in "Väterchen," p. 55.

[56]Ulrich Becher, Letter to Prof. H.-B. Moeller, Austin, Texas, 24 March 1977, p. 1.

[57]Ulrich Becher, Letter to Prof. H.-B. Moeller, Austin, Texas, 24 March 1977, p. 1.

[58]Letters on behalf of Becher's application for an Emergency Visa by Alexander Roda Roda and Helga v. Löwenstein. Ulrich Becher File, Deutsche Bibliothek, Frankfurt. I am indebted to the Deutsche Bibliothek for permission to peruse these materials.

[59]A similar response is noted by L. L. Matthias, another German exile whose works are critical of the United States. He calls his years in Latin America "von entscheidender Bedeutung" for his opinion. L. L. Matthias, Die Kehrseite der USA (Hamburg: Rowohlt, 1964), p. 7.

[60]Cazden, pp. 137-138. Cazden credits Hermann

Kesten with this quote.

[61]The founders of Aurora included Ernst Bloch, Bertolt Brecht, Ferdinand Bruckner, Alfred Döblin, Leon Feuchtwanger, O. M. Graf, Heinrich Mann, Berthold Viertel, Ernst Waldinger, F. C. Weiskopf, as well as Wieland Herzfelde. See Cazden, p. 129, footnote 56.

[62]Ulrich Becher, Letter to Prof. H.-B. Moeller, Austin, Texas, 3 June 1978, p. 1.

[63]Ulrich Becher, Letter to Prof. H.-B. Moeller, Austin, Texas, 24 March 1977, p. 5.

[64]Ulrich Becher, "Junge deutsche Dichter für Aufhörer" Weltwoche (Zurich), No. 1609 (11 September 1964), pp. 25 and 29. Becher refers to this article in his letter to Prof. Moeller, 24 March 1977, p. 5.

[65]Ulrich Becher, Letter to Prof. H.-B. Moeller, Austin, Texas, 24 March 1977, p. 4.

[66]Ulrich Becher, Letter to Prof. H.-B. Moeller, Austin, Texas, 24 March 1977, p. 6.

[67]Ulrich Becher, Letter to Prof. H.-B. Moeller, Austin, Texas, 24 March 1977, p. 11.

[68]Ulrich Becher, Letter and questionnaire to Prof. H.-B. Moeller, Austin, Texas, 19 October 1976, p. 2.

[69] Ulrich Becher, Der große Grosz, p. 18.

[70] Cazden, pp. 77-78.

[71] Ulrich Becher, Das Profil (Reinbek bei Hamburg: Rowohlt Taschenbuch Verlag, 1973); Ulrich Becher, New Yorker Novellen (Zurich: Benziger, 1974); Ulrich Becher, "Happy End," Männer machen Fehler (Reinbeck bei Hamburg: Rowohlt Taschenbuch Verlag, 1970).

[72] "Zuckmayer to Kesten, 3. Oktober 1940," Hermann Kesten, Deutsche Literatur im Exil. Briefe europäischer Autoren 1933-1949 (Munich: Verlag Kurt Desch, 1964), pp. 156-157.

[73] Ulrich Becher, Personal interview with Nancy Zeller, 17 September 1978.

[74] Dedication to 1969 Aufbau-Verlag edition of New Yorker Novellen; Letter from Becher to Helga v. Löwenstein of 19 August 1945 in Nachlaß or file of posthumous papers of Prinz z. Löwenstein No. 79, Series 1 (Munich: Institut für Zeitgeschichte), n.p.

[75] Ulrich Becher, Letter and questionnaire to Prof. H.-B. Moeller, Austin, Texas, 19 October 1976, p. 2.

[76] Ulrich Becher, "Die Seine fließt nicht

durch Paris. Porträt eines literarischen Kriegsverbrechers," Freies/Neues Deutschland, 3, No. 8
(July 1944), 27-28.

[77]Ulrich Becher, "Ahnung und Versprechen
(Am 29. August 1939 an Max Hermann-Neisse)" Freies/
Neues Deutschland, 4, No. 10 (September 1945), 21.

[78]Ulrich Becher, "Das arme Licht," Aufbau
(NY), 4, No. 1 (5 Januar 1945), 20.

[79]Ulrich Becher, "Ein 'innerer Emigrant':
Der Typ Frank Thiess" Aufbau (NY), 11, No. 47 (23
November 1945), 6.

[80]Ulrich Becher, "Ein Nachwort zum Nürnberger Prozess" Das andere Deutschland, 8, No. 131
(1 December 1946), 6-8, and No. 132 (15 December
1946), 8-9.

[81]Ulrich Becher, "George Grosz' 'Dreißigjähriger Krieg gegen den Krieg,'" Das andere Deutschland, 9, No. 133 (1 January 1947), 14-15.

[82]Ulrich Becher, "Der Rosenkavalier," Das
andere Deutschland, 9, No. 152 (15 October 1947),
12-14.

Chapter III:

Post-1944 Biography and Reception

It was the opportunity to return to his
home continent, to a German-language country, to
participate in the reconstruction of German culture,
to gain an audience for his works, and to put an end
to his unemployment and the other miserable conditions of exile that caused Becher to leave New York
in 1948.

The book version of his play, Bockerer, was
published in 1947 by the Universitätsbuchhandlung
A. Sexl in Vienna. Because the play was being produced in Vienna in 1948, Becher decided to return to
Europe. He had written the play in 1946 in New York
jointly with Vienna-born actor Peter Preses: its
origins go back, however, to anecdotes Preses told
in his Zurich exile in the late 1930s about a butcher
Preses knew personally who tried to resist Nazism.
Among Preses' listeners were Becher and Friedrich
Torberg (Kantor Berg). Torberg allegedly later turned Preses' anecdotes into short stories.[1] Preses re-

quested that Becher help him write a play in the form
of a Volksstück based on the life of this one-man anti-
Nazi party. Because established theaters had refused
the play, Bockerer opened in late 1948 under the
direction of Günther Haenel with Fritz Imhoff in
the title role at the Neues Theater in der Scala,
a new theater in Vienna initiated by the Austrian
Communist Party. Imhoff, an operetta star, established himself overnight as a great folk actor and report-
edly considered Bockerer the greatest role of his
life.[2] The play had eighty performances plus a tour,
a feat in post-war theater history equaled only by
Zuckmayer's Des Teufels General. Heinrich Mann and
Robert Neumann predicted that Becher's play would
triumph in Germany; but although several theaters and
prominent actors expressed a desire to produce the
play, the Vienna production remained the sole stage
version until 1963.[3] Bockerer was seen by many critics as a response to the Qualtinger play Herr Karl,
which blamed middle class Mitläufer for the Nazi
take-over of Austria and thus offended many influential people in post-war Austria. In contrast,
Becher's Bockerer is a model of passive resistance.
The long run of the play indicates its appeal to

Austrian audiences. Yet, the very qualities that endeared it to the Viennese opened the play to West
German charges of whitewashing the Austrian record of
support for the Nazis. However, neither this criticism
nor the fact that the play is written in dialect fully
explain the reluctance of German and Swiss theaters
to present Bockerer.

Factors contributing to the play's neglect
are to be found in extra-literary events. First of
all, there was a general tendency in Central Europe,
not only in literature but in all fields, to deni-
grate or even reject the potential contribution of
the returning exiles. In politics this was evident
in the career of Willy Brandt. Literary exiles often
chose to avoid returning to Germany for this very
reason. In addition, in the case of Becher, the return was rather late, forcing him to compete with those
who had decided to come back earlier and had already
reestablished themselves. The tenor of the post-war
theater had been set by Zuckmayer with his Des Teufels General and by Merz-Qualtinger with Herr Karl.
In the critiques Bockerer is compared to these more
famous earlier plays, as well as to Brecht's Schwejk
im Zweiten Weltkrieg, which was produced after Bock-

erer. Critics find Bockerer superfluous, arguing
that its themes are similar and better expressed in
the other plays. In addition, some of the most influential post-war critical organs were headed by
people whose political affiliations implied opposition to the themes of Becher's works.

One of these critical organs was the CIA-
supported Forum, published by Friedrich Torberg.
Torberg had little reason to present a favorable
picture of Ulrich Becher. In the New York courts
he had sued Becher, Preses and their publisher,
Berthold Viertel of the Austro-American Tribune,
for plagiarism after the initial production of
Bockerer, claiming the duo had based their play on
his short stories. Torberg was unable to win the
case. According to Becher, however, Torberg proved
victorious in his personal war against his adversary
by using his journal successfully to ban Becher's
plays from Austrian stages.[4] Following the original
production of Bockerer in 1948, performances of
Becher's plays in Austria have indeed been rare.
Bockerer was not performed in Austria again until
1963 when Österreichischer Rundfunk broadcast a new
television production with Fritz Muliar in the title

role. This production received the highest rating
of six on a public opinion survey to rate Österreichischer Rundfunk television plays, and it was subse-
quently broadcast in West Germany by Zweites Deutsches
Fernsehen.[5] The same year Walter Pohl, of the Basle
Stadttheater, directed a brief production of Bockerer
at the Landestheater in Tübingen, a theater which
had a moderately leftist political orientation at
that time.[6] Due to the late 1970s interest in the
Hitler era, as evidenced by the success in Germany
of the American television series "Holocaust," Bockerer and Becher have experienced renewed attention.
The revival of Bockerer by the Nationaltheater in
Mannheim under the direction of Jürgen Bosse and with
Adolf Laimböck in the title role opened in October,
1978, and ran through most of 1979. In April, 1980,
Bockerer finally returned to Vienna with the Volkstheater production directed by Dietmar Pflegerl. The
recent productions of Bockerer have proven so successful that one of the best known directors in Germany,
Boy Gobert of Berlin's Schiller Theater, has taken an
option on the play for the 1981/82 season.

      Bockerer tells the story of the seven years
of Hitler's thousand year Reich in Austria from the

Nazi takeover in 1938 to liberation in 1945 as seen
through the eyes of Karl Bockerer, a middle-class
butcher and the embodiment of Viennese charm and
wit. Becher shows how an individual might have
survived the horrors and resisted the fascism of
Hitler's Reich by using his wit, humor, and, when
necessary, physical strength to combat its tyranny.
He depicts the ordinary Austrian as possessing these
very qualities.

Although a collaborative effort, Bockerer
contains many of the themes and techniques developed
at greater length in Becher's later works. Throughout,
music is used to accentuate the plot. Bockerer re-
peatedly whistles the "Radetzky March," a technique
that helps identify him with Austria. Hitler's birthday (which also happens to be Bockerer's) is being
celebrated with a parade, trumpets, drums, and the
"Horst Wessel Lied." This martial music threatens
to drown out the quiet Viennese folk tune that Bockerer and his friend Hatzinger are singing to the
accompaniment of an accordion. As the parade passes
by, the folk song reasserts itself with greater authority, representing the eventual triumph of the
Austrian people over its foreign fascist leaders.[7]

Later in the play, Bockerer refuses to play "Wir
fahren gegen England":

> Des is ja ganz gefehlt. Schau, der Rosen-
> blatt is nach Amerika gfahrn, du fahrst nach
> Rußland; der einzige, der was in letzter
> Zeit nach England is, war der Heß, and der
> is net gfahrn, sondern gflogn. Glaub mer´s,
> Bua, ´s is scho besser, wenn mer dir a
> Weanerlied aufspieln zum Abschied. (115)

The character Hatzinger, never without his accordion
and always prepared to give forth with an Austrian
folk song, is a direct descendant of "der liebe
Augustin," who represents the Austrian people´s
powers of survival. Becher/Preses even make this
connection directly after Hatzinger survives the
bombing of his apartment building, but they extend
the comparison to Bockerer as well, and by implication to the Austrian people:

> Bockerer: D´Leut verreckn wie d´fliagn,
>   und der Herr Hatzinger stolziert um-
>   anander wie der liebe Augustin auf der
>   Pestgrubn, mit der Musi in der Hand.
> Hatzinger: (selbstgefällig) Na ja. Er
>   hat´s ja auch überstandn, der liebe
>   Augustin. Wie-r-i.
> Bockerer: Erschtens amal ham mer´s no
>   net überstandn, d´Pest. Und zweitens,
>   wann aaner der liebe Augustin hier is,
>   so bin i´s! (149)

As he did in his exile essay "Gefallene

Kamaraden der Freiheit," Becher also makes the connection between fascism and physical illness. Bockerer has developed a tumor that is being treated
with radiation. The tumor is located in the very
spot where his stormtrooper son had clubbed him with
a "Totschläger," and ironically because of the in-
jury, Bockerer is unable to give the Hitler salute
(122). This is an early example of the connection
Becher makes between fascism and cancer, which
will become a central motif in later works.

The entire play is, of course, a political
statement by example. Becher prefers to show the
effects of politics on the lives of individuals
rather than make openly political statements. Thus
it is significant that most of the play's explicit
political commentary occurs during the three bar-
room scenes. Here, as in other works, Becher's
"heilige Trinker" have the freedom of intoxication
with which to express their beliefs more eloquently
than they would in a sober condition. It is appropriate, too, that Becher uses the antithesis of
Nazi "Zucht und Ordnung," a drinker, to express his
views. The railroad man, Hermann, proclaims his communism thus:

> Sie sind ja beide anständige Menschen,
> aber im Grunde genommen, muß man heute mehr
> sein als ein anständiger Mensch . . . Einer
> allein kann's net dermachn. So wird sich
> nix ändern in dera Kasern, in der mir jetz
> lebn. Damit's anders wird, müssen mir mehr
> sein wia einer allaan. Viele, hunderte,
> tausende. Und a jeder muß imstand sein,
> alles zu riskiern. Alles. 's Tarockspiel,
> 's Kaffeehaus, d'Gmüatlichkeit, d'Freiheit
> und am End no--'s Leben . . . (46)

It is in a bar that Bockerer's son learns the truth
about the Nazi extermination squads in Poland where
he is headed. And it is in a bar that Bockerer gives
a cogent answer to the common excuse for Nazi crimes,
that those who committed them were "only following
orders":

> Den Schmäh kenn i. Führer befiehl, wir
> folgen dir! Sixt ja, wo er's hingführt
> hat! Am Urahl! Zum Abschlachten hat er
> s' gführt, der Herr Schicklgruber. Was
> haaßt denn, er is net gfragt wordn? A
> jeder is gfragt wordn. (119)

With these words Becher's protagonist denies that
surrendering one's conscience to another is a moral-
ly legitimate action. Everyone must face the moral
issue involved in the actions he takes.

We also see in Bockerer Becher's predilection for throwing together people of different backgrounds in public places. Here this is expressed

through the use of different German dialects. The
Nazis speak a Berlin dialect; the Austrians a Viennese dialect; and the refugees from the bombings
in other parts of Germany speak the dialects of
their region. Dr. Rosenblatt, on his return from
America, speaks an Americanized German.

Becher and Preses collaborated on yet
another play, again set in Vienna, but this time
in the seventeenth century, Der Pfeifer von Wien,
based on the legend of "der liebe Augustin."[8] This
play is the least politically oriented of all of
Becher's works. Thus it seems reasonable to assume
either that Preses' influence prevails here or that
the historical subject matter limited the political
implications. It is an attempt to portray

> die Zeitlosigkeit der Augustin-Figur als
> einer Art Symbol des ewigen Wieners. Ein-
> mal ist es die Pest, ein andermal der Krieg,
> vor dessen Hintergründen er sich abhebt.
> So, sollte man am Ende denken, wird es immer
> weiter gehen. Durch alle Zeiten hindurch.
> Bis auf die unserige.[9]

The 1950 Vienna Volkstheater production, under the
direction of Gustav Manker with Karl Skraup as the
piper, remains the only production of this play. However, it was used as the basis for a musical, Das

<u>Spiel vom lieben Augustin</u>, a version that Becher
rejects as a distortion of his original work.[10]

Although less engaged, many themes that can
be identified as Becher trademarks in <u>Bockerer</u> are
repeated in <u>Der Pfeiffer</u>. The entire play is set
in a bar; and the piper, forever drinking the innkeeper's best wine, becomes a saint or prophet to
the poor of Vienna. At one point, the piper extols
the virtues of wine:

> Der Wein ist ein Schlüssel zum Herzen, und
> man kann öfters mit dem Oktobersaft besser
> hinter die Wahrheit kommen, als der Scharf-
> richter mit seiner Folter. Der Wein macht,
> daß die Worte auf der Post reiten. Der Wein
> zieht den Vorhang auf, hinter dem manches
> Stückl verborgen liegt. (40-41)

and credits this quote to Abraham a Sancta Clara.
(41)

Another Becher theme is death, sometimes as
in <u>Bockerer</u> related to fascism, sometimes as the shad-
ow-side of life:

> Der Tod ist der endliche und letzte Arzt
> aller Schwach- und Krankheiten. Der Tod
> ist der Hafen, in den alle Menschen ein-
> laufen müssen. Der Tod ist gleich dem
> Schlaf. Der Tod ist der Widerhall des
> Lebens. Wie gelebt, so gestorben. (41)

And death has lessons for life. After climbing out

of the "Pestgrube," where he spent the night with corpses of various social position, the piper declares:

> Da ist mir das Sprüchel durch den Sinn:
> "Ob arm, ob reich/Im Tod alle gleich."
> Und ob man's eines Tags nicht bissel ab-
> ändern könnt: "Nicht arm und nicht reich/
> Im Leben alle gleich." (70)

Becher is also fascinated by the transitoriness of beauty, and we see in Pfeifer for the first time a character that will recur throughout his subsequent works, the fair-skinned reddish blond beauty who is always the first target of death.

Becher's solidarity with the downtrodden is another theme we find repeated in Pfeifer. To those who try to convince him of the need to change his rebellious ways, the piper replies:

> M-i-r? Was kann unsereinem schon viel mehr
> geschehn. Seit ich leb gehör ich zu den
> Schlechten Leuten und hab allerweil meinen
> Spass unterm Galgen gemacht. Taglöhner--
> Leerhäusler--Bettelmusikanten--Zigeuner,
> das Gesindel, das arme, war seinen Lebtag
> des Lebens nicht sicher. (86)

In addition to wine, and love of beautiful women, the piper must also have his music to survive. Again in this play music is a life force, expecially for the poor, and a symbol of the indomitable will of humans to survive.

The first of Becher´s independently authored plays was Samba, written in 1949 in Salzburg and produced in March, 1951, at the Theater in der Josefstadt, Vienna, under the direction of Franz Pfaudler.[11] The first German production took place in April, 1952, at Barlog´s Schloßparktheater in West Berlin with Ludwig Berger directing and Kaspar Neher as set designer. The Meiningen Theater introduced Ulrich Becher in the GDR with their production of Samba in December, 1954. While in the West discussion of Becher´s works was limited to journalistic newspaper critiques, a more scholarly treatment was written in the GDR after the Samba production. In fact, during the mid-1950s the dramas of Becher were almost alone among West German dramas to receive critical attention in the GDR.[12] This is especially remarkable given the official distrust of Westemigranten in the early years following the founding of the GDR.[13]

Drawing directly on his exile years in Brazil, Becher depicts the fate of a group of Europeans stranded in a decaying hotel in Brazil´s inter-

92

ior. There is an atmosphere of inactivity, resignation, despair, and hopelessness that only Kornau,
the young author, is able to overcome in the end by
insisting on his European humanist beliefs:

> Mein Vater: Berlin. Mama: Paris. Meine
> Frau: Wien, Bin ich nicht sehr Europa?
> . . . ich bin ungeheuer, ganz ungeheuer
> für das Leben. Hör zu, was ich heute nach-
> mittag geschrieben habe. "Das Leben eines
> einzigen unschuldigen griechischen Schaf-
> hirten ist mehr wert als alle Kunstwerke
> der Welt." (114-115)

By identifying his hero with Europe, Becher thus
holds out some hope for its recovery from the disease
of fascism.

Other characters in the play are not so
lucky; they are the indirect victims of the global
war. Monsieur Blaise dies of tuberculosis he contract-
ed "aus Protest gegen . . . La Paix de Munich" (67).
Hauptmann i.R. Franz Augustin, defender of the Austrian monarchy and last knight of the Occident, hangs
himself (like Ernst Toller) from his window sill
just before his arrest by the local police official,
Heredia. His crime has been the writing of letters
to various heads of state challenging them to duels
for what he sees as an affront to his honor and that
of the Hapsburg monarchy. Kornau's double, Parisius

("zwei Herzen und eine Seele," 119), is afraid to
risk his life and sinks deeper into the quagmire
of alcohol.

Samba mirrors Brazilian social and political conditions described by Becher in his essays
for Das andere Deutschland. In Heredia we see the
fascist Brazilian officialdom:

> Ordnung muß sei! E bißje militärisch Schliff
> un Schnick duut dene nix schade. Gucke Sie
> den Hitler an. E Herrevolk müsse mir aus
> dene Strunsköpp machen, e lateinisch Herre-
> volk! . . . Mei Vater war für de Kaiser
> Wilhelm, un ich bin für de Adolfo. (81-83)

Support for such sentiments comes, we learn, from
German plantation owners, emigrants from Wilhelminian
Germany, who bribe the officials for protection from
Brazil´s neutrality laws (62). The solidarity of
the exiles, whether monarchist or socialist, against
fascism is also evident in Augustin´s speech to Mana,
daughter of an Austrian army officer turned socialist:
"No, nix fier ungut, rot oder schwarzgelb, momentan
is uns beiden das Mal des Flichtlings auf die Stirn
gemeißelt" (72-73).

The social conditions in Brazil are pointed
out by Kornau in an attempt to justify his staying in
Brazil:

94

> Kornau: Man kann auch hier kämpfen.
> . . . Zum Beispiel dagegen, daß die Kin-
> der im Interior Blähbäuche haben vom
> ewigen Saubohnenfraß. Dagegen, daß die
> Säuglingssterblichkeit fünfzig Prozent
> beträgt. Dagegen, daß es ein paar viel
> zu Reiche gibt und Millionen von viel zu
> Armen. . . . Dagegen, daß siebzig Pro-
> zent der Bevölkerung verseucht sind.
> (102)

Two of the contagions in Brazil were present in earlier Becher works, alcohol and music,
narcotics of the poor against their intolerable
living conditions and tools of the powerful to provide a non-political outlet for frustrations of the
poor. Parisius succumbs to alcohol, while Kornau,
the genius artist, gains insight and inspiration
from intoxication (79-80). However, not even Kornau
can withstand the power of the samba, Brazil's
national dance. Everyone is overcome by its rhythms:
Mana and Kornau on their wedding day, Heredia while
he is arresting Augustin, the policeman standing
guard at the foot of the stairs, the innkeeper while
writing out a bill, and even the pall bearers:

> Seht Ihr's nicht. Sie können sich dem
> Sambagedudel nicht entziehen. Es elek-
> trisiert sie . . . Seht Ihr's jetzt--ja?
> Sie tanzen! (98)

Strongest evidence for the life-affirming power of

negro music is found in the "Vorspiel bei geschlossen-
em Vorhang" at the beginning of Samba. With music
alone, Becher suggests the history of Nazi conquest
at the beginning of World War II and then his exile
in Brazil:

> Anfang der polnischen Nationalhymne, drein
> jäh der Badenweiler Marsch dröhnt, das Polen-
> lied überschmetternd. Anfänge der norweg-
> ischen, dänischen, holländischen, belgischen
> Hymne, jedesmal vom Badenweiler Marsch über-
> schmettert. Die Marseillaise klingt auf,
> möchte sich behaupten, erstickt unversehens
> im gewaltig schmetternden, kesselpaukenden
> Marsch. Der rückt fort, und während er
> ferner und ferner dröhnt, kommt ein leicht-
> hüpfig verspielter Samba auf, jener brasil-
> ianische Volkstanz, eigentümlich mitreissend,
> reizvoll gemischt aus iberischen Volksweisen
> und dem Ritualgetön afrikanischer Negerstämme.
> Nach einigen Takten schweigt der zierlich
> pikkoloflötende gitarrende, von Flaschen-
> kürbisrasseln begleitet Samba. (9)

As depicted in the play, Becher uses the samba to
symbolize the untapped power and vitality of the
Brazilian people as well as to illustrate the reasons
for their powerlessness. Becher also uses music in
Samba in much the same way American films use background music, to intensify the action. After Kornau
returns from a visit to the Condessa, intoxicated by
her liquor, his newfound knowledge of the Makumba
cult, and the terrible beauty of the Brazilian jungle,

he explains his experience to Mana to the strains
of Tschaikovsky's B flat minor concerto. The background music intensifies his portrayal to the point
of melodrama (79). In the final scene of the play,
instead of samba music, everyone is whistling a German song "Die Vöglein im Walde . . .," emphasizing
Kornau's decision to leave Brazil to fight against
fascism (104-105).

In Samba Becher's social commentary is not
as central to the action of the play as was the case
with Niemand, where the characters were merely rep-
resentatives of their social class. The characters
in Samba are realistically drawn and well-motivated
individuals who also have views typical of their
social class. Against the historical backdrop of
World War II Brazil, Becher presents real people with
personal histories in order to examine the predica-
ment of European exiles caught between relief at having escaped and guilt at not taking an active part
in the opposition of Hitler. This consistent realism
manifests itself in Becher's style, which is much
more descriptive than the luxuriant verse of Bra-
zilianischer Romanzero. The Hotel Duque de Caxias,
the setting for the entire play, is described down

to the stuffing in the chairs and the mildew spots
on the walls; each of the characters, down to the
part in their hair. Before each act and each scene
and interspersed throughout the play we find details
of the action and clues to motivation. As in Bockerer this attention to detail extends to the language spoken by the characters. Blaise, the French-
man, nasalizes his German and uses French word order
and short vowels. Ernesto speaks a Berlin dialect
and Augustin the flowery, polite German of Austrian
aristocrats. Throughout the play are flourishes
of Portuguese and French.

The conflict of Samba, which is the central
conflict in most of Becher's work, centers around
Julius Kornau's shift from overriding concern with
his writing to his acceptance of personal responsibility in the fight against fascism. In the first
act, Kornau is glad to have escaped with his life and
his language: "Das ist beinahe das einzige, was ich
mir von drüben mitgenommen habe . . . die deutsche
Sprache" (39). He wants to devote himself to his
novel and forget about the war: "Bin froh, daß ich
weg bin von drüben. Hab keine Sehnsucht nach Henkern. Hab keine Sehnsucht nach Bomben. Ich will
arbeiten" (51). The opposing viewpoint is represen-

ed by Parisius, who fought with Göring in World War
I: "Wächter im elfenbeinernen Turm. Werter Bruder
Antifaschist, mit Träumern wie Ihnen ist noch kein
Krieg gewonnen worden" (51).

Kornau develops doubts about his position
in the course of the second act and at one point ad-
mits to having a guilty conscience (97). Blaise,
representing the pacifist viewpoint, argues against
Kornau's growing inclination to become personally
involved in the war: "Iesch 'abbe niescht Lust, zu
sterbän wie mein Vat'r im Feuär und Dreck. Niescht
einmal pour la liberté" (98).

By the final scene of the play, Kornau has
come to believe that art and the passivity of con-
templation cannot substitute for active political engagement. But it is not entirely clear that Kornau
has only thoughts for his fellow man: "Ich bin's
meiner spätern A-r-b-e-i-t schuldig. Wissen vom
wirklichen Leben, mehr als die andern! Mit Nur-
Phantasie schafft man Zerrbildern. So geh ich denn
lang nicht zuletzt wegen der lieben Wahrheit" (121).
It is a Heminwayesque attitude to the position of
the artist in society. While it is one possible solution to the conflict, one Becher found hard to reject

as evidenced by its recurrence in later works, it
is not the road Becher himself took. Other characters in Samba see Kornau as the victim of mis-
directed idealism and mobid curiosity, whose contribution to the defeat of fascism will be minimal and
suicidal. Mana, who feels Kornau is deceiving himself about his chances for survival, only replies
to his assertions that he will return, "Armer Juli"
(121). Samba clearly reflects the moral dilemma
that Becher, indeed most exile artists, had to face.

But Becher does not give us a clear answer
to the question of the proper form of political
engagement. Even though Kornau protests his hatred
of war to the very end, he undertakes, out of his
deep antifascist views, a dangerous underground mission, giving up a relatively secure, if enervating,
life with Mana, throwing away personal happiness,
in Mana's view, just to prove his manhood. This
theme recurs in Becher's next play, Feuerwasser as
well, but the conflict finds a somewhat different
resolution there.

Whereas Samba depicted the plight of Hitler exiles in Brazil, Feuerwasser, 1951, deals with
pre-World War II emigrants (including some non-Ger-

mans) who, for the most part, have become natural-
ized citizens. Feuerwasser is thus not directly
autobiographical, although some of the characters
are based on people Becher knew in New York.

> Wenn ich nachts nach der BOCKERER-Arbeit
> von P. Preses Wohnung zu meinem Penthouse-
> Kämmerlein West 86. Street beim River-
> side Drive zurückwanderte, kehrte ich
> stets bei CHARLIE BROWN (nicht in York-
> ville sondern Columbus Ave., ´Lucky Horse
> Shoe INN´) ein. Mein Spiel FEUERWASSER
> ist ein Epitaph auf den Barkeeper, der einer
> meiner besten Freunde wurde.[14]

Other characters based on real people are Laan von
Dorpe, priest turned drunkard, Polachek, the noble
tramp, and Charlie Brown´s southern belle wife, Rosalind.

Feuerwasser is set in the post-war year
1946, but war and its close relations, death and
murder, are still Becher´s subject matter, dealt
with this time less allegorically than in Niemand.
As in Samba, realism is achieved through detailed
descriptions of character and setting, taking up the
first five pages of the play. The Yorkville bar
setting again motivates the realistic mixture of German dialects, French, and English, plus assorted
curses and toasts in more exotic tongues. By re-

moving the autobiographical concern for the position
of the exile artist in society, Becher can concentrate on more universal questions.

The basic question posed by Becher in
Feuerwasser is: What can a socially engaged individual do in a world filled with injustice, ex-
ploitation and institutionalized violence to improve
the human condition? Becher's answer lies in his
political philosophy, which, on this point, shows
the influence of Nietzsche. Most individuals can do
little to affect the world around them in any significant sense. They are simply too weak to confront
the world. But Becher's strong individuals, like
Nietzsche's Übermensch, have the ability to bring
visible improvements to the world, even if it sometimes requires their fullest self-sacrifice. In contrast to Nietzsche, however, Becher is concerned that
this ability be directed towards improvement of the
lot of those who are weaker, rather than a rejection
of the weak and their values. In effect Becher has
taken the late nineteenth century's view of history,
as expressed in the works of Carlyle and Nietzsche,
regarding the role played by strong individuals in
the historical process and superimposed it on his

humanitarian, socialist concerns. The result is an
uncomfortable synthesis.

Feuerwasser presents this amalgamated political philosophy in graphic form. The war has
brought violence back to the streets of America;
jobless veterans, grown accustomed to daily killing,
find peace too boring.[15] Charlie Brown, barkeeper
of Gay Moose Head Tavern, ex-boxer, Lincoln-Brigade
member in Spain, keeps order with ironic banter,
reasoning, threats, or, if need be, with his fists,
i.e., any form of non-lethal persuasion. However,
when Sepp O´Brian, called Hund, robs Charlie´s
friend, Charlie hits Hund over the head with a
metal-based bottle, fully intending to kill him.
Charlie despises war, even though he fought in two
wars; but he would not hesitate to murder in defense
of his friends. To do away with this apparent con-
tradiction, Becher distinguishes between the imperson-
al, indiscriminate, and institutionalized killing
called war and personal violence by an individual
willing to take full responsibility for his act.
That Becher is not quite comfortable with this distinction is shown by the ending of the play: Charlie
does not actually kill Hund but arranges to have the

police catch him in the act of killing Charlie.
Becher´s message is that the individual must be willing to sacrifice everything, even his own life, for
the betterment of society, but only after trying
everything else.

Becher also differentiates between the
criminality of Hund and that of the petty criminals
in the bar. For Charlie, Becher´s spokesman in this
play, Hund represents the worst kind of criminal
because he turns murder into business. "Er setzt
dir auch wegen [sic] paar Talern das Messer an die
Kehle" (151). Moreover, Hund betrays his class by
stealing from the poor: "Du warst ein unheiliger
Räuber. Du nahmst den Armen und gabst den Reichen.
Den Einflußreichen, die du bestachst" (273). For
the same reason, lack of class solidarity, Charlie
condemns Joe for stealing Nelly´s purse, but excuses
his own theft from his employer on the grounds that
his employer can afford the loss and besides, he
is only following the rules of capitalism:

> Zur Geschäftspraxis dieser Händlerwelt
> gehört die Beutelschneiderei genauso wie
> die Heuchelei, die Unbarmherzigkeit, die
> Marktschreierei, das Organisationstalent
> und die Knickrigkeit. (214)

104

Charlie also condemns the political views
represented by Hund: "fromm faschistisch wie gewisse
Irenkreise hier; glühender Bewunderer von Pater Cough-
lin und Caudillo Franco" (151-152). A description
of Hund's crimes suggests a comparison with the mass
killings of Jews by the Nazis:

> Dein ganzes Leben ist eine Kette von Un-
> taten gewesen . . . Erpressung, Bestechung,
> Ausbeutung, Vergewaltigung, Verstümmlung,
> Morddrohung--und Mord. Am laufenden Band.
> (273)

And what makes Hund (and Nazism) even more dangerous is
the fact that he considers himself to be a "good"
man:

> die selbstgerechten frommen Gangsters.
> Die biedermännischen Amokläufer, die fort-
> gesetzt den Segen des Allmächtigen auf ihre
> Greueltaten runterbeschwören. (275)

And finally Hund is seen as "der Feind an sich" (289),
symbol of everything worth destroying in society.

Becher gives another solution to the problem of living in modern society, a solution more
suitable for ordinary mortals, not capable of making
the same sacrifice as the "Übermensch" or "Halbgott,"
Charlie (141). That solution is alcohol, Feuerwasser,
white man's poison for the Indians. In his literary

portrait of Becher, Arnold Künzli equates alcoholic

intoxication with the Dionysian:

> . . . der Rausch ist bei Becher--so unheim-
> lich in seinen ganzen Werken auch immer ge-
> bechert wird--nie ein Besäufnis um seiner
> selbst willen, sondern immer ein Mittel,
> in einer gottlosen Welt Schönheit, in einer
> stupiden Welt die Weisheit, in einer lang-
> weiligen Welt den Sinn zu finden.[16]

In Becher's works music, especially folk

music or primitive beats such as the samba, jazz, or

boogie woogie, is alcohol's constant companion, it-

self an intoxicant, but one that reveals the potential

vitality of the poor. In Feuerwasser, as well as in

Becher's other New York bar settings, a gaudily lit

jukebox provides the ubiquitous rhythms. There is

also at least one seduction scene to further enhance

the Dionysian elements.

For the poor, firewater, music, and sex

are a replacement for the Christian God and offer

even more comfort, because they are at the same time

a confirmation of life (219). However, in another

typically Expressionist theme, only a chosen few--

Charlie in Feuerwasser or Kornau in Samba--gain in-

sight or inspiration from their confrontations with

the Dionysian. Weaker souls--Parisius in Samba or

106

the priest in Feuerwasser--are consumed by its fires and end in insanity or death. These two opposing types of effects produce an ambiguity in Becher's works. The Nietzschean Becher tolerates intoxication and sensuality as a means to an artistic end. The socialist Becher condemns intoxication and sensuality as "opiates of the masses," and the title of the play itself calls to mind the early colonist's manipulation of the Indians by means of alcohol. The island of Manhattan is one example of such abuse; its low price is attributed to the drunken condition of the Indians who sold it (250).

> O Manhattan, billig erworbenes Eiland und
> dennoch teuer erkauft;/Insel der Unseligen,
> bevölkert von Millionen Feuerwasserköpfen/
> Aus Feuerwasser bist du geworden/In Feuer-
> wasser wirst du vergehen . . . (250-251)

By 1951 when Feuerwasser was written, other characteristics of an Ulrich Becher play had become standardized. The characters: displaced persons in the waiting rooms of fate; the message: a pugnacious humanism; the themes: the two-sided effects of al- cohol, music, and sex on man the animal, the politi- cal responsibility of individuals, and the contagious effects of war on society.

Feuerwasser was Becher's fourth play and
the original productions were better received versions of these themes. It was first performed in
November, 1952, at the Deutsches Theater in Göttingen
under the direction of Heinz Hilpert with Carl Rad-
datz as Charlie and Win Kristin, Carl Zuckmayer's
daughter, as Charlie's wife, Rosalind.[17] Kurt Meisel
played Charlie in the Austrian production at the
Volkstheater of Vienna in April, 1954. Fritz Wisten
directed the DDR production at the Volksbühne Berlin in 1955 in which Franz Kutschera played the lead.
A film version of Feuerwasser, originally planned by
the West German branch of Columbia, was stopped indirectly by Columbia boss Harry Cohn.[18] Only in
July, 1978, did Zweites deutsches Fernsehen broadcast a slightly shortened version, screenplay by
Karl Wittlinger, with Wolfgang Staudte directing and
starring Hans-Helmut Dickow as Charlie and Helmut
Qualtinger as Hund.

Samba and Feuerwasser were published together with a third play, Die Kleinen und die Grossen,
as Spiele der Zeit in 1957 simultaneously by Rowohlt
and Aufbau Verlag. Die Kleinen und die Grossen, a
fantasy dealing with the atomic age, was never pro-

108

duced and therefore did not receive the same kind
of reception as the other plays. However, it was
discussed in the GDR by Werner Mittenzwei along with
three other West German plays, as an example of the
antiatomic movement of the late 1950s.[19] Mittenzwei
considers Die Kleinen und die Grossen the best of
these plays because it focuses on the role of the
common man, rather than on that of the illustrious
scientist, in the fight for peace. He also finds the
form of this play, i.e. the "Zauberposse," suitable
for the subject matter, because it allows a connection to be made between past and present humanitarians
by making plausible the anachronistic introduction
on stage of historical characters, such as Columbus
or Spinoza.[20]

In spite of Mittenzwei's positive evaluation, Die Kleinen und die Grossen aroused no other
critical interest even in the GDR at the time of its
appearance.[21] This lack of interest can best be explained by the history of thaws and frosts in East-
West relations and the corresponding dogmatism in
the interpretation of Marxist cultural ideology. The
early "Volksfront" years with their emphasis on cooperation by people of various political views did not

really affect Becher, who had returned as the fact of a divided Germany was being institutionalized. During the time Becher's plays were being produced in the GDR, i.e. 1954 and 1955, the antiformalism of socialist realism which began in 1949 was still the dominant critical mode. A brief thaw in 1956 allowed criticism of the existing GDR literature via introduction of Western models, but was followed by repressive measures in 1957, during which Wolfgang Harich, the editor of Aufbau was imprisoned. As will be seen later, these events coincided with the almost total cessation of Becher's reception in the GDR.

Thus the publication of Spiele der Zeit in 1957 is most likely a result of Becher's previous acceptance in 1954 and 1955, given impetus by the brief thaw of 1956. However, even this publication was not sufficient to insure continued acceptance. Mittenzwei's article in 1961 appeared at a time when West German drama was no longer welcome on GDR stages.[22] When the boycott was finally lifted in 1964, the theme of Die Kleinen und die Grossen was no longer en vogue and a new generation of West German playwrights was making its influence felt. Thus, the untimely publication of Die Kleinen und

die Grossen precluded its production in the GDR,
the only country which could conceivably have welcomed such a concept.

Aside from Samba and Feuerwasser the only
other Becher play produced in the GDR was Mademoiselle
Löwenzorn, written in 1949 after Becher saw the Basler Fasnacht.[23] The premiere in West Berlin's Schloßparktheater in March, 1954, was directed by Ludwig
Berger and starred Bertha Drews and Gisela May. Two
other productions of this play are recorded: the
East German production in June, 1955, in Leipzig's
Schauspielhaus (Director Rudi Kurz, with Lola Chlud
and Gerd Fürstenau) and in 1957 at the Stadttheater
in Basle (Director W. Duvoisin with Margrit Winter
as Mademoiselle Löwenzorn). This is the only one of
Becher's plays to be awarded a prize; in 1955 Becher
received a DM 3,000 prize from the German Theater
Society (Deutscher Bühnenverein) in Cologne for
Mademoiselle Löwenzorn. The play was first published in a Spanish translation by Mariano S. Luque in a
collection of modern German plays published in 1960
by Aguilar, Madrid, Teatro alemán contemporaneo,
alongside plays by Brecht, G. Weisenborn, Zuckmayer,
and Borchert. Finally, in 1968 Aufbau in East Ger-

many published a collection of Becher's plays entitled Spiele der Zeit II, containing Niemand, Makumba, and Mademoiselle Löwenzorn, and an essay on
the origins of these plays, "Aus der Spielmacher-
schule geplaudert."[24]

Becher calls Löwenzorn a "border play" and
means more than geographical borders; moral and historical "borders" are included:

> Es spielt an einer Dreiländerecke; ziem-
> lich kurz nach dem Ende einer ganz und gar
> kriminellen Epoche, 1933 bis 1945, an der
> Grenze der Jahrhundert-Halbzeit. Und es
> möge zeigen, daß nach Absolvierung der bis-
> lang kriminellsten Epoche der Geschichte alle
> durcheinandergeworfen sind und jeder be-
> waffnet ist, an die Grenze des Kriminellen
> gedrängt, ein potentieller Mörder oder
> Töter . . . (Spiele II, 320)

Before the curtain goes up, Mademoiselle Ziselin,
owner of the Hotel zum Löwenzorn in Basle, is shot
by someone in a cat costume during the "Morgenstreich,"
an early morning parade in carnival season. The solving of the crime is not, however, the focus of the
play. After an initial interrogation scene, the rest
of the play is a flashback that reveals the motivations each one of the characters could have had to
commit the crime. We learn that Ziselin's cousin,
the hairdresser Paupaule, is in need of money and,

112

as his cousin's last living relative, stands to in-
herit the Hotel Löwenzorn. Madame Nairobi has been
asked to leave the hotel, even though her sick child
needs to be close to a nearby clinic, because Ziselin
is jealous of her. Metzle the hunter and the wait-
ress Poldi, who has been fired for flirting, would
like to remove the obstacle to their love affair,
and that obstacle is Ziselin. The lady has managed
to alienate all of her guests with her tyrannical
behavior, her "Führernatur" (Spiele II, 243). Even
those who have no reason to kill her did have motivation to kill the person who was standing next to
her, the icehockey trainer, Lamm, and could thus
have accidently hit Ziselin. Dr. Till Ulen had lost
his wife and Nebelsteiner his peace of mind at Au-
schwitz where Lamm, alias Lämmers, had been a high-
ranking SS man. All of these persons had the potential to become murderers, and most of them justify
their intents by referring to the necessities of
wartime:

> Gemusäus: Entsprich es den Datsachen, daß
> Sie im Kriegsjahr Einundvierzig in den
> Bergen um Grenoble einen Angehörigen
> der Vichy-Miliz mit einer Bistole an-
> geschossen haben.
> Nairobi: Ja . . . Es war Krieg. Heißer
> Krieg.

Gemusäus: He nu, . . . hier jädenfalls
      scheint der heisse Krieg nicht auf-
gehört zu haben . . . (<u>Spiele II</u>, 288)

Thus, as in earlier plays, the murderousness
of war continues into peace. In the final scene
we learn who committed the crime, but not as the result of the painstaking investigations into the motivations of the characters. The servant, Domenico
Aprile, confesses in a letter to the police inspect-
or to the shooting of Mademoiselle Löwenzorn because
of her 30 years of insults: she told her guests
that he stank, like all Sicilians. Aprile has returned to Sicily to join a Mafia clan. From <u>Feuer-</u>
<u>wasser</u> we know Becher´s views on organized crime:
the Mafia is a peacetime relative of fascism.

What is important to Becher is not the
unraveling of the crime, but the fact that each of
the characters at Hotel Löwenzorn is capable of murder: as the inspector says, the hotel is "Ein W-e-
s-p-e-n-n-e-s-t. Justament, als wäre jädr mit einr
Waffe zur Welt gekommen, auch die Weibsbildr" (<u>Spiele</u>
<u>II</u>, 292). "Der ganze Stall voll verkappter Mörder"
(<u>Spiele II</u>, 304). The flashback technique removes
the emphasis from the crime to the motivating fac-

tors leading up to the crime. Having Aprile con-
fess to the shooting in a letter also helps to make
the solving of the shooting secondary, as does the
fact that in the final scene Mademoiselle Löwenzorn
is back at her switchboard issuing commands to a
new Sicilian servant just as if no shooting had
happened. The final scene is identical to the first
scene of the flashback: "das Fatum einer ewigen
Wiederkehr in der Diaspora unserer Zeit."[25] In
addition, Becher quotes Büchner's Woyzeck, another
play that examines the causes of crime.

The carnival setting in Mademoiselle Löwenzorn is seen somewhat differently by Becher than the
carnival in Samba:

> Ihr (Basler) Fasnachtskult . . . bietet ihnen
> alljährlich die explosive und purgative
> Möglichkeit, ihre . . . Vergangenheit im
> Wortsinn spielend zu bewältigen. . . . Weil
> sie einen nur drei Tage währenden militanten
> Monsterspuk zu spielen verstehn, haben sie
> sich erspart, den militanten Monsterspuk
> zweier Dreißigjahre-Kriege erleiden zu
> müssen. (Spiele II, 321)

Instead of being a narcotic of the masses and thus
a tool of the ruling class, carnival in Basle is an
outlet for warlike emotions, sublimated war. This
idea of the purgative aspects of play can be trans-

ferred to Becher's theory of drama, and has been
done so by Becher himself in the essay "Das Theater
--Die Welt." Here Becher defines theater as "ein
magisches Ablenkungsmanöver, das weglockte vom
Vernichten."[26] However, the Basle carnival seems to
have no effect on the residents of Hotel Löwenzorn.
Perhaps this is because the nature of war has changed:

> DER KRIEG, trotz seiner grausigen Kehr-
> seite, hatte nichts von der kosmischen
> Anonymität einer Atombombe oder eines Fern-
> raketengeschosses; er konnte als schillernder
> Pfau daherkommen, er konnte prunken und
> musizieren; selbst den Spuk belebten Farbe
> und Rhythmus (das waren noch Zeiten!).
> (Spiele II, 322)

The result of modern technology is a cosmic fear with
which we humans are unprepared to deal. According to
Ulen, "das Atomspaltungsirresein tyrannisiert die
Gemüter" (Spiele II, 249). This fear makes the Jew
Nebelsteiner pretend to deafness and lameness:

> Sein Mimikry. Gejagte Tiere schauspielern
> gründlicher. Sie stellen sich tot. Kluger
> Instinkt. Die modernste Methode, unsre
> Zeit unangefochten zu passieren, mag sein,
> als Toter maskiert. (Spiele II, 303).

At the end of the play Nebelsteiner is preparing to
return to post-war West Germany to preach the gospel

of anti-atomism:

> Vormals hatte der Mensch Angst vor Gott und
> seinem geheimen Walten. Das konnt eine
> heilige Angst sein. Heute herrscht die Angst
> des Menschen vor dem Menschen und seinen
> geheimen Waffen. Eine unheilige Angst,
> . . . dennoch . . . die einzige letzte
> große Hoffnung. Nur die Angst kann uns
> retten. Von ihr zur Freiheit ist ein sehr
> weiter Weg. Den die Späteren gehn müssen.
> (Spiele II, 305)

There is only one answer to the possibility of inevitable destruction by atom bomb and that is an end to war: "Die alte alte Trommelei? Sie muß aufhören" (Spiele II, 305).

From a shooting and the ensuing investigation in Mademoiselle Löwenzorn, Becher moved to the story of a murder more directly connected to World War II in Der Herr kommt aus Bahia. The play, which was later revised and renamed Makumba, is the story of the murder of a man in the interior of Brazil who portrayed Adolf Hitler as a live effigy in a victory parade at the end of World War II. This story, based on an article in a New York newspaper[27], becomes a vehicle for Becher's political commentary and can be seen as a parable of Nazism. Becher reveals in his essay "Aus der Spielmacherschule geplaudert" the origins in reality of each component

in the play.[28] Shortly before the end of his exile
in Brazil, Becher met a Makumba sorcerer who introduced him to the origins and ritual of the cult, which
combines African black magic with Christian mysticism.
In the harbor district of Rio, Becher caught sight of
a figure on whose appearance he was to base the character of Padre Antonio, the fullblood Indian priest,
representative of the vitality of primitive peoples,
who, as a true Christian, tries to help the impoverished and exploited natives with more than words:

> Er sah im Wortsinn fabelhaft aus und beweg-
> te sich mit der fremden Anmut eines Rot-
> wilds. Sein Gesicht war selten ebenmäßig
> und wie aus Mahagoni oder dem verschollenen
> Edelholz Brasil geschnitzt. Und aus den
> obsidianschwarz, ja wie Lavastein leuchtenden
> Augen blickte mich etwas viel Älteres an
> als die Römische Kirche. Und dies viel
> Ältere lebte. (Spiele II, 326)

The Indian represents the vitality of primitive peoples.

It is not surprising that this Christian
priest joins forces with the only other person who is
interested in the welfare of the natives, the Communist organizer, Hannibal Cascadura, whose name means
"hard headed": "Jeder, der sein Gewissen erleichtern
möchte, indem er diesen Massen zu helfen sich müht,
kann als Kommunist gebrandmarkt werden und ins Ge-

fängnis wandern" (<u>Spiele II</u>, 325). Becher gleaned
a final **component**, the strange robbery-murder of a
Japanese peach salesman, from a 1943 Rio newspaper.
Except for the victim's nationality, the play's version of this incident corresponds to the newspaper
report. A band of robbers, upon finding a travelling
salesman pinned in his burning vehicle, decided to
shorten the unfortunate wreck victim's suffering by
cutting his throat and taking his money as a fee for
their efforts at mercy killing. Of course, the fact
that Becher's travelling salesman becomes a Japanese
peach merchant allows Becher to draw parallels between the wreck victim's fiery death and the death of
thousands of Japanese by atomic fire at Hiroshima.

Both versions of the play are replete with
the themes of Becher's earlier works but with far more
emphasis on the dangers of the atomic age and with some
attempts to satirize the Communist party line. His
concern for the poor, disenfranchized, exploited peasants
is still obvious in his sympathetic portrayal of the
mixed-blood <u>cabóclos</u>, illiterate dirt farmers who practice secondary trades just to keep their families
financially afloat. Even in their abject poverty
there is hope for them, if they will revolt against

their revolting living conditions:

> . . . ihre sprichwörtliche Geduld, Paciéncia.
> Millionen Cabôclos sind sozusagen, ja,
> Patienten der Armut. . . . solche Esels-
> geduld [ist] langsam am Erlöschen . . .
> . . . eines Tags grade da hinten im Minen-
> staat . . . A libertade, die Freiheit. Und
> einmal wird der Cabôclo sich die Freiheit
> bringen, die Freiheit von Elend, Krankheit,
> Unwissenheit. (Spiele II, 90-91)

Religion is one source of comfort for these
poor people. In the form of Makumba cults, religion
replaces alcohol as the "opiate of the masses":
"Makumba gibt unsren Armen etwas Glanz, hilft ihnen,
ihre Armut leichter zu tragen" (Spiele II, 90). Although most of the play is set in a bar where everyone drinks, alcohol is only a secondary intoxicant
here. It is the black magic of Makumba, whose effects
are portrayed extensively in several scenes, that
represents the Dionysian theme. While Becher, through
the Communist Hannibal Cascadura, views religion,
indeed all opiates, as a tool of those who would maintain the status quo, he seems to understand its appeal
and refuses to comdemn those who practice it:

> Eine Welt, die der Schwarzen Magie der
> Wasserstoffbombe verfallen ist, sollte
> eigentlich keine Veranlassung haben, auf
> Makumba herabzublicken. (Spiele II, 91)

120

Belief in the power of the atom is just another form
of hocus pocus for Becher.

Indeed, for Ulrich Becher, the evil of
Hitler and fascism has turned into the cosmic evil
of the atom bomb. This anti-war, anti-religion, antiatomic bomb stance was what endeared Becher to the GDR
in the 1950s; he provided a literary expression for
their concerns of the time.[29] In Becher's sympathetic
portrayal of the Marxist Hannibal, there are remnants
of this pro-GDR stance. When Padre Antonio ridicules
Hannibal for his pronunciation of Marx's name, Hannibal replies: "Erstens ist Marschi nicht mein Gott,
sondern mein Mensch" (Spiele II, 106). And Hannibal
claims he raised a red flag at the train station,
not because his party ordered him to, but because he
obtained private pleasure from doing so. Hannibal,
not Padre Antonio, finds the "Blume des Lebens" that
saves a child's life.

Makumba, the revised version of Der Herr
kommt aus Bahia, is especially interesting, because
it illustrates Becher's later attitude toward communism in the 1960s when he made the revisions. In it
Becher satirizes the party line. Hannibal Cascadura,
whose hard-headed adherence to the teachings of Marx

121

have cost him his right eye (making him a leftist
with leftist vision), follows his party's instructions
even when they make little sense. Hannibal cannot
explain world events to his girlfriend, Eros, who
represents the elemental force of sex, until she
has received instruction in "historical materialism;"
ironically, Eros cannot even read (Spiele II, 101).
Hannibal proclaims his party's solution for the sorry
condition of Brazil: "Unsereins würde euch dazu
zwingen, zu reparieren--den ganzen Minenstaat zu
reparieren. Und wer nicht mitmacht, den verschicken
wir nach Sibirien" (Spiele II, 102). That would not
bother the cabóclos, because they think Siberia is a
brewery in São Paulo. Hannibal appears at a Makumba
ceremony to hand out leaflets to the illiterate
cabóclos advertising a meeting in distant Rio to
organize anti-atom bomb peace demonstrations. It is
a useless attempt to raise their consciousness, but
as Hannibal perceives it: "Agitprop. Ich bin ein
Apparatchen, siehst du. Das funktioniert, wenn's
Die Partei so will" (Spiele II, 135).

Der Herr kommt aus Bahia (Makumba) was clearly the most controversial of Becher's plays. Heinz
Hilpert, the famous and successful director of the

122

Deutsches Theater in Göttingen, had wanted Becher to write another play for his theater after the successful production of Feuerwasser. According to Becher, Hilpert was rather enthusiastic about the script of Der Herr kommt aus Bahia (Spiele II, 330). The premiere took place in July, 1957, an unfortunate time for a premiere in a country where the theater season usually begins in the Fall. Becher, who had been unable to work with the cast before the dress rehearsal, was pleased with the stage design of W. Preetorius and with most of the actors. However, the lead character, the Makumba sorcerer and jungle gangster Orestes Goyano, was played by Martin Hirthe as a wild west outlaw, "statt Vaterfigur aus einem Guß jenseits von Gut und Böse zu geben . . . (Spiele II, 330). Becher worried that the total loyalty to and dependence of Goyano's henchmen on their fierce chief was not motivated by Hirthe's portryal of the character. They must both love and fear Goyano. The climactic moment before Goyano's murder, when he returns from the victory parade in which he has portrayed Hitler, turned into a cabaret parody of Hitler.

> Da Studenten bereits Generalprobe sahen,
> kaum Jugend im Theater, vorwiegend Genera-

tion, die Nazismus getragen; Unruhe im Saal,
Flüsterzischeln, entrüstetes Räuspern. Pre-
mierenbesucher, die Schlußbeifall spenden
wollten, wurden von anderen angefaucht:
Klatschen Sie nicht, sonst kaufen wir nicht
mehr bei Ihnen. Hilperts Fazit: Gewisse
Leute hier scheinen noch Hitlerbild unterm
Bett hängen zu haben. (Spiele II, 330-331)

The critics, even those who had kind words
for other plays, were unanimous in their dislike for
Der Herr kommt aus Bahia. After twenty performances
at the Deutsches Theater, Becher withdrew the original
version and years later published Makumba in Spiele der
Zeit to correct what he came to see as mistakes after
the disaster of Der Herr kommt aus Bahia. However,
Makumba has never been produced.

In Makumba Becher's revisions of Der Herr
kommt aus Bahia are aimed at explaining the Brazilian
milieu to make the action of the play understandable.
Becher also wanted to blur and fictionalize the parallels to Nazism by investing the setting with a fairy-
tale timelessness and by "Verfremdung der Hauptfigur
bei ihrem letzten Auftritt" (Spiele II, 331), perhaps
in response to the general anti-exile tendencies noted
earlier. Many of the negative critiques of the play
were based on Becher's emphasis on milieu or atmosphere
to the neglect of the story line. Becher comments to

124

young playwrights in this regard:

> Siebt eure Erfahrungen und Erlebnisse, seien
> sie noch so stark, einmalig, seltsam, hütet
> euch davor, euer Spiel damit zu hypertroph-
> ieren, zu überfüllen. (Spiele II, 328)

As a result of these concerns, Makumba has been streamlined by the removal of three characters: two travelling piano tuners from Germany and Goyano's wife, Empress Maria Theresia. Makumba contains no phonetic imitations of Brazilian speech and few Portuguese words or sentences to distract the German-speaking audience, an astonishing fact considering the Babylonian cacophony that prevails in Becher's other works. In addition, Becher has affixed a Prolog to Makumba, which serves two purposes. The Prolog is a frame for the story which helps to alienate (in Brecht's use of the term) the parallels to Nazism, and it explains the remaining bits of Brazilian milieu, such as odd names or customs, that might cause confusion.

1957 was not only the year of the disastrous reception of Der Herr kommt aus Bahia, Becher's last play until the 1970s, it was also the year in which his first fictional prose since the early 1930s ap-

peared signaling yet another shift in Becher's reception. Becher began work on what many critics consider
his masterpiece, the New Yorker Novellen, in 1945,
while still in exile in New York.[30] The publishing
history of these three novellas, including "Der
schwarze Hut," "Nachtigall will zum Vater fliegen,"
and "Die Frau und der Tod," is as full of adventure
as Becher's biography and characterizes his fate
in the literary marketplace.[31] During a summer vacation at the home of Hubertus Prinz zu Löwenstein in
New Foundland, New Jersey, Becher began work on "Nachtigall." In 1950 in occupied Vienna, Becher located
three men who founded a tiny new publishing house,
Continental Edition. With the publication of Becher's
novellas in 1950, Continental Edition folded; Willi
Weismann lost his money, another partner landed in a
mental institution, and the third was arrested for
his work on the news agency New China and learned
dentistry during his stay in jail. After this grotesque false start for his first prose work Rowohlt
printed an edition of 50,000 entitled Die ganze Nacht
(1955), minus "Der schwarze Hut," which was thought
to be too bitter an indictment of the American "Bild-
ungsbürgertum" who supported Nazism directly or indi-

126

rectly to risk its publication for a West German public indoctrinated by Adenauer policies and infatuated
with the Marshall Plan, "Wirtschaftswunder," and their
Atlantic alliance. Only 5,000 copies of this edition
were sold.

In the GDR the situation was somewhat different. The publication of Becher's works must be
seen against the framework of thaws and frosts set
out earlier, in particular the events of 1956 and
1957. The early months of 1956 brought a general
thaw in cultural policies as a result of the Fourth
German Writers Congress in January and above all
the Twentieth Congress of the CPSU in February. At
the former, GDR writers openly discussed the failings
of GDR literature and at the latter Chruschev institut-
ed the policy of de-Stalinization.[32] During the thaw
Becher's Novella "Der schwarze Hut," considered
provocatively avantgarde in the GDR, was accepted
for publication along with Weyrauch's "Bericht an die
Regierung" as the inaugural volume of the "Tangenten-
Reihe," a series of Western prose works. Unfortunately
for Becher the tide was already turning in late 1956
after the Hungarian uprising, and the Tangenten series
was discontinued in 1957 after official critical or-

gans rejected formalistically experimental prose as revisionism. This was also the year that Wolfgang Harich was imprisoned for promoting revisionist theories. After the period of intolerance for any form other than socialist realism had passed, i.e. by the time of the Sixth German Writers Congress in May 1969, Aufbau Verlag published a new, limited edition exclusively for the GDR of all three Becher novellas in 1969.[33]

Until Benziger Verlag in Zurich adopted Becher's works, there was no Western edition of New Yorker Novellen, though the GDR version could be found in libraries. To test the water Benziger first published "Der schwarze Hut" in paperback form in their modestly priced "Benziger-Reihe," but it went unnoticed. Only in 1974 did Benziger publish the entire cycle of novellas in hardback, albeit in a minuscule edition of 3,000 of which only a little over half was sold.[34]

Though Becher's publications during his stay in New York were scanty, politically motivated, and primarily non-literary in nature, his exile experience there provided material for much of his fiction, including the New Yorker Novellen. While

128

most critics seem preoccupied with the content of
these stories, the fates of emigrants in the big
city,[35] others view these novellas as the graphics
of George Grosz translated into prose.[36] The various
editions have all been dedicated to Grosz, and as with
Niemand, Grosz's life and art appear to be the inspiration for both the content and form of New Yorker Novellen.

    "Nachtigall" contains an only slightly fic-
tionalized account of Grosz in America, as well as
an uncomfortably accurate portrait of another member
of the Berlin Dada group, Richard Hülsenbeck. In
the alcoholic, left-wing Theodosi Boem, Becher traces
Grosz's development from social caricaturist of 1920s
Berlin to the apocalyptic Boschean visionary of the
late works, including the artist of the "hole," of
ominous landscapes and of the stickmen, called "Hornissenmenschen" in the novella (NYN, 11-13, 47, 63-64,
81, 89). Becher has invested his other protagonist,
Hans Heinz Nachtigall, with Hülsenbeck's psychological
problems, the borderline schizophrenia of an artist
who cannot justify his leaving Germany behind to accept the American dream of money and success. Dr.
Med. Nachtigall, former head of the "Zipp-zipp-ka

Bewegung" (e.g. Dada) and respected author of travel books, is unable to continue his literary career in exile.

> Er bemühte sich um Mitarbeit an den beiden deutschsprachigen Gazetten New Yorks. Die eine, angestammtes Organ der Deutsch-amerikaner, stand in jenen Tagen hitlerischer Machtentfaltung dem 'Bund,' der deutsch-amerikanerischen Naziorganisation nahe und lehnte die Mitarbeit von Hitlergegnern schnöde ab. Die andre, ein Wochenblatt, das die Interessen der deutschjüdischen Immigration vertrat, erteilte ihm eine höfliche Absage. Sie war mit Beiträgen von jüdischer Seite überlaufen; für einen Nichtjuden war er zu wenig prominent, um durch Mitarbeit als "Renommiergoi" den Ruf des Blattes zu fördern. Da er kein Jude, kein Nazi, kein Katholik, kein Mitlgied einer protestantischen Sekte war, gewährte ihm niemand Unterstützung. (NYN, 22)

This passage reflects more than a trace of Becher's bitterness over his own lost years in New York as well.

Through a series of fortunate circumstances, Nachtigall becomes a wealthy Park Avenue psychiatrist and American citizen, John Henry Nightingale. One side of his personality, Nachtigall, forever wants to return home to his father, who has managed to survive the war. However, the American side of his personality, Nightingale, fears that his father has turned into one of Boem's "Hornissenmenschen," fulfillment of Boem/Grosz's apocalyptic vision:

> Neunzig--nach all dem Krieg--Flüchten--
> Leiden--Hungern, nach all den Greueln und
> Entbehrungen, die er mit angesehn, zugelas-
> sen und durchgemacht hat--Neunzig. Er kann
> nicht mehr wie ein Mensch aussehn, Hans
> . . . Ausgemergelt zum Skelett--vergreist,
> verdorrt--verbittert, verbost--zerlumpt,
> verkommen--nein, nicht mehr wie ein Mensch
> . . . Wie (keucht)--ein Hornissenmensch!
> Wie einer von denen, die Boem gezeichnet
> hat--. . . (NYN, 105)

In a dialogue in which the two personalities argue

aloud, Nightingale finally talks Nachtigall out of

returning to Germany; it is a script-like passage

dotted with stage directions, showing the influence

of Becher's simultaneous work on Bockerer.

"Nachtigall will zum Vater fliegen" also

contains its many comments on the plight of the exile,

especially the exile artist, which reflect Becher's

own experiences in the United States, and most cer-

tainly Hülsenbeck's and Grosz's ambivalent, almost

schizophrenic attitude to their adopted country, one

that typifies the experience of many exiles. On the

one hand, writes Nachtigall/Nightingale, exiles have

every reason, even a duty, to love America, because

it offered a chance to rebuild their lives and even

achieve greater success than would have been possible

in Germany. Americans have many good qualities:
youthful vitality, pragmatism, friendliness; but
they also have many faults, such as their material-
istic life style, emphasis on money as a measure of
success, and their lack of tradition (NYN, 18, 28-
29, and 71-72). Artists like Boem/Grosz found little
respect for their achievements in the United States:

> Kunst war in den Staaten Geschäft; Künstler,
> die keine Geschäftemacher, waren keine
> Künstler. Daß Boem durchs Medium seiner
> genial pamphletistischen Graphik ein Spit-
> zenkämpfer gegen die Nazis und ihre Steig-
> bügelhalter gewesen war und mit knapper Not
> ihren Fängen entkommen, hatte nicht gezählt.
> Man hatte sich genügt, ihm mit burschikoser
> Herzlichkeit die Schulter zu klopfen und
> ihn respektlos ´good boy´ zu nennen, oder
> gemunkelt, er sei ein Linksradikaler ge-
> wesen, und ihm nicht minder kordial den
> Rücken gekehrt. (NYN, 16)

The remaining two novellas in New Yorker
Novellen are less directly involved with emigrants,
although Becher always includes at least one character of German heritage to motivate the use of a
German-English mixture. This and other techniques
which originate with the dramatist Becher are evident
in his prose. The two stories take place on two
extremely dramatic days--"Der schwarze Hut" during
and after a cocktail party in Greenwich Village on

May 5, 1945, Victory in Europe Day, and "Die Frau
und der Tod" in a Manhattan bar the night of the
bombing of Hiroshima. The party and bar settings
allow Becher to bring together an international mixture of memorable characters, some bordering on
caricature. The plot moves forward naturally in
"Der schwarze Hut" with the progression of the black
hat from owner to owner, and, in "Die Frau und der
Tod," with the movement of Slocum and his beautiful
lady through the streets of "Hell's Kitchen." Both
stories are filled with dialogue and the descriptions
of settings and body movements similar to the parenthetical stage directions in plays. All three novellas, including "Nachtigall," have a classical dramatic
structure. Their ten chapters can be divided almost
uniformly into three "acts" with a climax coming in
chapter nine and the epilogue, usually very short,
in chapter ten, a structure shared by Becher's plays
Feuerwasser and Der Pfeiffer von Wien.

If "Nachtigall" can be considered fictionalized biography of Hülsenbeck and Grosz, "Der schwarze
Hut" and "Die Frau und der Tod" are graphics translated into prose, images typical of Grosz's work.
Indeed, these two stories are excellent examples of

"wechselseitige Erhellung der Künste," the attempt
by an artist in one medium to duplicate the artistic
effects of another medium. The cocktail party scene
with its predominantly dark hues (everyone is in
mourning) dotted with bright splashes of color (Klop-
stock´s glimmering red auricles, Rossi´s ockercolored
face, Altkammer´s inflamed evil eyes, Higgin´s orange-
haired hands and head) is visually reminiscent of
Grosz´s early cafe and street scenes. Grosz´s dada-
ist collages appear combined with his cityscapes of
The City, Germany, a winter´s tale, and Dedicated to
Oskar Panizza in the "Times Square" montage of "Die
Frau und der Tod." We are caught up in "den träg
sich hinwälzenden, myriadenstimmig summenden Mahlstrom
sommerlich gekleideter, schwitzender klebriger Masse"
in Times Square, "diesem nimmermüden Jahrmarkt aus
Stein und Licht" (NYN, 279).

   But the similarities are more than just
visual. Like Grosz, Becher expresses his political
sentiments by juxtaposing incongruent elements. News-
boys hawk papers telling of the explosion of the first
atom bomb; neon lights flash ads for alcohol, cigar-
ettes, and amusement centers.

   Hinten schossen Soldaten und halbwüchsige

Bengel auf Tontauben und in Schienen hin-
herhampelnde Japanerpuppen . . . Rechts im
räumigen Eingang tat sich die SCHIESSGE-
WEHRHOCHZEIT beschriftete Attrappe eines
Juxphotographen . . . Links im Eingang
ein Verkaufsstand, drauf eine Formation
fabrikgemachter Bronze-Heilande . . . zu
Füßen lagen zierliche Imitationen ver-
schiedener Mordwerkzeuge zum Verkauf.
ATOMBOMBEN MOMENTAN AUSVERKAUFT. (NYN,
280-281).

In the middle of the square, a crowd gathers around
an imitation Statue of Liberty, stopping traffic at
the feet of the goddess and setting off a frenetic
horn-honking concert (NYN, 283). There is a peanut
as tall as five men, a gigantic mouth blowing smoke,
and over it all, the "Ruppertbierhimmelsauge" sees
everything (NYN, 284). The movie theaters' marquees
advertise a selection of murder and horror films
(NYN, 288-289).

Becher's prose has also drawn inspiration
in the use of the grotesque from his friend's paintings. Many of the characters are given animal traits,
a technique used by Grosz in his paintings to show
their dehumanization. In "Der schwarze Hut" Dr.
Klopstock is described as having a "Hofhundebell-
stimme;" Pepe-le-Moco in "Die Frau und der Tod" has
a bulldog face with rodent teeth and from behind
he has the neck of a young dachshund. The Russian

is called a wrinkled rat; Slocum whinnied like a colt; the men in the bar stare at the lady, their heads lowered like steers; Petit-Gaston is an ugly little swine.

However, the women are more dehumanized than the men for, as in Expressionism and in Grosz´s paintings, they are seen almost exlusively through the eyes of men as dolls, marionettes, beautiful animals (especially birds), or carnival masks. The only human alternatives for Becher´s women are nymphomaniacs, prostitutes, terminally ill Camille figures, or vaguely-defined wifely types. The only women in these works who receive more than cursory treatment are the classical beauties, symbols of "Anmut" (the fittingly-named Helene in "Der schwarze Hut") or beauty (the unnamed "Schöne" in "Die Frau und der Tod"). Becher often calls to mind famous paintings by Botticelli, Titian, and especially Baldung, whose beautiful young maidens in the clutches of death aid the reader in visualizing these women. However, such women are destined to end in madness or terminal illness, because for Becher (and Grosz) "Schönheit ist etwas sehr Gefährliches, verdammtnocheins, sie kann zum Wahnsinn anstiften" (NYN, 226).

Becher rarely expresses his leftist-orient-
ed criticism of American society explicitly, but implies it in his characterizations or in his descriptions. Most frequently this criticism is expressed
in Grosz-like caricatures emphasizing a particular
physical or psychological feature to the point of
grotesqueness. Almost every character and feature
at the cocktail party in "Der schwarze Hut" is a
caricature: shabby Dr. Klopstock with his uncon-
trollably loud voice, the result of his concentra-
tion-camp-imposed deafness; Alois Altkammer, hyper-
elegant snob, Wall Street broker, bisexual and Hitler imitator; Madenfriedrich, son of a wealthy
New England family, who carries leeches in a snuff-
box to help drain an inflamed wound; red-haired drunk-
en Irish painter James Higgins, married to twins.
These figures continually sing "Don´t Fence Me In"
in a setting in which all of them are fenced in by
their mutual hatred. On the wall overlooking the
entire scene, a surrealistic Higgins portrait of
Altkammer´s dead wife "lächelte kindlich-sphinxisch
herab" (NYN, 145); holes in the portrait beneath
the breasts allow a view of a stormy sea and sinking
ship symbolizing her death and that of the decadent

bourgeoise society she represents.

Becher´s criticism is put into words in
Dr. Klopstock´s evaluation of the cocktail party.

> Hatte er sich verstricken lassen in die
> verantwortungslose Hysterie einer bei leben-
> digem Leib verwesenden Gesellschaft, in
> jenen ausgelassenen Totentanz der Noch-
> Lebenden, der seine Taubheit heute abend
> umgaukelt hatte wie ein allen Sinns ent-
> ratener, pompös-konfus-skuriller Stummfilm
> den ein teuflisch-zynischer Regisseur ge-
> dreht hatte zu seinem einzigen Pläsir: dar-
> zutun die vollendete Würdevergessenheit des
> bürgerlichen Menschen? (NYN, 172)

From short stories dealing with exile experiences in New York, Becher moved to a novel about
the events and motivations that led to exile. On
the surface Kurz nach vier contains all the elements
of a bestseller: intrigue, adventure and sex.
Zborowsky, post-war Viennese art professor, is
travelling to Rome to visit an old friend. During
a sleepless night in noisy, tourist-filled Piacenza,
his Hemingwayesque past is recounted in cinematic
flash-backs which present the pre- and post-war
Austrian literary scene, the Spanish civil war, and
the guerilla warfare of the Yugoslav partisans woven
together with the story of Zborowsky´s love for Lola
Aguirre who is murdered by Spanish Falangists.

But Kurz nach vier is more than an adventure-

138

packed love story. For the more reflective reader
familiar with the German literary scene, Becher's
first novel becomes a paradigm for the experiences
of an entire generation of Germans who, like Becher,
were just coming of age when they foundered on the
political rocks of the 1930s, "die havarierten
Europäer," "die leergeschossene Generation," as
Becher calls them. The novel's love story and
Zborowsky's successful attempt to lay to rest the
spectres of his past can be seen as a comment on
Germany's "unbewältigte Vergangenheit." In addition,
Becher's playful use of language, more of a hind-
rance to the casual reader, appeals to the literary-
minded, as in Zborowsky's transformation into Leutnant
Skizze: Zborowsky becomes Boro, his childhood nickname, which in turn becomes Borrón, his Spanish nom
de querre, transforms the nickname into the Spanish
word for sketch which in turn leads to the German
word Skizze, also a play on "schizoid." Interspersed
throughout the book are sentences in languages other
than German: American English, Italian, Spanish,
French, Czech. Becher's style, many elements of
which are drawn directly from the Expressionists,
also stands out: abrupt, staccato sentences with

capricious word order, or run-on stream-of-consciousness prose, theatrical dialogue, and set descriptions. He intensifies Kuropatkin´s betrayal of Zborowsky by references to similar betrayals in other literature: Prospero-Caliban in Shakespeare´s Tempest, Romulus and Remus, in Latin legend the twin founders of Rome, plus the entire Doppelgänger legacy of Romanticism.

To illustrate more concretely the elements of Becher´s prose style, a brief textual analysis will be performed at this juncture on the following exemplary passage from Kurz nach vier:

> "Und die Platten und Mappen?" beharrtest du, um endlich zu erfahren, daß des Himmler Geheime Staatspolizei sie konfisziert hatte samt und sonders, eingeschmolzen, eingestampft. Mitte deiner Dreißiger standst du, der so früh begonnen, mit leeren Händen, da existierte kein Radiernadelkritzer von dir, kein Blatt, kein Kupferblech, keine Kalkschieferscherbe, aber du existiertest, Franz Zborowsky. Totalen Krieg überlebt hattest du und warst da (Bewußtsein, das von der jugendlichen Intelligentia Frankreichs alsbald zu einem Credo erhoben wurde), da in der letzten Stunde eines globalen Massakers und der zugleich ersten eines neuen Zeitalters, in der die Menschenerde ihren ersten künstlichen Leibwind hinausknallen ließ in den Kosmos. Ja, wie der Historie erster Atombombenpilz im Himmel sich blähte über japanischer Hafenstadt, gedachtest du, . . . Moritz Schlands und seiner Prophezeiung--37

Twice in the first line Becher´s general tendency
towards abbreviation is apparent, in the lack of a
verb and question word in the question and in the
use of a subordinate "um-zu clause" instead of a
new sentence. The "du" address form is an element
of the stream of consciousness narrative, in which
the thoughts of a protagonist are expressed directly
instead of through a narrator. This "du" form is
used throughout the passage.

Line two contains the unusual word order
of an archaic, poetic genitive, "des Himmler," which
helps to heighten the alliteration of "s" and the
rhythm of the following line, in which the verb placement has again been altered for emphasis of the expressive verbs "eingeschmolzen, eingestampft."

The second sentence of this passage, beginning at the end of line 3, has three examples of
ellipsis: the missing preposition "in" and article
"der" before "Mitte," the missing helping verb "hat"
in the dependent clause in line 4, as well as the
single incidence of the word "da" to serve both as
the separable prefix of "dastehen" and in the parti-
cle construction with the verb "existieren." In
addition to the ellipsis, this sentence also con-

tains the parallel repetitions of the verb "existieren" in lines 5 and 7, as well as the paratactical
repetition of "kein" and the alliteration of "k"
in lines 5 and 6. These stylistic elements help
to accelerate the tempo of the sentence and to emphasize the repeated elements as well as Becher´s word
creations, "Radiernadelkritzer" and "Kalkschiefer-
scherbe."

Further examples of ellipsis occur in line
7 (the missing article before "Totalen Krieg"), in
line 11 (the lack of the word "Stunde") and in line
13 (a missing article in the genitive construction
"der Historie erster Atombombenpilz"). The word
"da" in line 10 is a paratactical repetition of "da"
in line 8, as is the triple repetition of the word
"erst" in lines 11, 12 and 13. Inverted word order
occurs in line 7, emphasizing the object "Totalen
Krieg," and in the placement of the prepositional
phrase "über japanischer Hafenstadt" outside the
verbal parenthesis in line 14, as well as in the inverted genitive construction in line 13. The rhythm
of lines 13 and 14 is also stressed by the alliteration of "Historie - Himmel - Hafenstadt." Besides the
use of the "du" address form, the parenthetical in-

sert in lines 8 and 9 is characteristic of the stream
of consciousness narrative. Yet another paratactical
device is the antithesis of the phrase "letzten
Stunde" in line 10 and the phrase "ersten Stunde"
in line 11.

It is the inclusion of such stylistic features discussed above, i.e. elliptical devices,
parataxis, and general manipulation of language,
as well as the inclusion of cosmic themes, such as
the striking metaphor in lines 11-13 comparing the
atom bomb to a cosmic fart, which point to Becher's
stylistic indebtedness to Expressionism. On a
semantic level there are other indications in Kurz
nach vier, such as Becher's skillful implementation
of cinematic transitions, e.g. flashback and fade-
in/fade-out, or his inclusion of bits and pieces of
the protagonist's world in the form of newspaper
headlines, articles, songs, letters.

Becher's style in the above passage is
typical for Kurz nach vier and for much of Becher's
prose work as well. Likewise the thematic content
of Kurz nach vier is typical of Becher's oevre.
Becher has managed to combine an adventure-love
story of high literary quality believably with his

political views by entangling the life story of his protagonist, Zborowsky, with twenty years of European history. Many themes from earlier works are repeated here. The main protagonist is a moderate leftist artist working for the socialist cause and against all anti-socialists: "Er haßte die Faschisten aller Schattierungen mit Vehemenz, sie bedrohten sein Werk und seine Liebe." (23)

Embodied in Zborowsky's odyssey is the dilemma faced by Becher's generation; but in contrast to Becher's earlier works, in which separate characters represented the opposing viewpoints, one character, Zborowsky, contains both sides of the debate. For a generation with traditional Western morality that placed value on peace and relief from suffering, the emergence of the evil represented by National Socialism created a situation in which a choice had to be made between the inaction of flight (exile) and the ethically abhorrent actions of violence (personal involvement in the war). Particularly for one who had adopted the tenets of German Socialism in the 1920s with its anti-war emphasis, the logical choice was that of inaction or flight. Any support of a war was support for the capitalist merchants of war

144

who used the bodies of the workers both to produce
their war machines and as victims of the very machines
they had built. Much of 1920s pacifism was the result of very real horrors experienced first-hand
during World War I; pacifists resolved never to let
such a thing happen again. In addition, Nazism seemed so gigantic an enemy that any one person's sac-
rificing his life in a war against it was a futile
waste of time and energy; there was enough injustice,
poverty, and starvation in the world to battle. On
the other hand, within this same socialist perspective
there were arguments in favor of war. Nazism threat-
ened the achievement of socialist, indeed, of humanist
ideals. Any violence used to defeat Nazism was clearly less pernicious than the violence represented by
Nazism. Unless everyone were willing to sacrifice
his life to defeat this evil and restore freedom and
democracy to the world, Nazism would surely prove
victorious.

For the socialist artist the dilemma was
even more acute. In addition to the valid arguments from the socialist perspective, the artist
was torn by his role as both member and observer
of society. To reject war the artist had to believe

in the primacy of his work. But what was his work,
if not based on experiences shared with the community
for whom the artist produced? Art becomes mere arti-
fice, if not based on experience. Thomas Mann's
early views as propounded in "Betrachtungen eines
Unpolitischen" and his official declaration of unity
with the anti-fascist cause in his letter to Bonn
University in 1937 represent the two extremes of
the dilemma.

Ulrich Becher's biography reflects his
decision to use his art in the fight against fascism. In effect Becher has tried to take the middle
road, to maintain his integrity both as an artist and
a socialist. But it is clearly an unsatisfactory
choice, one that Becher is uncomfortable with, because he feels compelled to argue his case anew with
each new book. In Samba Becher's sympathies are on
the side of action; Kornau leaves behind his work
and his bride to join the underground in order to
salve his conscience and provide material for his
future writings. Kornau's alter ego, Parisius,
chooses to remain in exile, partly out of fear,
partly because he sees Kornau's suicidal mission
as futile. The same conflict plagues Nachtigall,

but it is expressed as oedipal guilt; Nachtigall cannot return to his father, who stayed in Germany through all the hardships, because he feels guilty for having escaped to a life of physical and financial security. The result of this inner conflict is schizophrenia.

In Kurz nach vier Becher again tackles this thematic complex. In spite of strong pacifist tendencies, Zborowsky joins the International Brigade in the Spanish Civil War, and later fights with Yugoslav partisans. However, Zborowsky's participation is due more to circumstance than conviction. He has gone to Spain primarily to locate his fiancee and becomes involved in the war only after he discovers that she is dead. He joins the Yugoslav partisans only because the partisans capture him as he is deserting his service as a "Strafsoldat" in the German army. Zborowsky wavers between his art and his cause, between reflection and initiative. At times he believes in the political power of art:

> Fantasie schaffte und machte mich freier
> als die andern in einer Epoche eisigsten
> Zwangs und schenkte mir das Feuer zur
> Initiative. . . . Schöpferische Künstler
> verfügen über andre Waffen [als Pistolen]
> (53)

But when Zborowsky is faced with direct personal
violence, as when he views the machine-gunning of
a group of teenagers, he is no longer able to believe in the political efficacy of art. Indeed,
his only recourse is flight from the threatening
situation.

> . . . infiziert mit unerträglichem Leiden,
> dessen Wüten sich allein zu heilen vermochte
> durch Amoklauf, das hieß: qualvollen Selbst-
> mord oder Flucht. Als Leidensbekämpfer
> wählte ich Flucht . . . (54)

However, Zborowsky discovers flight cannot be a
political alternative because avoidance of one political position assumes adoption of an opposing
political position. Zborowsky runs from the horrors
of Nazism, to join the Yugoslav partisans in their
campaign against Nazism. Even in post-war Europe
Zborowsky finds similar political choices: he decides in favor of action when he shoots a former
concentration camp commander.

The double ending of Kurz nach vier demonstrates the schism. Zborowsky learns of his friend
Kuropatkin's betrayal and resolves to kill him. In
his fantasy, Zborowsky carries out this resolve and
thus purges himself of the need for revenge. Then,

in the final scene, Zborowsky discards the Luger
pistol he has carried with him since his fighting
days, forgives Kuropatkin, and ends his personal
war: "die Waffe war versenkt. Seinen Krieg,
Zborowsky hatte ihn versenkt bis auf weiteres . . .
Doch nur dies: bis auf weiteres" (211). Even with
this rejection of personal violence, the last words
indicate that only a truce has been concluded; no
commitment to a final peace has been made.

    Zborowsky´s forgiveness of his friend is
a recognition of a new morality, a relativized morality, drawn from the philosophy of his teacher
Moritz Schland (based on the Viennese empiricist
Moritz Schlick) and in part from Einstein´s new
relativized universe. The entire moral dilemma
would not be so acute were it not for exponential
advances of technology, which has increased the
evil of war to cosmic proportions. In the face of
this cosmic evil, the atom bomb, it is impossible
for any existing morality to provide an answer.

> Wir alle müssen lernen, daß das mechan-
> istische Weltbild einen Riesensprung er-
> litten hat . . . daß die Erde keine Ma-
> schine, zwei mal zwei nicht unbedingt vier,
> das Absolute nicht ist, nicht Ewigkeit der
> Zeit, nicht des Raums Unendlichkeit. Wenn
> wir derlei begreifen lernen, können wir uns

> sehr langsam zurechtfinden in einem nagel-
> neuen Weltbild, kongruent der Höhe heutiger
> Forschung, zum Mitinhalt einer Ethik, die,
> gemessen an allem Vergangenen, auf ebenso
> stratosphärischer Höhe schreitet. (17)

The universe is continually expanding and is under

a "Galgenfrist." As an inhabitant of the earth,

Zborowsky thinks it important to take sides, espe-

cially as a champion on behalf of the world's vic-

tims; "die politische Rotverschiebung," i.e., leftist

politics, most clearly emphasizes this duty. However,

as a child of the universe, he realizes the relative

inefficacy of our political actions; nothing can alter

the inevitability of the end of the universe.

> Die Heutigen, sie hatten genug explodieren
> lassen im Ersten und Zweiten Krieg und im
> Nachkrieg der Experimente mit Atombomben.
> Was eine besondre Situation and den besondren
> Moment betraf, wär man ein Tropf, wollte
> man sich, wär's auch nur mit einem einzigen
> Lugerpistolenschuß . . . der Herde der ex-
> plosionstollen Pyromanen beigesellen.
> (210)

Therefore, at least on a personal level, forgiveness

and understanding must be the foundation of a new

morality, one that sees violence as necessary, yet

futile. Such a belief must lead either to madness

or resignation.

This schizophrenic dilemma receives a

double treatment in <u>Kurz nach vier</u>. Not only does
the character Zborowsky waver between the two poles
of action/inaction, as Nachtigall in "Nachtigall will
zum Vater fliegen," but Becher also uses a <u>Doppel-
gänger</u> motif, as he did in Samba. Zborowsky's double,
his "Wahlzwilling," is his friend and betrayer,
Kostja Kuropatkin. As a manufacturer of the condoms
much in demand by the German army, Kuropatkin cooper-
ates with the Nazis, because doing so is good for
business. In their school days, Kuropatkin and
Zborowsky had been a team, with Kuro playing the
clown, presenting almost a caricature of Boro. Kuro
imitates Boro's mannerisms and beliefs, but in such
a way as to mock them, because he both hates and loves
Zborowsky. "Haßliebe--einer der ältesten Motoren,
die das Menschenherz bewegen" (146). Becher compares
the two to Castor and Pollux, Romulus and Remus,
Prospero and Caliban, all literary models for the
theme of betrayal and murder of one brother or friend
by his twin. Kuropatkin can also be seen as Zborowsky's guilty conscience. Although it is clear that
Zborowsky was never unfaithful either to his fiancee
or to the Spanish leftists, Kuro's rumors could not
have caused the damage they did had there not been

some element of truth to them. Kuro has pointed
to Zborowsky´s flaw, the flaw of inconsistancy.
Becher sees inconstancy as the Achilles heel of
liberal intellectuals: wavering between theorizing
about politics and actual involvement in politics.
Zborowsky wavers between his art, which he sees as
a political statement, and personal involvement in
the causes he believes in. And there is some guilt
involved in deciding for art, because it represents
the safer road. Kuro is an extreme example of "playing it safe" to the point of cooperation with and aid
to the enemy. Kuropatkin is able to harm Zborowsky
by claiming that Zborowsky is capable of deception;
just as Kuro is only pretending to support the Nazis,
he accuses Boro of pretending to be a leftist out
of opportunism to gain recognition for his art.

      Zborowsky admits to his fear of physical
suffering as his reason for flight. Related to this
theme of flight is the theme of forgetting. Zborowsky
quotes Freud:

> Endlich muß auffallen, daß das Schuldbewußt-
> sein viel von der Natur der Angst hat, es
> kann ohne Bedenken als "Gewissensangst"
> beschrieben werden . . . (179)

152

Just as Zborowsky flees physical suffering, his mind
flees from mental suffering caused by his guilty
conscience into a state of forgetfulness. Zborowsky
forgets his knowledge that his fiancee has been murdered, rationalizing this failure to face the truth
by claiming that survival of a brutal epoch only
seems possible if one forgets.

> Um die Millionen Zwangstode faschistischer
> Kriegswillkür: das große Tabu. "Gewissen
> ist, was man am gewissesten weiß"--man will
> indes nicht wissen. Man verwechselt Erin-
> nern mit Vergessen. Man klammert sich ans
> große Tabu des Verdrängens und Vergessens
> einer gesamten apokalyptischen Epoche, Tabu,
> dessen Verletzung entstehn lassen würde
> das Schuldgefühl . . . Die Geisteskrankheit
> Europas. (181)

However, forgetting only seems to be the
answer. In reality, it leads one to try to destroy
all reminders of the truth, as when Zborowsky tries
to destroy first the camp commandant and later Kuropatkin, thus adopting the very methods he reviles.

Woven throughout Kurz nach vier are themes
from other works as well as interesting biographical
references. Sex and alcohol are again present in
their function both as narcotics and as means of
insight. Zborowsky is a heavy drinker who requires
three fourths of a bottle of Sliwowitz or ten mugs

of wine in as many minutes to fend off the memories
that his artistic sensibilities threaten to dredge
up. However, when Zborowsky finally learns the
truth about Kuro's betrayal, it is alcohol that paves
the way for insight: "Das Doppelgetränk putschte
ihn jäh auf zu einer Überwachheit, in der sich Ver-
drängtes empordrängte" (140-141). Zborowsky's love
for Lola releases him from the Dantean vision of his
art by its timeless quality (31). However, it is
sex with an old girlfriend that helps Zborowsky first
to conjure up Lola's image and then to recognize
that Lola has no reality outside of his own memory,
that she is dead. Sex helps to release Zborowsky
from the delusion that he may one day still find
Lola alive.

Becher's view of women remains the same.
Lola embodies Becher's idea of love and beauty, which
condemns her to death. Alma is the generous "Dirn."
The other women in Kurz nach vier, die Schneideritza
and Leonore von Grunau, are only brief sexual inter-
ludes, hardly characters at all, more fortunate amen-
ities among the discomforts of concentration camp
and guerilla fighting life.

Uns die Füße zu wärmen, steckten wir sie in

154

Kuhfladen. Mir selbst blühte das Glück,
mich zudem wärmen zu dürfen an der Schneideritza. (59)

In the love scene Becher completely
dehumanizes Alma by referring to her as "das Wesen"
and by couching the entire scene in metaphor.

Ein Pirat, der nach langer Irrfahrt, ohne
Widerstand zu finden, einfuhr in den sich
ihm in altersloser subtropischer Üppigkeit
darbietenden Hafen, in den er schon einmal
eingedrungen war . . . Keine üble Rückkehr,
wenn´s auch die eine große Heimkehr nicht
war . . . Immerhin Seeräuberromantik, über-
aus lohnenderweise praktiziert. (173)

The sexual act depersonalizes Alma; she is transformed into "woman" and as such conjures up all the
women Zborowsky has made love to: "aber die Stimme
des Atems war anonym wie die Stimme des Winds.
Stimme des Atems, die allen gehören konnte" (174).
Finally, Alma becomes Lola; in making love to this
image of his lost love, Zborowsky is finally able
to exorcize Lola and admit that his "süßer alter
Wahnsinnszweifel," that Lola was not dead, was a
delusion.

Kurz nach vier also contains many autobiographical references. The description of Zborowsky upon his return to Vienna after the war is also

a description of Ulrich Becher: "Mitte deiner Dreiß-
iger standst du, der so früh begonnen, mit leeren
Händen, da existierte (nichts von dir) . . . aber du
existiertest . . ." (69). The critical opinions of
Zborowsky echo the opinions of Ulrich Becher in the
post-war years:

> Er hätte mit 26 berühmt sein können, wenn
> nicht sein Landsmann Hitler dazwischenge-
> brüllt hätte . . . Nun ist er an 40--die
> von Faschismus und Zweitem Krieg mehr als
> dezimierte, teils aufgeriebene junge Gen-
> eration kommt erst mit 40 ans Licht. Mit-
> schuld dran trägt wohl sein Standort Wien
> . . . (83-84)

In addition, comments Zborowsky makes about the post-
war literary situation in Vienna and about his 1948
trial for attempted murder can be seen as Becher's
indictment of Friedrich Torberg, the man who charged
Becher with plagiarism in 1948:

> Die Kulturoffiziere der Sowjets, wenngleich
> sie deinen "kosmopolitischen Formalismus"
> bekrittelten, deinen "zeitweilig bis in
> Mystische ausartenden Pessimismus," begeg-
> neten deinem Wirken mit etwas wie mißbil-
> ligendem Wohlwollen. Die Kulturinstanzen
> der französischen und britischen Besatz-
> ungsmacht förderten dich mit Maß . . .
>
> . . . Aber die "Amerikaner" boykottierten
> Zborowsky. Unter den Fittichen der ameri-
> kanischen Besatzungsmacht zurück kehrte ein
> Handvoll jüngerer mediokerer, vorwiegend
> jüdischer-bürgerlicher Wiener Intellek-

156

tueller, die vorm Zweiten Krieg in die
Staaten emigriert waren und dort nicht re-
üssiert hatten, verkrachte Literaten . . .
ausgehungert nach billiger Macht und ramsch-
barem Erfolg, remigrierend ausgerichtet
nach dem Exerzierreglement und Katechismus
des "Komitees Für Unamerikanische Machen-
schaften" . . . auftretend . . . als "Um-
erzieher," "Theater- und Presseoffizier"
. . . Ex-Emigranten und Ex-Nazis machten
einander hoffähig. (70-72)

An jenem Kaffeehaustisch der Jasomirgott-
gasse wurde dir der Prozess gemacht, noch
ehe der amtliche gegen dich eingeleitet war
. . . die Jasomirgottbande . . . die In-
stinktarmut und Fantasielosigkeit jener, die
dem Massenmord rechtzeitig entwischst waren
und nun, verkleidet als Hyperamerikaner, an
einem Lästertisch hockten mit ihrer Brüder
Henkern . . . (73)

Kurz nach vier received the widest recognition of any Becher publication, with a cumulative
circulation from various editions approaching 180,000
copies sold up to the Benziger edition in 1975.[38]
However, only 18,200 of these copies represent German-language editions, an interesting comment on
Becher's reception problems in Germany, that only
10% of the total circulation of Kurz nach vier was
in the German language. The remainder can be credit-
ed to Russian, Slovak, French, Italian, Yugoslavian,
Polish, and Ukrainian translation. The German editions include the 1957 Rowohlt hardcover (13,000
copies), the 1975 Benziger hardcover (3,200 copies),

and the 1978 Rowohlt paperback (2,000 copies).

Becher followed the success of Kurz nach
vier with a more modest effort, Das Herz des Hais.[39]
This short novel was first published in serial form
in the Frankfurter Allgemeine Zeitung in December,
1958. The paperback edition by Rowohlt published
in 1960 had an edition of 42,000 but received little
attention at the time because it was in paperback
form. Twelve years later, Benziger began republishing the works by Becher that were deemed to merit more
attention; and Benziger's first choice was Das Herz
des Hais. This 1972 hardcover edition of 5,000 has
sold only 2,000 copies to date.

After the labyrinth of political and artistic expression of Kurz nach vier, Das Herz des Hais
appears lighter reading because it focuses on the
love story for its own sake, instead of using love
as a symbol or metaphor for Europe's repressed past,
as in Kurz nach vier. The 11-year-old marriage of
mismatched artist couple from Basle, Lulubé and
Angelus Turian, falls apart during a vacation on
the volcanic island of Lipari. Angelus, true to
his name, is a gentle man, an understanding and
patient husband, but also singularly untalented both

in his art and in satisfying his wife. Lulubé, calling
to mind Wedekind's Lulu, is his opposite in every
way: dark complexion, black eyes that glow with
excitement, enthralled by bull fights, carnivals,
and volcanic islands. But this vital woman is asexual:

> In der deutschen Schweiz sind die Frauen
> sächlich. Erst das Altern oder das Alter
> beehrt man mit dem Attribut der Weiblich-
> keit. In der patriarchalisch-demokratischen
> neutralen Schweiz ist die blühende Frau ein
> Neutrum. (7)

Das Herz des Hais tells of Lulubé's transformation from asexuality to "true womanhood." We
learn that her predilection for danger and death, as
evidenced by her attraction to bull fighting , is the
result of having witnessed her drunken father knock
out her mother's eye during a beating. "So wuchs
das Lulu in der kaum bewußten Vorstellung auf, daß
Grausamkeiten zur Tagesordnung der Zivilisation ge-
hörten" (9). Lulubé is entranced by the spectacle
of the bull fights, but her husband makes the mistake of sympathizing with the murdered bull and shed-
ding a few tears.

Becher's hatred of suffering is expressed
in the description of the dying bull's gaze:

> Es war kein Blick der Dankbarkeit, den
> das Wesen der bunten Überzahl seiner Folt-
> erer und Mörder schenkte, sondern der eines
> sehr jungenhaften maßlosen fürchterlichen
> Staunens, Staunens darüber, daß man ihm all
> dies (so kunstvoll ertüftelte) mörderische
> Leid zugefügt hatte. (14)

And Becher cannot resist opining that the Spanish
Republic would have never been conquered if it had
not tried to outlaw bull fights, which Becher suggests
is a more acceptable outlet for the violence in human
nature than is war.

Lulubé purges her passions in the carnival
rituals of Basle. She is the best drummer in all
Basle; so when Angelus tries to become a drummer at
the advanced age of thirty-two, he cannot help but
fall short of his wife's expectations. During one
carnival, Lulubé sees the man she should have married in the carnival mask of a wild man, and warns
Angelus that if she would ever leave him, it would
be for such a wild man.

It is just such a man that the Turians
meet on their trip to Lipari. John Crossman, whom
the Turians call Cromagnon due to a misunderstanding,
is the "new cave man," Lulubé's wild man. Becher
gives him an anti-fascist father who was murdered by
Mussolini's forces on Lipari, which opens the floor

to one of Becher's favorite themes, the equivalence
of war, fascism, and the atom bomb. It is after
expounding on these dangers that Crossman declares:

> Ich glaube, es ist heute schwieriger als
> früher ein Mann zu sein. Eine Schwierig-
> keit, die besonders die Frauen zu spüren
> kriegen. Der Mann muß ein stärkeres Herz
> haben als früher . . . ein Haienherz . . .
> (58)

The image of the shark's heart is purposely
ambiguous. Sharks are not the most sympathetic of
creatures, and Becher equates them with the fascists
who killed Crossman's father. On the other hand,
the shark's heart, which refuses to stop beating
even when cut out of the body, becomes a very positive
image of the inextinguishable life force. Becher
equates this will to live with masculinity: "Dieser
Hai ist das unanzweifelbarste Männliche" (152). This
is one more example of the two-sided power of the
Dionysian, to destroy life on the one hand while
affirming it on the other.

It is upon confronting this force in Crossman that Lulubé is transformed from an asexual "Es"
into a woman. But she is not the woman formed from
Adam's rib; this image is too much a part of the
patriarchal Judeo-Christian tradition. Lulubé be-

comes instead Aphrodite, goddess of love and beauty. In addition, Lulubé is cured of her obsession with bull fights and learns the quality of mercy. Still, she leaves her husband to follow her wild man: "Ich suche einen Mann, der Deine Herzensgüte als Gutheits- vernunft im Kopf hat und dazu das Herz eines Hais" (170). Lulubé becomes the only lovely woman to sur- vive a Becher novel, precisely because she is able to accept the dual nature of the Dionysian.

In 1956 after his father's death, Becher moved to Basle, where his mother still lived. In 1959, the year after the publication of Das Herz des Hais, Becher's friend and mentor George Grosz died of a heart attack at the bottom of a stairway in Berlin. Two other friends and patrons died the following year: Paul Hühnerfeld, cultural editor of Die Zeit, in an automobile accident and Ernst Rowohlt, Becher's discoverer and publisher. The deaths of these two men was not only a personal loss for Becher, but also meant that he was now without support in the publishing circles of West Germany.

Between 1958 and 1969 Becher did not pub- lish another new work of fiction. Instead, he wrote various essays about his famous friends and enemies

162

which appeared in Swiss and German newspapers. The
earliest of these remembrances was a piece on Grosz,
"Der Maler des Nichts als Cowboy" in the Frankfurter
Rundschau, October, 1962, depicting Grosz's reception
in America and explaining the presence of a Grosz
museum in Arizona. In July, 1963, a poem about
Grosz, "Böffs einsame Nacht auf Hillair-Farm," was
also published in the Frankfurter Rundschau.

The following year an essay appeared that
has been called Becher's phillipic against Rudolf
Walter Leonhardt, then the new cultural editor for
Die Zeit.[40] In this essay, "Junge deutsche Dichter
für Aufhörer," Becher takes issue with comments by
Leonhardt in his book Junge deutsche Dichter für
Anfänger concerning the value of literature written
by emigrants. Becher accuses Leonhardt not only of
irresponsibly denigrating works by exile authors but
also of purposely avoiding reviewing Becher's works
in order to condemn them to obscurity. Leonhardt's
work itself is evidence of the general anti-exile
sentiment that prevailed in the post-war years.

Further essayistic publications during
this eleven year period 1958-1969 include portraits
of Alexander Roda Roda, the actor Helmut Qualtinger,

and Ödön von Horvath, as well as a reprint of Becher's
reminiscences on the book burnings first published
in 1943 in Das andere Deutschland.[41] In addition,
a short autobiographical article appeared in 1965
describing Becher's efforts to publish in Brazil
where speaking and writing German during the wartime period were forbidden.[42]

In 1962 Rowohlt published two works by
Becher, Der große Grosz und eine große Zeit, a speech
held at the opening of a Grosz exhibit in the Akadamie
der Künste in West Berlin, and a collection of Becher's
Brazilian poetry, Brasilianischer Romanzero, most of
which had already been published elsewhere in the late
1940s.[43] This edition is dedicated "Dem Andenken
Pauls," indicating just how deeply Becher felt the
death of Paul Hühnerfeld. Both works were published
in 1,000 copy editions.

Thus during the twelve years from the publication of Kurz nach vier in 1957 to the publication of Murmeljagd in 1969 the name and works of Ulrich Becher the novelist and dramatist slipped from
the consciousness of the reading public. Outside
of seven newspaper articles, no new work appeared.
The one-time telecast of Bockerer in 1963 by Öster-

reichischer Rundfunk did equally little to enhance
the public's awareness of him, and the 1962 Rowohlt
publications were published in editions too small
to be of any significance. Even the 42,000 copies
of Herz des Hais had little lasting impact, in part
because they were in paperback and in part because
they appeared early in this interruption of Becher's
publishing career. The effect on Becher's reception
was not unlike the effect of his exile in Brazil
and the United States; this time, however, the period
lasted even longer and was not brought about by any
external events.

Yet Becher had been writing during those
eleven years, just as he had in exile, and in 1969
Rowohlt published a 4,000-copy first edition of what
has been called Becher's life's work, his masterpiece,
the 570-page Murmeljagd. A 15,000 copy paperback
edition followed in 1974.[44] Ironically, Murmeljagd
was published the very year Rowohlt was not represented at the Frankfurt Book Fair because of the infamous
Balloon Affair; Rowohlt had printed 50,000 copies
of the antistalinist memoirs of Eugen Ginsburg for
the German Defense Ministry which were delivered to
the GDR via weather balloons. Rowohlt's cooperation
in this affair prompted a boycott by its stable of

leftist authors.[45]

Murmeljagd contains all the themes of all
the preceding Becher works: the neuroses of the
shipwrecked European who wavers between action and
inaction; the contagious quality of war which leads
to death even in the midst of peace; the Dionysian
powers of music, alcohol, and sex; the detailed dis-
cussions of political alternatives, local customs,
artistic and literary gossip. In addition, the formal elements are familiar, although heightened by
the sheer length of Murmeljagd: the dramatic prose
with its dialogues, onomatopoetic imitations of dialects and foreign speech, and emphasis on stage settings; the flashbacks occasioned á la Proust by sound,
sights, and smells; the orthographic emphasis via
hyphenating, italicizing, capitalizing that Becher
adopted from Dos Passos; the plethora of exotic names
and places. One familiar with all of Becher's works
gets the impression that he has gathered the forces
that merely have been in training in the other works
for one gigantic attack on the demons of his past.
All of the themes and all of the stylistic peculi-
arities are not only present but seem to reinforce
one another. If the author's intent was catharctic,

166

however, that aspect of the work clearly failed, because Murmeljagd is not Becher's final novel to deal with these themes.

The plot of Murmeljagd can be told in a few sentences. Albert Trebla, whose name reads the same backwards and forwards, World War I fighter pilot, socialist, and Viennese journalist, escapes on skis across the Alps to neutral Switzerland after the fall of Austria in 1938. The events of four weeks of his exile are narrated with flashbacks from forty years of Austrian history: Trebla is as old as the twentieth century, and his biography is designed to mirror the history of a whole country. The idyllic peacefulness of "die tote Zeit," off season for tourist-oriented Engadin where Nietzsche went insane, seems illusory in contrast to the reports of the more horrible reality of Nazi concentration camp murders and the brutality of the transport trains. Incited by the paranoid conviction that he is the target of a Nazi plot, Trebla rushes headlong from one imaginary trap to another, victim of the justifiable paranoia of his generation.

Trebla identifies with the marmot, the skittish ground dweller who runs at the slightest hint of danger:

> Ich war klein, pelzig, weich, leicht ver-
> wundbar, indes eins hatte ich für mich;
> ich war schnell. Der Kreuzung Murmelmensch.
> Ich wurde gejagt. Nicht wissend, von wem.
> Ich war ein unseliges einsames unbewehrtes
> abgehetztes Murmelmenschlein, allein und
> elend auf weiter Flur, allein mit meinem
> wesenlosen Verfolger. (129)

Feeling the need for self-defense, Trebla begins to carry his pistol with him and sees himself as the hero of a murder mystery or a gangster film. After learning about the deaths of his best friend and his father-in-law, Trebla decides to take the offensive:

> Zum Henker mit den Henkern! Man muß es auf
> sich nehmen! Die Henker zu henken mit eig-
> ner Hand! Nicht im Genre einer "Flucht
> nach vorn," sondern als listenreicher
> Leidensbekämpfer, als ein von seinem Im-
> perativ Geleiteter . . . zu handeln wie eine
> Schillerfigur! (344-345)

He plans to shoot the two blond Austrians whom he suspects to be Nazis, but realizes he has succumbed to the distorted thinking of his epoch when he discovers one of the young men is a deaf-mute:

> Verwirrt vom Zwangsaufenthalt im Zerrspiegel-
> Kabinett einer kriminellen Epoche hatte
> ich einen Halbkretin für einen auf Sonder-
> kommando gedrillten Herrenlümmel genommen,
> im Wortsinn aus Ver-Sehn; infolge eines
> chaplinesken Versehens. (415)

168

Trebla is brought back to reality only on the book's
final page, as his wife Xane, who has witnessed Trebla's final hallucinatory act, confronts him with
the absurdity of his behavior. She knows her father
is dead, but refuses to poison herself with sadness,
especially given the reality of her three-month old
pregnancy. Thus, after all the death and fear, real
and imagined, the novel ends with a reaffirmation of
life, hope among all the hopelessness.

One new metaphor, comparable to the carnival
metaphors of Samba, Mademoiselle Löwenzorn, and Herz
des Hais, is the Prater motif that runs throughout
the novel, substituting an amusement park for the
carnival. Two of the novel's books are entitled
"Geisterbahn I" and "II," in which the fortress-like
house of Henrique Kujath becomes a spook house as
Trebla learns of various deaths. This image is then
transferred to Trebla's entire exile experience in
Switzerland. The labyrinth of the Geisterbahn becomes the image of the mundane horrors of exile:
the bureaucratic foul-ups, unexpected dangers and
narrow escapes, the ghosts of the past and the mon-
sters of the present and the knowledge that, even if
one survives one ordeal, there is another shock on

the way. The Hall of Mirrors is a graphic representa-
tion of the optical illusions of exile, the inability
of telling friend from foe and of finding the real
exit out of the labyrinth of problems. The marionettes of the Prater Kasperltheater and the mechanical
shooting-gallery figures are identified in Becher's
fantasy with the manipulated fates of the exiles who
expect atrocities as part of everyday existence and
for whom the normal lives of most of us are so abnor-
mal as to be absurd. The winking, blinking and
bubbling of the Prater with its continuously rota-
ting Ferris wheel and whirling swings becomes synonymous
for an age divested of real meaning, "das Zeitalter
der Illusionsfabrikanten" (248); and the only way to
survive such a world is to develop the resiliency
to withstand any dangers along the way:

> Heute stecken wir in 'ner neuen Inquisition
> mitten drin, nur dasse diesmal mehr eilig
> als heilig ist. Du m-u-ß-t dich darauf
> gefaßt machen, daß wir a-l-l-e, ob groß
> oder klein, mit oder ohne Zaster, Held
> oder Schlemihl, berühmt oder namenlos,
> jeden Augenblick in die Klemme kommen
> können. In die allerletzte Klemme. (245-
> 246)

Murmeljagd almost brought long-expected fame
to Ulrich Becher; it was widely reviewed, even called

worthy of a literary prize,[46] and translated into
French (Editions du Seuil) and English (Crowns, New
York). The Rowohlt printing of 4,000 copies was,
however, never completely sold, which explains why
Rowohlt refrained from publishing additional hard-
bound editions of Becher´s "masterpiece."

Nonetheless, in 1970 Rowohlt published a
paperback version of Becher´s first prose work, Männer machen Fehler, adding new stories written during
or about Becher´s exile experiences in Brazil and
the United States.[47] Unlike other books by Becher,
this paperback edition received two printings, 15,000
copies in 1970 and 4,000 more in 1974, of which 1,000
copies remained unsold. Sales of 18,000 hardly indicate a bestseller in the paperback market. However,
Männer machen Fehler obviously benefited from the exposure Becher´s name gained during the critical discussion of Murmeljagd.

The stories contain much that is familiar
to the reader of other Becher works. In two new
stories from Männer machen Fehler we see the two
sides of Becher´s New York exile. "Katharinapolka,"
set in 1944, portrays the guests in a bar in "Hell´s
Kitchen." It includes all the types we find in

Charlie's bar in <u>Feuerwasser</u>: drunken GI's, tough
guys, dandies, flirtatious or withdrawn women, a
bartender who has seen everything, plus a vistor
from the beyond (named Kilroy) who tells a ghastly
tale of war. The ghostly soldier's entire company
has been boiled alive in a bath of quick lime, water
turned into fire. The image is clear: this Hell's
Kitchen bar represents the living hell of the exploited poor in capitalist America who are being consumed
by alcohol and war. The other story, "Happy-End,"
reflects the gossipy, intellectual Village-existent-
ialist scene in 1955, a scene related to Becher by
Grosz in a letter; Becher's fantasy gives substance
to this Grosz anecdote. The fictional characters
are portrayed within a circle of celebrities, such
as Maxwell Bodenheim, Ben Hecht, Ezra Pound, and
George Grosz, with Becher himself reporting the events
as if writing a memoir, although Becher left New York
in 1948. It is the story of the origins of artistic
inspiration. A pianist experiences the two extremes
of love: a tortuous sexual love for an incomparable
beauty and a soothing, homely love for a plump Czech
widow. The pianist goes on to fame and fortune in
America; the beauty goes through several husbands

172

and turns up later as the cosmetically preserved wife of
an American serviceman; the Czech widow becomes a
fat street-lady in Greenwich Village. She commits
suicide after her happy reunion with the pianist, who
achieves an "Atombomberfolg" in Carnegie Hall. Again,
Becher situates the source of artistic inspiration
within the Dionysian. The pianist's sexual contacts
help him to ever greater success, while destroying
weaker souls.

"Er wollte sie nicht haben," Becher's
shortest short story, describes the suicide of a
Brazilian farmer who has just learned he has leprosy.
Another more recent story from this collection, "Das
kurze Leiden," deals with another incurable illness,
cancer. A middle-aged man receives the notice of his
former high school teacher's death and is obsessed
with reliving his youth through memory. But a second
chance at life is unobtainable and attempts to relive
one's life lead to death. Thus the death of the
school teacher leads to the death of the protagonist
in the story. The contagiousness of death is one of
Becher's favorite themes, in other works seen in connection with war. Incurable diseases such as cancer
or leprosy seem to fascinate him and represent more

than just shocking images of death. Cancer is not simply another disease, it is an "unerforschte, unheilbare Zivilisationskrankheit" linked with Western, especially American, civilization. It is an image for that innate characteristic of capitalism that brings about its own destruction when confronted with death in its variants of war, World War II, fascism, the atomic bomb.

"Die Flieger" is Becher's most poetic short story. A squadron of fliers is forced to land to wait out a storm, a dangerous proposition since fliers are far more vulnerable on the ground than in the air. At least the story seems to be about a squadron of fliers with their modern jets. Only in the final paragraph does the reader realize that this squadron is a formation of swallows flying south for the winter. The reader realizes in retrospect that what he thought were animalistic metaphors for machines were in reality the opposite.

Becher continued in 1971 and 1972 to publish essays in the Frankfurter Rundschau, Weltbühne, and in Basle's National-Zeitung. These essays include articles on George Grosz, Ödön von Horvath, Alfred Kerr, and Roda Roda.[48] Also in 1972 Benziger began

174

republishing Becher's novels with small editions of Herz des Hais (5,000 hardback copies of which 2,000 were sold) and Der schwarze Hut (2,200 paperbacks of 990 were sold).

In the five years after Murmeljagd Becher worked stimultaneously on several projects. The first of these to come to fruition was Das Profil, published by Rowohlt in 1973 in paperback in an edition of 18,000 copies. The novel is dedicated "Meinem alten Freund H-M, L-R," Heinrich-Maria Ledig-Rowohlt, Becher's publisher, indicating that in spite of problems with the company dating from the late 1960s Becher still honors his long-standing relationship with Rowohlt.

Das Profil is based on an anecdote Becher heard from Grosz concerning the series of Grosz interviews by Richard O. Boyer for the New Yorker series "Profiles" in 1943.[49] According to Grosz, Boyer had pretended all during the interviews, which stretched over several weeks, that he was a teetotaler. But on the day of the last interview, Boyer succumbed to Grosz's offer of whisky and the result was a drunken binge similar to the one described in Becher's novel.

Das Profil is set in September, 1959 (not
1943), so as to enable Becher to make some pronouncements on the coming decade of the 1960s (or the previous decade in terms of the publication date). During a week of interviews with the famous German emigrant artist, Altdorfer--a slightly fictionalized
Grosz character--a reporter for the "Manhattan Review," Dennis P. Howndren, reveals his astonishingly
detailed knowledge of Altdorfer's past as well as
of the CIA and its activities. At first Altdorfer
suspects Howndren of being a CIA agent who is trying
to trap him, a former left-winger, into expressing
incriminating (i.e., left-wing) political opinions.
Howndren seems to have too much inside information
on the luminaries of the leftist German emigration
and his leading questions on political matters are
suspiciously frequent. In fact, Howndren seems
fixated on politics and the men who make history:
"Die Weltgeschichte wird von Menschen mit Profilen
gemacht."[50] In the first two sections of Das Profil, entitled "Seancen" and "Dinner Party," Howndren
profiles several men who made history, chiefly the
Dulles brothers and Stalin. Allen Dulles, head of
the CIA, is portrayed as the real power of the west-

ern world, driven by a mission to destroy Communism
any way short of nuclear war. Allen Dulles´ "Sendungs-
bewußtsein" is a "Krankheit mit pestartigen Folgen"
(43) as deadly as the cancer from which John Foster
Dulles died. Indeed, it is a kind of political cancer that had led the CIA into involvement in the
overthrow of governments in Iran and Guatamala to
keep these countries from turning socialist. Howndren predicts (the story is set in 1959) that the
1960s will be "Ein Kalenderjahrzehnt politischer
Schizophrenie" (45) in which the CIA will be involved in assassination, conceivably even of an American
president if he should be too leftist.

        For Becher, from the perspective of the
early 1970s, those turbulent 1960s were strikingly
similar to the Weimar Republic. He sees in the CIA
a growing right-wing revolution comparable to Nazism.
It is entirely possible, although Becher denies it,
that some characteristics of Howndren are based on
Sinclair Lewis, whose It Can´t Happen Here (1935)
dealt with the possibility of just such a fascist
revolution in the United States. Howndren can also
be seen as a spokesman for the group around Grosz
at Aurora Verlag, and for Becher as well, German

literary exiles who continue to suffer from their
personal experiences in exile. Becher's sympathy
is clearly on the side of these slightly insane
Cassandras:

> Außerdem . . . hat er recht. Weil Dennis
> ein Gerechter ist. Und die h-a-b-e-n recht.
> Auch wenn sich's . . . zu ihrer Zeit--so
> ansieht, als seien sie plemplem . . . Die
> Don Quichottes, die Letzten Ritter . . .
> sind manchmal die Vorreiter . . . die Vor-
> läufer . . . die Vorcrawler . . . die Vor-
> kriecher der Revolution. Der wirklichen
> Kämpfer von morgen. (145)

Once again these insights into the political
nature of the time are connected with the Dionysian.
Sections III ("Es geschieht") and IV ("Lichter") detail the results of Altdorfer's insistence that
Howndren have a drink. Howndren, a reformed alcoholic who has been abstinent for some months, starts
an all-night binge that can only be described as
grotesque and very similar to some American paintings of George Grosz, such as The Wanderer (1943),
No Let Up (1936), or The Survivor (1944). Each of
these paintings presents a solitary male figure
plowing his way through a swamp-like landscape filled with fallen trees and mud. In an effort to escape those who are trying to calm him down, Howndren

178

flees through a similar landscape, disrobing along the way, to end up naked on top of the cabin of a yacht, raving about creating a new Cabinet for the United States. In this pose he is compared with a statue of Neptune in Bologna that represents persecution mania for Altdorfer (138).

The dramatic structure of Becher's prose is very obvious in Das Profil; Becher himself points it out in a quote from Abbe Galiani on the first page of the book:

> Nie könnte ich etwas anderes schreiben als Dialoge oder Komödien in Prosa. Das geselligste Volk auf Erden kann nicht denken, ohne zu sprechen. (6)

Immediately following this motto, Becher lists "Zeit, Ort und Personen" as if the book were a play. There are five title sections divided into chapters like acts and scenes in a play. Das Profil could be a play with four acts and an epilogue.

Das Profil, written more than twenty years after New Yorker Novellen, contains much the same constellation of themes as Becher's earlier New York works. This fact alone testifies to the intensity of the exile experience and the existential questions posed by it. However, the answers given in Das Pro-

No let up 1936
pen and ink drawing
no. 63 in *Interregnum*

180

fil are less nihilistic, more resigned. The sexa-
genarian Becher seems to have acquired, along with a
permanent residence and a secure income, a kind of
good-humored resignation to the ineffectuality of
the engaged artist.[51] The artist is still a priv-
ileged seer who prophesies the peril inherent in a
corrupt and exploitative society, but this threat
no longer demands immediate personal sacrifice. Instead of an "Übermensch," the artist has become an
anti-hero, a Don Quixote with at most the hope that
his message will be heard.

In 1974 Becher returned with Williams Ex-
Casino to the same complex of themes found in earlier
works.[52] This novel is Becher's most straightforward-
ly autobiographical piece of fiction. It was written simultaneously with Profil, and shares with it
many of the expected themes and viewpoints, although
it differs in the emphasis given each theme. Profil
emphasizes the role of the artist in society; Williams
Ex-Casino on the other hand highlights the inescapa-
bility of politics in the modern world.

Written during a serious illness by a man
in his sixties, the novel is also preoccupied with
unfulfilled dreams, infirmity, disease, and death.

The main character, Hitsch Kandrian, commercial artist from Zurich, has been incapacitated by an accident during a 1961 summer vacation in Nice. He is forced to sit with his bandaged leg or limp with the aid of a cane, an unpleasant prospect in a tourist-filled, automobile-filled city. So he sits in street cafes and bars with a drink in one hand and binoculars in the other, observing some very suspicious-looking goings-on. It is the bloodiest summer of the French-Algerian War and Hemingway has just committed suicide in Sun Valley, Idaho. The name Hemingway surfaces as a leitmotif throughout the entire novel in conjunction with death and dying. Kandrian's wife and son have left him in Nice to fly back to the deathbed of her mother in Zurich, and Hitsch expects a phone call or telegram any moment informing him of his mother-in-law's death. And on their trip to Nice the Kandrians only narrowly escaped being involved in an automobile accident.

Therefore, it is not implausible for Kandrian to develop suspicions based on his observations. He becomes a witness to a plot to assassinate the Algerian representative to the peace talks. Yet even when his suspicions are confirmed, Kandrian does

nothing to prevent this murder. He is side-tracked
by his hypochondria and a "linksbürgerlicher Ehe-
bruch;" and he submerges himself in alcohol, melan-
choly reminiscences and intellectual game playing
in order to repress his consciousness of failure.
Unlike his hero Hemingway, Hitsch Kandrian, as most
later Becher protagonists, is a weak, neurotic, and
miserable man who makes mistakes. In spite of his
outward show of worldliness and his success with
women, this Becher man carries within him a trauma
of fear, that can become paranoia as in Murmeljagd,
or in Hitsch's case, hypochondria and inability to
act.

> Demut ist Hochmut./Sogenannte Nächsten-
> liebe fantatisierter Haß./Mut ist umge-
> kehrte Angst (vor der Höhle)./Angst./
> Angst./Angst./Todsünde./Todsünde./Tod als
> Ewiges Leben./Tod./Tod./Tod./Du sollst
> nicht töten./Töte./Strafe./Strafe, um nicht
> gestraft zu werden,/vielmehr: um selber
> gestraft zu werden./Totschlagen: Das,
> was den Tod nicht als/als/einzige Erlösung
> empfiehlt. (109-110)

In order to avoid facing his fears, Hitsch contents
himself with the role of passive observer: "Ich
eine Kamera namens Kandrian . . ." (173). Thus,
Becher's protagonist has moved from daring activist
in the early plays to a schizophrenic torn between

action and inaction in New Yorker Novellen and Murmeljagd to a totally resigned and passive anti-hero
in his last two prose works.

Williams Ex-Casino was chosen by a Darmstadt jury as book of the month in May, 1974. However, Williams Ex-Casino is also significant because
it was the first of Becher's novels to premiere with
Benziger. Thus the 3,600-copy Benziger hardbound
edition indicates strained relations between Becher
and Rowohlt. A Rowohlt spokesman admitted that there
had been disagreements in the early 1970s, but would
not specify the nature of these disagreements and refused to release the Rowohlt-Becher correspondence.[53]
Peter Keckeis of Benziger reports in an article in
Basle's National-Zeitung that, as the result of an
argument, Becher was considering publishing in Switzerland, his adopted country.[54] Becher himself expressed
dissatisfaction with Rowohlt on numerous occasions,
partly because the Balloon Affair discussed above
led Rowohlt to cut back on their planned publications
and their entire advertising budget.[55] One of the
cuts was the West German edition of Becher's Spiele
der Zeit II, which was supposed to be published simultaneously by Aufbau and Rowohlt. In addition,

184

against the conventional wisdom of the publishing industry, Das Profil was never published in a hardbound edition, and thus did not receive the critical examination and advance publicity Becher thought his due. Prior to publication of Das Profil Becher's opinion of Rowohlt was quoted in a Viennese newspaper:

> Rowohlt hat (Das Profil) angenommen, aber
> wir streiten noch wegen Auflage und Honorar.
> In letzter Zeit haben einige Autoren Rowohlt
> verlassen. Vielleicht muß ich's auch. Ver-[56]
> lage erinnern mich immer an Fleischfabriken.

Becher also expressed his opinion of the publishing industry in general in his 1974 two-act play, Biene gib mir Honig, which satirizes the business practices of Germany's largest publisher, Bertelsmann.[57] Thus in the early 1970s when Becher could have been exploiting his connections in the German publishing industry in order to reestablish his name after a long absence, he chose instead to take his work elsewhere. A more prominent author could have underscored his demands by such tactics; Ulrich Becher on the other hand could not afford a total break with Rowohlt.

Since the Benziger first edition of William's

Ex-Casino, Rowohlt has only issued paperback editions
of Becher's works. In 1974 Rowohlt brought out a
paperback version of Murmeljagd (15,000 copies),
while Benziger countered with a hardbound New Yorker
Novellen (3,000 copies). The following year, 1975,
saw the two publishing houses vying once again for
the public's attention, Rowohlt with a paperback
Williams Ex-Casino (15,000 copies) and Benziger with
a hardbound version of Kurz nach vier (3,200 copies).
It is unclear whether this competition between Rowohlt and Benziger was intentional; however, four
publications in two years can only have helped Becher's
name recognition.

In 1976 Becher announced that he was working on a new novel that would bring him into the
1970s for the first time. Excerpts from this novel,
entitled "Abseits vom Rodeo," were published in Poesie,
a fledgling Swiss literary journal.[58] The ten-page
excerpt shows a continuation of themes that have
characterized other Becher novels. The proposed chapter titles alone imply a direct connection with the
idea of exile: "Flucht," "Asyl," "Fight," "Verführ-
ung," "Auskunft." On the first page we are introduced
to Harry Neuwinter, twenty-five year old foreign ex-

change student at Columbia who is running from
Vice-President Spiro Agnew's silent majority because
he is one of those who were never silent at all (27).
As a "Blitzrefugie" (29) Neuwinter ducks into the
nearest bar and disappears from the face of the earth.
We learn he has taken part in a Vietnam protest march
and was singled out for punishment by a squad of hard
hats, although he cannot understand why they should
have chosen him. The bar, Old Child's Tavern, appears
to be inhabited exclusively by blind people and their
guide dogs. There is the requisite strawberry blonde,
a Grace Kelly look-a-like who curses the rodeo parade
outside in "eine Art Singsang, in der Resignation und
Empörung kontrastierten" (35). She advises Harry to
forget his fear: "Heutzutage lohnt sich's doch gar
nicht mehr, vor irgendwas Angst zu haben. Denn sonst
können Sie ja vor Angst kaum mehr laufen" (36). These
two quotes contain the essence of Becher's current
style and subject matter: he writes with a tone of
resigned indignation about the terrifying aspects of
capitalist society.

In 1976 Becher was awarded a prize for his
collected prose works by the Swiss Schiller Foundation. In that same year a West German television

company took an option on Feuerwasser. This television production was finally broadcast on July 24, 1978, by Zweites deutsches Fernsehen and received a respectable 17% of the audience although almost total critical rejection.[59]

In 1978 Benziger published SIFF, a collection of essays, most of which had already appeared in one newspaper or another. The title SIFF was an acronym used as a radar code by the U.S. Navy in World War II meaning "selective identification of friend and foe." Some of the essays in SIFF were originally published during Becher's exile by Das andere Deutschland or Alemania libre/Freies Deutschland.[60] The rest of the essays in SIFF appeared from 1960-1971 as articles in the Frankfurter Rundschau, the National-Zeitung (Basle) or Weltwoche (Zurich). "Stammgast im Liliputaner-café" (1961) details Becher's brief friendship with Ödön von Horvath. "Grand Old Man des deutschen Theaters" (1960) honors Heinz Hilpert, who produced two of Becher's plays in Göttingen. In "Finnegan's Wake" (1960/1970) Becher eulogizes his friend and publisher Ernst Rowohlt who died in 1960. Becher wrote "Aus Stein Leben schlagen" in 1967 as a sixtieth birthday pre-

sent for and about Fritz Wotruba, Austria's most
famous sculptor. "Vindobonus der Gefürchtete" (1971)
is a satire on Friedrich Torberg. "In memoriam Hohner-
Baby" (1970) traces the influences on Ulrich Becher
from his childhood to the time of his exile in Brazil.

FOOTNOTES

[1]The history of the Torberg controversy was related in a personal interview with Ulrich Becher. I have not been able to ascertain which Torberg story was based on Preses' anecdote.

[2]P.V., "Doppelte Tragik des 'Bockerer,'" Frankfurter Rundschau, 12 February 1963, n.p.

[3]P.V., "Doppelte Tragik," n.p.

[4]Ulrich Becher, Personal interview with Nancy Zeller, 17 September 1978.

[5]"Literarische Notiz über Ulrich Becher," Frankfurter Rundschau, 25 October 1963, n.p.

[6]Letter to Nancy Zeller from the Landestheater Tübingen, 3 December 1979.

[7]Ulrich Becher, Peter Preses, Der Bockerer: Tragische Posse in drei Akten (Munich: Thomas Sessler Verlag, 1975), p. 30. All further references given parenthetically in text.

[8]Ulrich Becher, Peter Preses, Der Pfeifer von Wien (Munich: Thomas Sessler Verlag, no date). All further references given parenthetically in text.

[9]Ulrich Becher, as quoted in Siegfried

Melchinger, "Anmerkungen zu einer Theaterwoche,"
Die Presse (Vienna), 7 October 1950, n.p.

[10]Composer Robert Stolz used Pfeiffer von
Wien as the basis of this musical, Becher insisted
in a personal interview that Stolz´s version distorts
the message of Pfeiffer with waltz music and popular-
ized lyrics. While he accepted royalties from performances of Das Spiel vom lieben Augustin, he required that he not be listed as the author.

[11]Ulrich Becher, Samba in Spiele der Zeit
(Hamburg: Rowohlt Verlag, 1957). All further references given parenthetically in text.

[12]Otto F. Riewoldt, Von Zuckmayer bis Kroetz:
Die Rezeption westdeutscher Theaterstücke durch Kritik
und Wissenschaft in der DDR (Berlin: Erich Schmidt
Verlag, 1978), p. 12, 81, 101-105, 110, 112-114. Riewoldt reports that the only review of a West German
play in the 1951 volume of Weltbühne was on Samba
(Riewoldt, footnote p. 81).

[13]Konrad Franke, Die Literatur der Deutschen
Demokratischen Republik (Munich: Kindler Verlag,
1971), p. 26, 30.

[14]This quote and the information directly
following from Ulrich Becher, Letter to Professor

H.-B. Moeller, Austin, Texas, 24 March 1977, p. 6.

[15]Ulrich Becher, Feuerwasser in Spiele der Zeit (Hamburg: Rowohlt Verlag, 1957), p. 141. All further references given parenthetically in text.

[16]Arnold Künzli, "Ulrich Becher--Dichter havarierten Europäertums," Nationalzeitung (Basle), 3 March 1957, n.p.

[17]Ulrich Becher, Letter to Prof. H.-B. Moeller, Austin, Texas, 24 March 1977, p. 8.

[18]Ulrich Becher, Letter to Prof. H.-B. Moeller, Austin, Texas, 24 March 1977, p. 9. Becher refers to Cohn's refusal to produce anything that hinted at criticism of the U.S. or sympathy with Russia, due to pressure from the McCarthy committee. See Lillian Hellman, Scoundrel Time (Boston: Little, Brown, 1976), p. 67-76.

[19]Werner Mittenzwei, "Deutsche Dramatik gegen die Atomkriegsgefahr," Frieden und Sozialismus (Berlin: publisher not cited, 1961), p. 201-260. Cited in Riewoldt, p. 81, 112.

[20]Riewoldt, p. 112-114.

[21]A scene was published in Aufbau 11/12 (1955), p. 1069-1077.

[22]Riewoldt, p. 120.

[23] Ulrich Becher, Mademoiselle Löwenzorn in Spiele der Zeit II (Berlin-Ost: Aufbau Verlag, 1958).

[24] Ulrich Becher, "Aus der Spielmacherschule geplaudert," Spiele der Zeit II (Berlin, Weimar: Aufbau Verlag, 1958). All further references to this volume given parenthetically in text.

[25] Jürgen Rühle, "Karneval der Heimatlosen," Sonntag, 9, No. 17 (25 April 1954), 4.

[26] Ulrich Becher, "Das Theater--Die Welt," Blätter des Deutschen Theaters in Göttingen, 8, No. 129 (1957/1958), 210.

[27] Ulrich Becher, Spiele der Zeit II, p. 327.

[28] Ulrich Becher, Spiele der Zeit II, pp. 323-327.

[29] Riewoldt, p. 101.

[30] Ulrich Becher, New Yorker Novellen (Zurich: Benziger Verlag, 1974). All further references given parenthetically in text.

[31] Valentin Herzog, "Schicksalnächte in New York und Basel," Nationalzeitung (Basle), 30 November 1974, n.p. All information concerning the publishing history comes from this article.

[32] Franke, p. 66-77.

[33] Franke, p. 162.

[34] All publication and sales figures come from letters to the researcher from Rowohlt Verlag, 23 February 1979, and from Benziger Verlag, 21 December 1978.

[35] Arnold Künzli, "Ulrich Becher-Dichter havarierten Europäertums," Die Kultur (Munich), 15 December 1959, n.p.

[36] Ernst Alker, Profile und Gestalten der deutschen Literatur nach 1914, ed. Eugen Thurnher (Stuttgart: Alfred Kröner Verlag, 1977), p. 229.

[37] Ulrich Becher, Kurz nach vier (Zurich: Benziger Verlag, 1975), p. 69. All further references given parenthetically in text.

[38] See Note 34.

[39] Ulrich Becher, Das Herz des Hais (Zurich: Benziger Verlag, 1972). All further references given parenthetically in text.

[40] Ulrich Becher, "Junge deutsche Dichter für Aufhörer," Weltwoche, No. 1609 (11 September 1964), 25 and 29.

[41] Ulrich Becher, "Ein lächelnder Zentaur," Frankfurter Rundschau, 25 September 1965, n.p.; "Der Gewaltinger," Frankfurter Rundschau, 14 May 1966, n.p.; "Gefallene Kameraden der Freiheit," National-

194

zeitung (Basle), No. 45, 28 January 1968, n.p.

[42] Ulrich Becher, "Man muß sich nur auf einen kleinen Dreh verstehen," Frankfurter Rundschau, 27 February 1965, n.p.

[43] Ulrich Becher, Der große Grosz und eine große Zeit (Reinbek bei Hamburg: Rowohlt, 1962) and Brasilianischer Romanzero (Reinbek bei Hamburg: Rowohlt, 1962).

[44] Ulrich Becher, Murmeljagd (Reinbek bei Hamburg: Rowohlt Verlag, 1974). All further references given parenthetically in text.

[45] "Blinder Moment," Spiegel, 23, No. 38 (15 September 1969), 206.

[46] Hans Bender, "Gejagt wie ein Murmeltier," Deutsche Welle broadcast of 25 June 1969.

[47] Ulrich Becher, Männer machen Fehler (Reinbek bei Hamburg: Rowohlt Verlag, 1970).

[48] Ulrich Becher, "Das romantische Gelüst," Frankfurter Rundschau, 17 January 1970, n.p.; "Miniplay X. v. Y. Ein Traum für Sigmund Freud," Frankfurter Rundschau, 27 March 1971, n.p.; "Im Loch: Ein Cowboy. Eine George-Grosz-Anekdote," Frankfurter Rundschau, 12 June 1971, n.p.; "Es war einmal ein freier Kritiker," Weltbühne, 25 (1971), 787-790;

"Roda Roda-der lächelnde Zentaur," Weltbühne, 15
(1972), 457-460; "Zu Gast im Terminus (Horvath),"
Nationalzeitung (Basle), 16 November 1974, n.p.

[49]Richard O. Boyer, "Demons in the Suburbs,"
The New Yorker, 19, No. 41 (27 November 1943), 32-42;
"The Saddest Man in all the World," The New Yorker,
19 No. 42 (4 December 1943), 39-48; "The Yankee
from Berlin," The New Yorker, 19, No. 43 (11 December
1943), 37-43.

[50]Ulrich Becher, Das Profil (Reinbek bei
Hamburg: Rowohlt, 1973), p. 22. All further references will be given parenthetically in text.

[51]Personal interview with Ulrich Becher,
17-18 September 1978. In addition to royalties,
Becher receives income from the occasional sale of
paintings inherited from his mother.

[52]Ulrich Becher, Williams Ex-Casino (Reinbek bei Hamburg: Rowohlt, 1975). All further references will be given parenthically in text.

[53]Researcher's interview with Mr. Heepe
from Rowohlt Verlag, December, 1978.

[54]Peter Keckeis, "Abenteuer," National-
zeitung (Basle), 15 December 1973, n.p.

[55]"Blinder Moment," Spiegel, 23, No. 38

(15 September 1969), 206. Authors of Rowohlts "ro-roro-aktuell-Reihe" were particularly upset by their publisher´s participation in the "Balloon-Affair."

[56]Quoted in "Bald wieder in Wien," Die Presse, 10 March 1972, n.p.

[57]Günther Mehren, "Zu Tode gelacht," Frankfurter Rundschau, 2 March 1974, n.p.

[58]Ulrich Becher, "Abseits vom Rodeo: Auszüge," Poesie: Zeitschrift für Literatur (Basle), 4, No. 3 (December 1975-January 1976), 27-36. Although announced for publication in 1976, this novel has never appeared.

[59]Telejour, 24 July 1978 (Allensbach: Teleskopie Gesellschaft für Fernsehzuschauerforschung, 1978), n.p. "Telequota" measures the percentage of all households with television sets. Thus, a 17% rating for Feuerwasser means 17% of all households with television in the Federal Republic were tuned into the ZDF broadcast of Feuerwasser from 9:20 to 11:00 p.m. This compares with 16% for the ARD broadcast Farbige Britten and 14% for the ARD broadcast Bitte, umblätten which together filled the same time slot as Feuerwasser. Figures for the Drittes Programm were not given, but they are assumed to fall

below the other networks. Earlier that same evening,
from 8:30 to 9:30 p.m., an ARD broadcast of Anna
Karenina garnered 38% of the potential audience.
The later hour for the Feuerwasser broadcast probably
accounts for some loss of audience.

[60]This is true for "In der Alpenkatakombe,"
"Wir wollten sie nicht mehr sehn" (a reworking of "Ein
Nachwort zum Nürnberger Prozess"), "Der grosse Grosz
und eine grosse Zeit" (a combination of several articles
on Grosz), "Die Seine fließt nicht mehr durch Paris"
(Becher´s criticism of Ernst Glaeser), and the two
essays on Roda Roda, "Reiter und Writer mit der roten
Weste" and "Erinnerung an einen lächelnden Zentauren"
(originally as "Väterchen" in Freies Deutschland, 4,
No. 12 (Nov./Dec., 1945), 55.)

CHAPTER IV:

Assessment of Newspaper Criticism

The past two chapters have provided a summary of Becher's life and works, along with some initial indications of how those works were received.
For Werkimmanent criticism an exclusive focus on the
works themselves would be sufficient. For reception
aesthetics the public view of Becher's works is the
primary concern.

Previous chapters provided the background
information necessary for proper evaluation of the
secondary material discussed here. Because virtually
the only public statements which reflect Becher's
reception are newspaper critiques of individual works,
and because the judgments drawn in these critiques
vary from work to work and even from one publishing
date to the next for the same work, it is necessary
to have a very clear idea of the nature of each work
before proceeding to a discussion of the critiques
themselves. In addition, this chapter is to lead
to the development of theses about Becher's reception,
many of which will emerge directly from Becher's

publishing history discussed earlier.

The following chapters deal with the statistical analysis of the critiques of Becher's works. Thus, this chapter also serves as a bridge between the narrative discussion of Becher's works and that statistical analysis by presenting a narrative discussion of the raw material of the analysis, the critiques. Even without the statistical chapters to follow, this chapter and the three previous ones could form a complete discussion of Becher's works and their reception. However, organized in the current manner, this chapter leads into a type of analysis that is rather unusual in literary criticism, namely the statistical testing of theses, deemed a necessary addendum to the full implementation of reception aesthetics.

In order to provide the reader with a full understanding of the role book critiques play in forming the public reaction to a literary work, the first part of this chapter will deal with the nature of German book critics and critiques. Once that is complete, a discussion of the roughly 500 critiques available on Becher's works will be undertaken on a work-by-work basis. Finally, themes will be sum-

marized from this discussion, as well as from information gleaned from the previous two chapters. These
themes will form the first statement of the hypotheses
to be tested in the following chapters.

From the standpoint of reception aesthetics,
there are several reasons why professional newspaper
criticism is especially suited to the task of examining an author's reception. As discussed in Chapter I,
reception aesthetics focuses on the role of the reader
in the literary process, and professional critics must
always first become readers before they can become
evaluators of a work.[1] More importantly, professional
critics occupy a special place among all readers, because it is precisely the critic's function to develop
a concretization of a literary work and to incorporate
it into the system of prevailing literary norms. The
professional critic's evaluation, by its very nature,
brings about a confrontation of the qualities of the
work with the literary criteria of his time.[2] Because reception aesthetics is most concerned with the
changing reception of a work, it must, from a purely
methodological standpoint, search out those subjective
views which show this confrontation of individual work
and literary norm most clearly (Vodicka, 99).

Often, professional critiques provide the literary historian with the only clues to the reception of a work, because critics are usually the only readers who record their reactions to a work in a preservable form, namely the written word (Vodicka, 75). Another positive quality of professional criticism is that critics justify their opinions with arguments and examples which provide indications of the critic's literary value system.

The most serious drawbacks to the exclusive use of critiques would be that not all sources are of equal quality and it is not always possible to obtain all critiques. Thus, any evaluation of the history of a work's reception depends on the quantity and quality of the critical sources (Vodicka, 81).

It is not enough to take critical opinions at face value. Any investigation of criticism must include the context of that criticism, i.e., it must separate the subjective views of the critics from views that represent a literary norm. To do this one must learn something about the critics, in this case about German critics. What educational background do they have? What are their political persuasions? How do they view their jobs? What is the power structure of the German press that allows one critic's opinions to become more influential than others?

Fortunately, a number of fairly recent studies are available to help answer such questions, products of the post-war German interest in American marketing research and perhaps the late 1960s' anti-Springer movement, as well. One work in particular, Peter Glotz' Buchkritik in deutschen Zeitungen, is extremely valuable for this investigation because it deals only with literary criticism, whereas the other available sources are more general.[3] Glotz bases his observations on information collected from lengthy questionnaires sent to a sample of newspaper critics in the Federal Republic of Germany. Although his survey of thirty-eight papers cannot claim statistical validity, it does reflect important tendencies, especially since the conclusions about critics and cultural editors drawn from the survey are united with evidence about the other three factors in the communication process, i.e., the medium, the content, and the readers.

From the questionnaires Glotz learned that newspapers in the Federal Republic of Germany can be divided into three groups and this division has implications for an understanding of the type of criticism that appears in each type of paper. These three groups are supraregional papers, local papers, and group papers.

Editors of the cultural sections of supraregional (überregionale) publications such as the Frankfurter Allgemeine Zeitung, Die Welt, Süddeutsche Zeitung, Die Zeit, Christ und Welt, Rheinische Merkur, Sonntagsblatt, Allgemeine Sonntagszeitung, Echo der Zeit, Der Spiegel, Welt am Sonntag, Frankfurter Rundschau and the Stuttgarter Zeitung, are so homogenous both in their educational backgrounds and their literary values that it is understandable why they can be viewed as a clique. At the time of Glotz' interviews, all the cultural editors in this group had academic backgrounds or the equivalent, most having obtained their doctorates in some literature. Thus, the editors of this group are specialists. In addition, most of these men belong to the generation that was just entering the profession at the end of World War II (Glotz, 106), and are thus roughly equal in age.

Group two consists of local newspapers (standortgebundene), within which Glotz distinguishes between those with a circulation over 120,000 and those with a smaller circulation. While there are only thirteen supraregional newspapers, there are over one hundred local newspapers. Examples of newspapers in this group are the Westdeutsche Allgemeine, Münchner Merkur, Recklinghäuser Zeitung, and the Düsseldorfer Nachrichten. Within this group there are three typical education backgrounds: 1) the "classical" route as an intern, 2) the "academic" route, alone or in conjunction with an internship, and 3) the "individual" route over various other professions to journalism. Although all of these educational backgrounds are represented in group two, the classical dominates. There is no homogeneity in the ages of this group of editors (Glotz, 108).

The remaining newspapers Glotz terms group newspapers (Gruppenzeitungen), those which are the press organs of religious or political groups. This includes such newspapers as Vorwärts or Deutsche Volkszeitung. Some of the papers included by Glotz in the first group are clearly group papers as well (Christ und Welt, Rheinischer Merkur). However, in regard to their cultural sections, such papers more closely resemble the universality of the supraregional

papers. Because group papers are the press organs
of minorities, the backgrounds of the editors reflect the changing fates of the minorities. Thus,
the individual educational route is dominant among
editors of the cultural sections of group newspapers
(Glotz, 109).

Regardless of their educational backgrounds,
editors in all three groups were unanimous that an
academic background is desirable in their professions,
while members of group two emphasized the desirability
of additional practical experience. All groups rejected the study of journalism but members of group
one were most blatantly opposed to what they saw as
"hard journalism:" "Feuilletonleute sind ja auch
nicht nur Journalisten, sondern doch schon mehr"
(Glotz, 112).

The Glotz questionnaire also explored the
self-image of cultural editors. Glotz distinguishes
between three possible journalistic attitudes: 1)
the monologue--the communicator ignores his audience;
2) the publicistic attitude (publizistisch)--the
communicator wants to influence public opinion; and
3) the communicative attitude--the communicator wants
to articulate a range of opinions. According to this

scheme, Glotz found that the cultural editors of
supraregional newspapers view themselves primarily
as teachers of educated readers and thus prefer either
the monologue or the publicistic attitude. The editors of the local newspapers have a more communicative attitude, but either do not believe their readers are interested in literary criticism or do not
have the resources to present criticism their readers
would find interesting. The cultural editors of group
newspapers, by the very nature of their roles as
spokesmen for special interest groups, see themselves
as propagandists for their cause and review basically
that literature that relates directly to their sphere
of interest.

Implicit in the editors' self-image is their
image of their readership. Journalists who write
critiques for the supraregional papers feel they
are providing a service for an exclusive minority of
educated and informed readers. They never feel obliged to write for the so-called "average" reader,
either because they do not perceive it to be their
duty or more frequently because they do not feel the
"average" reader appreciates or understands good literature (Glotz, 116). The critique sections of many

of these newspapers are actually literary journals on newsprint aimed at a small circle of the "initiated" (Glotz, 80-81).

As Glotz points out, this image of the reader is not based on a systematic communications marketing analysis. Research on readers is conducted only by a few large papers in West Germany, and the results are usually reserved for the advertisers. Even when market research is conducted, it rarely includes questions on book criticism, and is often suspect methodologically. As a final difficulty, users of the results are obliged to keep the names of the respective newspapers secret (Glotz, 101).

The smaller newspapers either cannot afford scientifically valid market research or still harbor deep prejudices against the reliability of marketing analysis, preferring to rely on experience or intuition (Glotz, 131-132). Often the only information about readers comes from letters to the editors, and such letters are rare to the editors of book criticism. The result of this situation is that only a minority of editors of book criticism knows with authority who its readers are.

In order to obtain a better idea of readers

of book criticism, Glotz uses information from general
surveys on readers conducted by the DIVO-Institut
Gütersloh. From these surveys, four separate Kom-
munikationsräume are discernible (Glotz, 62-65).
Area 1 consists of the 28 per cent of FRG citizens
who own no books. This group contains mostly, though
not exclusively, Volkschule graduates who have become
blue-collar workers and whose only reading material
consists of sensational literature (Heftchenromane,
Illustriertenromane). Area 2 constituents are the
average members of the large book clubs who read
mostly light fiction (Unterhaltungsromane) or popular
non-fiction (Sach- und Fachbücher). Since 36 per cent
of book owners are members of book clubs, area 2 is
very large (Glotz gives no exact percentage of the
population). Area 3 consists of the educated non-
experts, high school and university students and their
teachers, usually middle class. Readers in this group
are familiar with realistic fiction and would be at
ease with discussion of content, but could understand
with explanation a more literary discussion of structural aspects, as well. Glotz gives no estimate of
the size of this group. Area 4 represents literary
experts, approximately 5 per cent of the population,

who are interested in literature per se.

The purpose of this brief investigation of readership analysis was to arrive to an estimate of the size of the population served by book criticism. By their own definitions, editors of the supraregional papers aim their critiques at the educated minority, the 5 per cent of the population who are interested in literature per se. Their critiques represent a discourse for experts. For Glotz this attitude represents an "Aristokratismus" which is inconsistent with the function of newspaper book criticism, which he believes should be communicative, i.e., should allow the reader to decide for himself on the basis of objective information (Glotz, 43).

The situation becomes more problematical when one investigates the critiques that appear in other groups of newspapers. Local newspapers which are financially able to do so model their criticism on supraregional newspapers, in spite of the fact that they view their readers as average. The majority of local newspapers, however, have no systematic literary criticism and simply use the texts that are sent to them by the publishers or news services. Often the editors admit that their book critiques are just filler for blank space left by ads (Glotz, 165). Group newspapers rarely include book critic- ism, but when they do, their political persuasions are less applicable than their aesthetics, which they adopt intact from the supraregional papers (Glotz, 143).

The result is a vicious circle. The large supraregionals do not present critiques for the aver- age reader or refer him to the smaller, local papers. The local papers, on the other hand, view book critic- ism as the duty of the large, financially-strong papers, and declare themselves not responsible for or not capable of mastering such a high aesthetic task. Group newspapers either ignore literature or adopt the attitude of the supraregionals. Thus, according to Glotz, the media fail in their role as mediator between literature and society.

What emerges from Glotz's investigation is the predominance of a small group of newspapers in literary criticism.

> Die verschiedenen kritischen Positionen,
> die "Hauptrichtungen der Literaturkritik,"
> die es in einer Gesellschaft gibt, sind
> fast immer an der Diskussion weniger Organe,
> ja weniger Kritiker ablesbar. (Glotz, 13)

These papers include the supraregionals mentioned
earlier. The importance of these papers in defining
"good literature" makes it imperative that the aesthetic values of their cultural editors be investigated. The central norm cited by almost all cultural
editors in this group was linguistic and structural
innovation (Glotz, 143). Content was considered
secondary, if the author presented his material in
a new way. The viewpoints of formalist literary
criticism taking post-Modernist works as their norm,
predominate. Thus, it matters little what the political persuasions of either the editors or the authors
are, although, given the editors' backgrounds, there
is a general allergic reaction to totalitarian views.
But it is not because of their authors' political
views that the works of outspoken Third Reich or GDR
authors such as Eberhard Wolfgang Möller or Dieter
Noll are not discussed, but because their works are
seen as aesthetically inferior. Glotz does not seem
to consider exiles as a political group, and therefore does not view their wholesale rejection as exception to this rule. By basing his conclusions on
interviews with these cultural editors, Glotz has
taken their explanations at face value, ignoring the

consistent rejection of exiles by these critics as
a cultural-political phenomenon. According to Glotz,
"Der ´Boykott´ im Sinne eines gezielten ´Totschweigens´
ist selten und richtet sich nur gegen exponierte Aus-
senseiter" (Glotz, 143), against those who insist
on confronting the past or who refuse to play the
literary game. Any literature that does not fulfill
the aesthetic criteria of these editors is relegated
to the realm of Trivialliteratur, and it is a matter
of prestige that the supraregional papers never review Trivialliteratur (Glotz, 117).

Aesthetics affects as well the kinds of critiques that are written. Because literary criticism
in the supraregionals is primarily Fachgespräch, it is
lacking in contemporaneity (Aktualität), and thus the
themes which are considered appropriate are limited.
From 30-50 per cent of book critiques are concerned with
"schöne Literatur," while popular fiction, political
literature, and popular non-fiction are almost completely ignored (Glotz, 184). The form of the critiques
is determined by what is seen as the seriousness of
the subject matter, making the traditional review,
in which one critic expresses his opinions on a book,
the prevailing form. Only on rare occasions does one

find the interview with or portrait of an author or a text sample or multiple critical opinions used as the form of a book critique.

What then are the implications for this investigation of the critical reception of Ulrich Becher's works? Not only are the number and quality of critiques on each work important, the source of the critiques must be investigated as well and their relative influence weighed. Critiques by star critics in supraregional newspapers identified by Glotz must be considered more important because of their normative quality, whereas critiques in women's magazines, trade magazines, local papers must receive lesser weight.

Thus, for each critique the following categories of information must be noted, in addition to the above-mentioned points:

a) Name of the source and location (country)
b) Circulation
c) Political affiliations or leanings
d) Judgment expressed (positive, neutral, negative)

Before turning to a discussion of the critiques themselves, I would like to remind the reader of the major problems in Becher's reception as developed in the previous two chapters. The first, and most far-reaching, of these problems is, of course, Becher's exile. Cut off from his audience after the publication of his first work, Becher was unable to develop his fledgling reputation through his publications in exile. His frequent change of residence during the exile years also worked against the building of fame, as did his stay in Brazil, which was not a primary literary center and offered no market for German language works.

In addition, Becher remained independent enough that he never received the support of any group of exiles, and yet he was associated with the leftist Grosz circle and branded as a communist sympathizer by an influential group of conservative exiles. According to the German saying, "er setzte sich zwischen zwei Stühle" by being considered too engagé and insufficiently aesthetic for the conservative faction and too involved with the literary tradition of the bourgeoise past to satisfy the leftists and GDR critics.

The content and style of Becher's works were also affected by his exile experiences. On the one hand, exile cut Becher off from developments in German literature and traumatized him so that there

remains a clear connection to Expressionism in his
works. Thus, the expressionist style that Ulrich
Becher--in his own variation--shared with Wolfgang
Borchert and Arno Schmidt, may in part explain his
sporadic reception and may, as was the case with the
early Schmidt, have put him out of step with the late
1950s and 1960s mainstream. In addition, Becher's
subject matter was determined by his exile. Many
of his works, especially the ones set in Brazil
and New York, have little relevance beyond exotic
appeal for the average German reader because they are
based on experiences few have shared. Becher remains
dedicated to exile themes even in his most recent work.
However, until the recent revival of interest in
Nazism and its consequences as evidenced by the pro-
longed discussion of the American television film,
Holocaust, Becher's brand of Vergangenheitsbewältigung
was unpopular with the post-war generation which just
wanted to forget its recent past and get on with business. Unlike Böll, Grass and Lenz, who clothed their
criticism with post-Modernist stylistics, Becher
employed a narrative style which did not obscure
his concern with the past and criticism of the present. Being the "guilty conscience of German litera-

ture" is not exactly conducive to popularity.

Other problems lie in Becher's publishing history. By the mid-1950s Becher was known as a dramatist. His switch from plays to prose represented as well a change of audience and to some extent necessitated a rebuilding of his reputation, this time as a prose writer. Then, just as his reputation had been reestablished, Becher fell silent for almost the entire decade of the 1960s while writing his "masterpiece" Murmeljagd. German prose literature was fundamentally altered in 1959 by the publication of Günter Grass' Blechtrommel and Uwe Johnson's Mutmassungen über Jakob.[4] Perhaps it was this fact, the establishment of new forms for the novel, that caused Becher, after the modest success of his very traditional novel, Herz des Hais, to turn Murmeljagd into a 600-page mammoth which was in fact compared to Blechtrommel. Whatever the explanation, it is possible that his decade-long absence from the market hurt his reputation as well as the sales of Murmeljagd.

Another factor in Becher's waning fame surely must be his outsider position in the German book trade. Having chosen to settle in Switzerland, after Austrian

critics led by Torberg closed ranks against him and
GDR critics rejected his works as too bourgeoise,
Becher's only link to the German market was through
his publisher, Rowohlt. This probably would have
been a sufficiently strong link had Rowohlt shown
more interest in promoting his work. However, Rowohlt failed to publicize Becher's works, failed to
arrange lecture tours, published some works in first
editions as paperbacks, and did not attend the Book
Fair in 1969 when Murmeljagd was published. Becher's
consequent switch to a small Swiss publisher of hymn-
books, Benziger Verlag in Zurich, further weakened
his position in the market. In addition, Becher
himself worked against a favorable reception by his
reluctance to become involved in the promotion of
his books and his castigation of critics who did
not give his works the attention he felt they deserv-
ed.

In addition to reception problems caused
by external factors such as exile and publishing mis-
management, Becher's literary works have not been
entirely successful on the basis of aesthetic criteria
applied by many critics. Certainly aesthetic judgments play a central role, as Glotz's results have

shown, in newspaper criticism. The following section investigates various aspects of the aesthetic
judgments critics have made of Becher's works, dealing with formal elements such as style, language, and
structure, as well as with the critical reception of
the ideas or content of Becher's works.

Critical judgments have differed with the
differing works being discussed, and in Becher's case,
there appears to be a clear division with regard to
genre and time period as well. We have already noted
the considerable diminution of Becher's reception
after his decade-long silence, which coincides with
his switch from drama to novel. In regard to the
time period, whereas the initial productions of
Becher's dramas received almost universal praise
and were given special attention in the GDR, later
productions, like his prose works, met with more
resistance, usually on the basis of formal elements.

In the case of Bockerer the original 1948
Austrian production received little critical commentary in general and on formal elements in particular,
perhaps giving credence to Becher's charge of a boycott by Austrian critics. The only available critique
from 1948 is from a West German paper, and it is obvi-

ously based only on the knowledge of the script, not on the actual production of the play.[5] However, this critique anticipates all the issues raised by subsequent reviews of Bockerer. The question of whether the history of the Hitler-era is suitable subject matter for humor is brought up. This critic feels that Becher and Preses were talented enough to have discovered the proper mixture of tragedy and comedy. He also approves of the message of the play as represented by the main character, Karl Bockerer:

> In dem Karussell von Farce und stupider Verrohung harren Güte und Sinn für Gerechtigkeit in den Herzwinkeln schlichttapferer Menschen mutig aus . . . (J.Z.)

We know from the number of performances that this original Austrian production was very successful, and yet neither the publisher nor the author could provide copies of newspaper critiques pertaining to it. In the immediate post-war period no such luxuries as regular clipping services existed to help document reception. However, an equally plausible explanation could be that Bockerer was indeed boycotted by critics.

The 1963 Österreichischer Rundfunk broadcast appears to have had a greater impact on the Austrian press, although in Becher's overall reception, this

one broadcast made little or no impression during
Becher's long silent period. The Viennese press
unanimously declared Bockerer the perfect Volksstück,
and Fritz Muliar in the title role became an overnight sensation.

> Mit dem "Bockerer" haben wir also jetzt end-
> lich ein richtiges Volksstück bekommen, in
> dem uns ein Spiegel unserer tausendjährigen
> Vergangenheit vorgehalten wird. ("TV gestern
> heute," Kurier, Vienna, 28 January 1963)

Most Austrian critics approved as well of
the ideas represented by the main character. Some saw
in Karl Bockerer "das goldene Wiener Herz" which by
its loving nature resists the brutality of Nazism
(o.f.b., "Der Bockerer und die große Zeit," Neues
Österreich, 29 January 1963). This was a welcome
message for Austrians still smarting from the charges
of Mitläufertum leveled in the Merz/Qualtinger play,
Herr Karl. A less chauvinistic Austrian critic from
Radio Österreich sees in Bockerer the "Zusammenstoss
eines unbeugsamen kleinbürgerlichen Individualismus
mit der furchtbarsten kleinbürgerlichen Massenbewegung
unserer Epoche."

West German reviews of the same production
contain more reserved praise. Bockerer is no model of

passive resistance in their view, but a representative

of humanism who cannot help but come into conflict

with the inhumane ideology of Nazism (A.H., "Hitler

contra Bockerer," Ruhr-Wort, Essen, 23 November 1963).

Others show their approval by comparing the play to

works by Zuckmayer, Brecht, Ödön von Horvath, and

Nestroy ("Herrn Karls bewältigte Vergangenheit,"

Stuttgarter Nachrichten, 14 February 1963).

However, in considering the suitability of

form to content, the West German critical verdict is

no longer unanimous. The socialist paper Vorwärts

found the form suitable:

> Die Posse wird zum schauerlichem Ernst. In
> . . . Lächerlichmachen besteht . . . das
> Hauptverdienst des Stücks. Noch niemand
> hat . . . bisher das fürchterlichen Spieß-
> ertum der braunen Machthaber so erbarmungs-
> los deutlich gemacht, wie es hier geschieht.
> ("Zustimmung," Vorwärts, Bonn, 20 February
> 1963.)

But there were dissenting voices. Becher expressed

outrage at the vehemence of an attack in the Stutt-

garter Zeitung (15 February 1963) and received a month

later an official, printed apology by Siegfried

Melchinger in the same paper. The original critic-

ism, says Melchinger, was an allergic reaction typical

of the younger generation of critics to the use of

humorous forms in dealing with the Nazi past.

> Diese Art von Widerstand war eben zu wenig,
> wie sich gezeigt hat, und ich bin dagegen,
> daß sie uns heute vom Bildschirm her wieder
> als eine quasi optimale Möglichkeit vorge-
> führt wird, so daß sich jeder sagt: "wenn's
> wieder mal passiert, als Bockerer kommt man
> schon durch." (Stuttgarter Zeitung, 15
> February 1963.)

Another critic rejected Bockerer entirely

on the basis of form.

> Das soll eine dramatische Posse ein? Er
> war keine. Es war ein Sammelsurium von
> bitterem Ernst, billigem Kabarett und einer
> Art Schweijk-Figur. Die "dramatische Posse"
> war verzeichnet; sie malte zwar gelegentlich
> ganz schwarz und ganz weiß, aber hauptsäch-
> lich war sie so lau, daß man weder echte
> Dramatik noch echte Posse empfand. (Ric
> von Rijn, "Eine Posse?" Allgemeine Zeitung,
> Mainz, 14 February 1963.)

A milder criticism of Bockerer's form simply pointed

out the non-traditional use of a series of chronolog-

ically arranged scenes:

> . . . das keineswegs nach der "Hamburger
> Dramaturgie" gebaute, mit Bedacht in der
> Art von "comic strips" angelegte und den-
> noch gar nicht Kabarettistische Spiel . . .
> (p.v., "Doppelte Tragik des Bockerer, Frank-
> furter Rundschau, 12 February 1963.)

By the 1978 Mannheim production much had

changed in the theater. Bockerer could no longer be

rejected solely on the basis of non-classical form,
when Bilderbogen plays such as Brecht's Furcht und
Elend and tragi-comedies such as Dürrenmatt's Besuch
der alten Dame had themselves become classics. Thus,
only individual moral reservations remain in basically
positive critiques.

> [Eine Posse] . . . kann das Phänomen Hit-
> ler nicht erschließen. Wir Älteren verstehen
> nicht, warum gelacht wird. Es gab in diesen
> Situationen nicht im mindesten etwas zu
> lachen. (Edwin Kurtz, "Der Bockerer,"
> Rhein-Neckar-Zeitung, 10 Oktober 1978.)

One younger critic agrees with the point made in 1963
that it is only too easy for the real Bockerers of the
world to dismiss the seriousness of their behavior
during the Hitler years by viewing it as comedic.
Therefore, he feels the "Posse" is an inappropriate
form for the subject matter.[6]

However, most of the 1978 critiques ignore
the question of form entirely and concentrate on the
effectiveness of Bockerer's message, on the history of
its productions, and on the quality of the Mannheim
production. In comparing Bockerer to either Brecht's
Furcht und Elend or Schweyk, critics find Bockerer
inferior both in its description of the political climate and in the solutions offered. Whereas Brecht's

224

Schweyk rationally analyses and exploits the inherent weaknesses of the system in order to destroy it, Bockerer necessarily works against the system because his values are diametrically opposed to it. Critics see Brecht's attacks as more direct and precise, and therefore, more acceptable to them.

> (Bockerer ist ein) . . . in sich gekehrten und gerade deshalb mit besonderer Gefähr- lichkeit gelegentlich herausdonnernder Brocken von Mann, der das Richtige mehr ahnt und fühlt als weiß. Gerade das unterscheidet ihn von dem realistisch denkenden Schweyk.[7]

This critical acceptance of Brecht's solutions in addition to the success of Schweyk is also seen as one reason for the lack of success of Becher's play.

> Trotz der Sorgfalt (der Inszenierung) er- wies sich einmal mehr, wie gerade die An- klänge an Schweyk . . . dem Stück im Wege stehen. Dabei sind die Anklänge an den Brechtschen "Schweyk" mit dem Auftreten "Hitlers" gegen Schluß besonders mißlich. Man vergißt zu leicht, daß dieser Schweyk erst zehn Jahre nach dem Bockerer auf die Bühne kam . . . (Golitschek)

Most of the 1978 critics are full of praise for the Mannheim production. It is called "ein voller Er- folg"[8] and "ein theaterhandwerkliches Meisterwerk."[9] The naturalistic staging was considered especially

appropriate to the Posse form (Hans Peter Kensy,
"Konturen," Süddeutscher Rundfunk, October 11, 1978).
Mention was even made of the honorable motivations of
the Nationaltheater Mannheim in disinterring a for-
gotten play:

> Die Wiederaufführung ist darum weniger ein
> Tribut an die modische Hitler-Welle als ein
> Akt gesellschaftsbewußten Theaters, etwa im
> Sinne des Sozialpsychologen Wilhelm Reich:
> "Man kann den faschistischen Amokläufer
> nicht unschädlich machen, wenn man ihn nicht
> in sich selbst aufspürt." (Hans Jansen,
> "Bockerer ist unter uns," Westdeutsche
> Allgemeine Zeitung, Essen, 11 October 1978.)

One critic approvingly refers to the production as a
memorandum for the older generation, a history lesson
for the younger (Osterwald).

The most recent production of Bockerer in
April, 1980, at the Volkstheater in Vienna was a total
critical success. The critiques contain jubilant
praise for the rediscovery of a play which so perfectly fulfills the needs and expectations of the
audience, the theater, the actors, and the times. The
working-class audience of the union-affiliated Volkstheater could enjoy and identify with the realistic
folksy characters and the tragi-comic situations without
getting lost in abstract political theorizing. The

Volkstheater obtained a play tailored to its interests, i.e., genuine Volkstheater, politically engagé entertainment. The play contains a plethora of roles especially suited to ensemble actors. And finally, the content of the play appeals both to the generation which lived during 1938-1945 and to a younger generation which has found renewed interest in the period.

Only one critique even mentions the possibility that the comedic aspects of Bockerer could trivialize Nazism (Hans Heinz Hahnl, "Der standhafte Herr Karl Bockerer," Arbeiter Zeitung, 28 April 1980). The rest found the play perfectly suitable as a history lesson:

> In diese Aufführung sollte man ganze Schulen schicken. (Helmut Butterweck, "Erhellendes Lachen," Die Furche, 30 April 1980.)

> . . . ein Stück, daß . . . anschaulicher und sinnfälliger als jeder Geschichtsunterricht Vergangenheit bewältigt . . . (Rudolf U. Klaus, "Sieben Jahre 'Drittes Reich' in Wien," Wiener Zeitung, 29 April 1980.)

The reception of Bockerer shows clearly the initial positive evaluation of Becher's work up to the late 1950s, the more reluctant to negative evaluation of the next twenty years on the basis of formal considerations, followed by a renewed positive recep-

tion in the late 1970s due to renewed interest in the
Hitler era. Because only Bockerer and Feuerwasser have
been produced in more than one decade, they are the
only plays that can show a change in reception. The
rest of the plays serve to illustrate the reception
of the 1950s alone, and we shall have to turn to the
prose works to investigate the change in reception
indicated in the case of Bockerer.

With Samba Becher´s style, as distinct from
that of Preses, emerged. FRG critiques emphasized
Becher´s excellent characterization and welcomed his
plays as a sign of hope for the German-language theater, which was thought to be at an all-time low after
World War II.

> Eine seltene Genugtuung lag allein schon
> darin, einen deutschen Autor auf einer
> deutschen Bühne in einer deutschen Erstauf-
> führung begrüßen zu können.[10]

> Ihm gelingt eine Überzeugungskraft in der
> Schöpfung von Figuren. So war der Beifall
> . . . herzlich, mit einem Einschlag von
> Jubel darüber, einen deutschen Autor über-
> haupt zu finden, der so kräftig Personen
> auf die Bühne zu stellen fähig ist. (F.L.,
> "Ulrich Bechers Samba," Neue Zeitung, 8
> April 1952.)

These same critics felt that characterization and atmosphere, however well done, were not the
only components of satisfactory drama.

> Die Schilderung eines Zustands kann als
> durchaus realistisch bezeichnet werden.
> Aber es war ein Zustand nur und nicht im
> eigentlichen Sinne ein Drama. (Schwirten)
>
> Die Mängel sind typisch: Seinsschilderung
> statt Entwicklung, Milieu statt Aktionskurve.
> (W. Schimming, "Ein Bündel Schicksale,"
> Frankfurter Neue Presse, 9 April 1952.)

Thus, in the West Samba was judged exclusively from an aesthetic standpoint. Because Samba did not correspond to the critics ideal of good drama, it was judged inadequate. Most FRG critics expressed the hope that later works by Becher would correct this "failing" and establish him as a rare talent of the German theater.

GDR critics had more unreserved praise for Samba. Becher's characterization was described as being written with the hand of a poet (Jürgen Degenhardt, "Mit der Hand eines Dichters geschrieben," Sonntag, 12, No. 29, 21 July 1957, 8). His dramatic form is honored with the Brechtian term "epic:"

> . . . die dramaturgische Form: mehr episch
> als dramatisch aneinandergereihte Bilder,
> packend dennoch, lebendig in ihrer foto-
> grafisch präzisen Momentaufnahme von Mensch
> und Welt, Meinung und Zusammenhängen. Es
> ist eine sehr eigenwillige dramatische Form,
> Stärke und Tragkraft gewinnt sie nicht zu-
> letzt aus einem überaus realistischen Dialog
> . . ."

This critic aside, no Becher play can be considered epic theater in the Brechtian sense. To be sure, Samba and Feuerwasser contain epic elements. Becher uses the idea of a string of scenes, Bilderbogen, and he calls Feuerwasser a "Chronik." However, the effect on the audience is more traditional. Becher plays are closer to the aristotelian idea of theater of illusion in which the audience is asked to identify with the action on stage to bring about a cathartic resolution of a problem. In the reference system of GDR drama, Becher's plays are closer to those of Friedrich Wolf than to Brecht's antiaristotelian theater of alienation. Naturally, Becher's plays cannot be equated with the third type of GDR drama, the Bejahungsstück, which advocates strict adherence to the party line. Thus, while it was indeed praise to label Samba "epic," it was hardly an appropriate evaluation of Becher's dramatic form. But by far the strongest praise of GDR critics is reserved for the political and social commentary contained in Samba, which is seen as a rarity among Western authors.

> Angeklagt wird jegliche Gewalt dem Geist,
> dem Menschen, dem humanen Fortschritt gegen-
> über, angeklagt wird damit der Faschismus in
> jeglicher Form und Ausgeburt, wird der Krieg

230

in jeglicher Gestalt. Jede Dichtung Bechers
ist ein Bekenntnis zum Leben, zum Humanis-
mus, zum Frieden. (Kaltofen)

They also feel, however, that Becher unnecessarily
limits the effectiveness of his criticism by con-
centrating on middle class characters who never quite
reconcile their beliefs with political action.

The contrast between FRG and GDR receptions
of Samba is quite striking. Western critics concentrate exclusively on the aesthetic qualities of the
play and completely ignore the obvious political statement, preferring to see instead Becher's attempt to
recreate the "exile condition." GDR critics discuss
all aspects of the work with emphasis on the political
message, but without neglecting formal considerations.

Becher's next play, Feuerwasser, has the
same structure as Samba and like Samba was hailed in
the 1950s as a harbinger of the rebirth of German
theater. However, formal considerations played only
a minor role in the reception of Feuerwasser. Some
comments by West German critics on the play's form
questioned the appropriateness of the subtitle,
"Eine deutsch-amerikanische Tragödie."

Tragödie? Ach, nein. Aber ein Kriminal-
stück mit tieferer Bedeutung und stärkster

Charakterzeichnung in einem neuen Milieu.
(Felix Emmel, "Kaschemme der GESTRANDETEN,"
Frankfurter Abendpost, 2 December 1952.)

Another pointed out the "epic" nature of
Becher's dramatic structure, in which an epilogue
follows the denouement.

> Dieses Anhängsel ist für den novellist-
> ischen Hang des Verfassers Ulrich Becher
> noch bezeichnender . . . weshalb wir auch
> durchaus nicht die "deutsch-amerikanische
> Tragödie" sehen und hören . . . (Will Sering-
> haus, "Feuerwasser", Frankfurter Abendpost,
> 2 December 1952.)

Three years later, perhaps as a result of the FRG
objections, the GDR production of Feuerwasser bore
an altered subtitle, "Eine deutsch-amerikanische
Chronik in 6 Bildern." However, East German critics
preferred the term Milieu-Stück to Chronik which they
consider an epic theater term.

> . . . weil alle handelnden . . . Personen
> seines Stückes nur aus dem spezifischen
> Milieu zu verstehen wären. Es handelt
> sich um ein Milieu-Stück, das einen ganzen
> Komplex wirklichen Lebens zu umfassen ver-
> sucht. (Carl Andrießen, "Charlie Brown und
> seine Stammgäste," Weltbühne, 11, No. 4,
> January 25, 1956, 109-111.)

Testimony to the East German appreciation of Becher's
plays is the fact that no lesser a critic than Herbert

New York Soda Counter ca. 1936
Galerie Ilse Schweinsteiger (Munich)

Ihering compares Becher´s Feuerwasser to Brecht´s

Der gute Mensch von Sezuan. Ihering maintains that

Brecht and Becher share similar goals, but differ in

their artistic views and methods, primarily in Becher´s

preference for characterization over action.

> Figuren, die einer Zeit die Maske abreißen,
> aber kaum eine durchgehende Fabel. Hier
> trennen sich die Wege Brechts and Ulrich
> Bechers. Brecht hat immer eine dichterische
> Fabel, die Personen und Handlung, Sinn
> und Bedeutung kontrolliert. In Ulrich
> Bechers Stücken entlarvt sich das Milieu
> selbst. Die Personen schleppen ihr Schick-
> sal auf die Szene. Dort explodiert es,
> und die Explosionen reihen sich aneinander.
> Es ist die Technik der szenischen Knall-
> frösche. Brecht und Ulrich Becher--Das
> deutsche Theater ist nicht so arm an Werken
> wie diejenigen, die sie nicht spielen wol-
> len, angeben.[12]

The primary factor influencing the reception

of Feuerwasser was the believability, i.e. the psycho-

logical realism, of the characters and the situation.

The critics of the 1950s productions had experienced

the atmosphere of the post-war period and were gener-

ally more familiar with the problems faced by those

who had been uprooted. For this reason, the early

productions of Feuerwasser were evaluated as realistic

portrayals of the post-war climate.

> Man hat episodenlang das Empfinden, einen
> auf die Bühne transponierter neorealist-

ischen Roman mitzuerleben: so wuchtig-
dicht und dennoch psychologisch durchfeilt
ist das Ganze . . . (L. Tsch., "Feuerwasser,"
Frankfurter Rundschau, 15 December 1952.)

The well-known critic Friedrich Heer finds the char-

acters in Feuerwasser to be both "einmalige Menschen"

with their own very unusual backgrounds and at the

same time "Typen" who possess the same human frail-

ties as the people around us.[13] Thus, Becher's char-

acters are seen both as well-rounded individuals and

as standard-bearers of various moralities.

Jede dieser "Figuren" (Figur hier als Sym-
bolgestalt im Paracelsischen, vielleicht
auch im Jüngerschen Sinne) verdiente eine
Existenzanalyse: die Dramen und Tragödien
des alten Europa ließen sich an ihnen auf-
rollen. (Heer)

These early critics thus emphasize once again that the

artistic success of Becher's plays depend on his ability

to create characters who represent the many sides of

a moral dilemma, while maintaining their realism.

Er schafft Gestalten unserer Zeit. Kühn
und rücksichtslos wird diesen Menschen und
ihrem Leben die Maske abgerissen. Figuren,
die einer Zeit die Maske abreißen. (Ihering)

Ulrich Becher ist eine Art dramatischer
George Grosz. Wie dieser Maler, so pin-
selt er seine Szenen, saugt sich an ab-
seitigen Typen fest, stempelt sie auf die
Generallinien seiner Ethik . . . Ulrich
Becher's Menschenspezialisten-Dramaturgie

bewährt sich erneut. (Hermann Wanderscheck,
"Bechers Feuerwasser an der Volksbühne,"
Frankfurter Abendpost, 13 January 1956.)

Unlike the 1978 and 1980 productions of
Bockerer, the 1978 ZDF version of Feuerwasser did
not seem to profit from renewed interest in the
World War II period. Twice as many critiques were
negative as positive (18 to 8). Those that liked
the production did so on the basis of the play's
and author's reputation from the 1950s. They mention the period of post-war realism in the theater
which the play revives (kdh, "Realismus der Nach-
kriegsjahre," Augsburger Allgemeine, 26 July 1978).
Others feel that Becher is an interesting author
whose work deserves more attention (Ernst Johann,
"New Yorker Nachkrieg," Frankfurter Allgemeine Zeitung, 26 July 1978) and better directors (M.S., "Mit-
telmäßig," Nürnberger Nachrichten, 25 July 1978).

The negative critiques almost unanimously
rejected the play on the basis of believability.
While some lay the blame on the director and script
writer,[14] most simply do not believe the events and
characters of Feuerwasser.

Man sollte sich in Deutschland doch nicht
an Stücken aus dem amerikanischen Gangster-
Milieu versuchen. Sie wirken unecht, ge-

künstelt und konstruiert . . . da gab es
nur Typen, die Phrasen droschen. (Heide
Werner, "Schlag ins Wasser," Saarbrücker
Zeitung, 26 July 1978.)

Das Stück verschenkte Autor Ulrich Becher
mit flacher Naivität und papiernen Dialogen.
(-w-, "Feuerwasser," Berliner Morgenpost, 26
July 1978.)

Zum Stück reicht es nicht, nur zu ver-
schnulzter Kolportage. Die Dialoge sind
platt. Charaktere bleiben unerkennbar. Es
rächt sich, daß Becher nur geschwätzt, nicht
gestaltet hat. (Sd, "Kritische Gänge,"
Frankfurter Neue Presse, 26 July 1978.)

Das Milieu dieser "Tragödie" von Ulrich
Becher wurde nicht stimmiger. In welcher
Bar von New York, bitte, sprach man denn
ausschließlich deutsch? Wieso spricht "der
Hund" . . . gar Weanerisch? Trank man dort
in der Nähe des Broadways schon damals Cola
mit Bacardi? Soviel Unsinn in neunzig Minut-
en . . . (Horst Ziermann, "Prima Husten,"
Die Welt, Bonn, 26 July 1978.)

There are two explanations for this reversal
in the evaluations of Feuerwasser. The scriptwriter
of the television production, Karl Wittlinger, shortened Becher's stage script primarily by removing sections of the play that did not contain action. Charlie's lung damage from poison gas in World War I is
mentioned, but not his suspicions that Maurice could
have been responsible. The second bar scene, with its
emphasis on the inherent evils of capitalism compared
to Marxism and Charlie's single-handed battle against

these evils, has been completely cut, as has the
entire discussion of lack of medical care for the
poor, Petschek's belief in Marxism, and fascist tendencies in the United States. Thus Wittlinger has
removed the political and moral arguments which
provided motivation for the actions of these characters, and has placed more emphasis on the action
of the play, the shootings, stabbing, and larceny.
The 1978 version is, therefore, incomplete and essentially a different play altogether, one that does
not truly represent Becher's intentions. It is perhaps ironic that the lack of action in his plays
brought on the most criticism of Becher's dramas when
they appeared in the 1950s, but that removal of all
the other aspects of Feuerwasser caused a negative
reaction in 1978.

      The second possible explanation for Feuer-
wasser's negative reception in 1978 is that these
critics represent a younger generation unfamiliar
with the milieu of the play and unsympathetic to the
problems presented in post-war literature. They represent a generation of critics weaned on Werkimmanent
criticism and the esoteric philosophizing about language and reality typical of works of the 1960s.

They bring a different set of implicit expectations
with them, in Jauss' terminology, a different "Erwartungshorizont," against which they measure a play
that is inextricably bound up with a specific time,
place and way of thinking.

It is evident that an "Erwartungshorizont"
for Ulrich Becher's drama has been formed by the time
of the reviews on Mademoiselle Löwenzorn. The concretization of Mademoiselle Löwenzorn is identical
to that of the previous plays, in that no new elements
are introduced into the discussion. Becher's aesthetic strengths are seen to be characterization and description, but the plot is secondary to the message.
For East German critics this emphasis on the message
of a fighting humanism is Becher's saving grace. In
the West Becher's plays fail or succeed solely on the
believability, i.e., psychological realism of his
characters, because his political message is not considered a suitable topic for literary discussion. This
contrast is clear from the following quotes pertaining to Mademoiselle Löwenzorn, first the West German
quotes:

> Sicherlich geschieht nicht allzuviel in dem
> Stück, denn die eingebaute Kriminalgroteske
> ist nichts als dramatischer Vorwand. Aber
> dieses Nichts an Handlung wird ausgefüllt

> durch die Intensität der Charakterisierung,
> durch die scharfen Kurven der Dialoge . . .
> (E. Schw., "Mademoiselle Löwenzorn," Frank-
> furter Rundschau, 27 March 1954.)

> . . . episch und impressionistisch zugleich,
> lyrisch und detail-dramatisch gebärdet. Das
> ist Bechers originelle Art, für das Theater
> zu schreiben. Er sieht den Menschen bis auf
> ihre hohlen Zähne und ihre Ausdünstungen.
> Er leuchtet sie als Typen wie ein Röntgen-
> ologe ab. Er stellt ein physiognomisches
> Panoptikum als Krankheitsbild der Zeit hin.
> (Hermann Wanderscheck, "Bechers Mademoiselle
> Löwenzorn in Barlogs Schloßparktheater,"
> Frankfurter Abendpost, 12 March 1954.)

For then-GDR critic Jürgen Rühle Becher´s
plays represent the most the West has to offer in the
way of humanism. But Becher is limited by his concentration on bourgeoise characters. Rühle feels
that those limitations in Becher´s political views
also limit the form of his plays.

> So hängen dramatischer Bau und ideologische
> Aussage bei Becher wie bei jedem realist-
> ischen Künstler untrennbar zusammen. Auch
> daß sich seine Charaktere nicht entwickeln,
> daß die Fabel nur den lockeren Zusammenhang
> eines Bilderbogen, einer bunten Szenenfolge
> hat, ist durch das Fragmentarische seiner
> weltanschaulichen Position bedingt. (Jürgen
> Rühle, "Karneval der Heimatlosen," Sonntag,
> 9, No. 17, April 25, 1954, 4.)

However, another GDR critic feels that in Mademoiselle
Löwenzorn Becher has finally achieved the dramatic
unity of a self-contained plot.

240

> Hier ist es gelungen, was wir in unserer
> Dramatik erstreben: selbstverständliche
> Verknüpfung politischer Ereignisse mit
> einer interessanten originellen Fabel,
> synthetische Gestaltung unserer Zeit.
> (H.D. Sander, "Mademoiselle Löwenzorn,"
> Theater der Zeit, 10, No. 8, August 1955,
> 51-54.)

This is indeed high praise, and illustrates once again
the extent of Becher's acceptance in the GDR.

Of all Becher's prose works, his first post-
war publication, New Yorker Novellen, has received
the most consistently positive critical reception,
from the Weismann edition of 1950 to the Benziger
edition in 1974. Some critics consider this collection of four novellas to be Becher's masterpiece, better even than his novel Murmeljagd, which was touted
as his life's work.[15]

In contrast to the plays, which gained
favor largely on the strength of Becher's characterization and, in the GDR, because of his political message,
the prose works impressed critics from the outset with
their style and language. The only critique of the
1950 edition that was available is a library listing
which recommends the novellas as a complement to the
prose works of Dos Passos and Thomas Wolfe on the
basis of Becher's "ausdrucksstarke und vitale Prosa"

(Jürgen Eyssen, "Becher, Ulrich: Nachtigall will zum
Vater fliegen," <u>Buchanzeiger für öffentliche Buchereien</u>,
4, No. 40/41, 1.). Articles on later editions also
mention the initial positive reception of the 1950
edition by international critics, who saw the novellas
as one of the best accomplishments of German post-war
literature (Ekkehart Rudolph, "Lesezeichen," Süddeutscher Rundfunk, 26 February 1975). The lack of
early critiques is due primarily to the fact that
Weismann Verlag was tiny and soon went bankrupt and
that 95% of Rowohlt's records were destroyed by fire
in 1955, and are thus unavailable today.

   Five years after the Weismann first edition,
Rowohlt published two of the four novellas. A GDR
critique of the shortened Rowohlt edition still emphasizes Becher's psychologically masterful characterizations and pacifist, anti-Western content, but also
singles out his style for comment:

> Ulrich Bechers expressiver, neue Worbild-
> ungen schaffender Stil ist der Thematik
> und Atmosphäre seiner Erzählungen gemäß;
> die ungewöhnliche Bildhaftigkeit weist auf
> den Maler Ulrich Becher, ehemaligen Schüler
> von George Grosz. (René Schwachhofer, "Im
> Dicht der Einsamkeit," <u>Sonntag</u>, 11, No.
> 18, 29 April 1956, 8.)

With various shifts of emphasis, the points raised in

242

this quote become the accepted view of Becher's prose
style in New Yorker Novellen and for many of the other
prose works as well. The concretization of New Yorker
Novellen becomes the "Erwartungshorizont" against
which later works are measured.

The positive evaluation of Becher's works
in the GDR changed in 1957 with the controversial '
Tangenten-Reihe publication of "Der schwarze Hut,"
one of the novellas that had been omitted from the
1955 Rowohlt edition. While still admiring Becher's
dedication to antifascist, anticapitalist themes,
GDR critics find his style problematic. Instead of
a straight-forward realism, they claim, Becher skill-
fully employs expressionistic devices to evoke the
decadence of the society he describes in "Der schwarze
Hut." While he succeeds in reconstructing the
period through language, Becher becomes too abstract
and the result is an undialectical view of social
reality (Hans-Werner Braun, "Von den Schwierigkeiten,
das Wahre darzustellen," Bibliothekar, [Leipzig], 11,
No. 7, July 1957, 708-715). In this critique of
Becher's novella, one can observe the effect of the
cultural-political crackdown of 1957 in the GDR. Although there were many changes in GDR cultural norms

subsequent to 1957, Becher´s reception suffered irre-
vocably at this time. Spiele der Zeit II was published in 1968, but Becher never again received the same
level of critical attention. Essentially, the critiques of the 1957 edition of Der schwarze Hut mark the
end of Becher´s reception in the GDR.

What the East Germans saw as formal experimentation in 1957, Western critics rejected as affecta-
tion in 1972. While all the critiques of the 1972
Benziger edition of "Der schwarze Hut" are basically
positive, increasing objection to Becher´s expressionistic style and especially to his invented words,
is evident. These characteristics are seen as "man-
ieriert" (Peter Vodosek, "Becher, Ulrich: Der schwarze
Hut," Buchanzeiger für öffentliche Büchereien, 25, No.
292, June 1972) or mistaken for unintentional mis-
prints (Swiss library entry of July, 1972). One
Austrian critic also points out a thematic connection
with expressionism in Becher´s recurrent use of the
social outcast and his portrayal of the ugliness behind the refined mask of society (Johann Straubinger,
"Erzählende Literatur," Erwachsenenbildung Österreich,
April 1973).

Of the critiques of the 1974 Benziger edi-

tion of New Yorker Novellen only the Austrian critiques are consistently negative. The basis of this
negative evaluation is again Becher's style and use
of language. The gentlest of the Austrian critiques
compares his style to an obstacle race which whets
the competitive appetites of the reader (E.W. Skwara,
"Kurz und kritisch," Österreichischer Rundfunk, 19·
December 1974). This same critique praises Becher's
ability to treat autobiographical material and touchy
subjects with great literary skill. The most negative
of the Austrian critiques completely rejects the novellas on the basis of style:

> Vieles davon hat an Aktualität verloren und
> wird den Leser kaum berühren--überdies er-
> leichtert der zum Teil unbeholfene Stil und
> die eigenartige Sprache keineswegs den Ein-
> stieg in die dargestellten Ereignisse.
> Makabre Züge und ein seltsam anmutender Humor
> machen die Lektüre weder erfreulich noch
> amüsant, und schaffen in vielen langatmigen
> Abschnitten kaum eine interessante Abwechs-
> lung. (Sigrid Mühlberger, "Becher, Ulrich:
> New Yorker Novellen," Die Zeit im Buch,
> February 1975, p. 82.)

Another Austrian critic finds Becher's content un-
healthy for the youth of the 1970s; he objects to
fixation on themes of guilt for Nazism, to Becher's
negative heroes, and to his portrayal of alcohol as
a solution for misery (anonymous critic on österreich-

ischer Rundfunk, 6 December 1974).

In contrast West German critics have only kind words for Becher's style and language. His prose is called "sprachlich einfallsreich, leicht lesbar, bildhafte, schöpferische Prosa" (Werner Schwerter, "Grauen des Nachkriegs," Rheinische Post, 23 November 1974) and his language "zupackend, plastisch" (Ekkehart Rudolph, "Lesezeichen," Süddeutscher Rundfunk, 26 February 1975). Becher's Sprachkunst is seen as reason enough for Benziger Verlag to have faith in the success of the 25-year-old novellas and Becher himself is compared with E.M. Remarque (Köster, untitled, Berufsschuljugend und Buch, 1974). Several critiques find Becher's "am Expressionismus geschulte Sprache" a worthy model for younger writers.[16] Becher's relationship to George Grosz is also mentioned:

> Elend, Erbärmlichkeit, Ekel. Dies in eine Sprache gebracht, die so scharf, so lieblos engagiert die Umrisse des Erbärmlichen zeichnet, wie George Grosz es gekonnt hat. Schön vor Häßlichkeit. Die Figuren, die Anlässe und die Motive dieser Geschichten, die Gegenstände also bleiben auswechselbar. Die Manier der Mitteilung macht's. (Kramberg)

Many of the West German articles emphasize as well Becher's personal history or the reception history of his works. Those critics who mention

Becher's status as a permanent emigrant or his lack

of success in publishing are overwhelmingly favorable

toward his works.

For example, Swiss critics concentrate on

biographical influences on Becher's work, one even

maintaining that Becher's biography provides the

content of his works as well as the main theme, the

outcast of society.

> Becher selbst ist in mehrfacher Hinsicht
> zum Emigranten geworden: als Flüchtiger
> vor dem NS-Regime, als von Ost und West
> gleichermassen verkannter Autor--abzulesen
> gerade am Schicksal der einzelnen New Yorker
> Novellen--als ein im Literaturbetrieb schwer-
> lich Einzuordnender. Die Wechselfälle des
> Becherschen Lebens, zusammenzufassen unter
> dem Stichwort "Emigrantenlos," bestimmen
> auch den Inhalt seines Werkes. (Béatrice
> Leutenegger, "Gegen den falschen Optimismus,"
> Vaterland, 11 January 1975.)

Becher's second post-war prose publication,

and his first novel, was Kurz nach vier, published

by Rowohlt in 1957. Again, Rowohlt files contained

only a few critiques of this early edition. Without

exception these few critical articles concentrate

on the formal aspects of the novel, such as Becher's

language or structure, leading one to conclude that

this was indeed the focus for most, if not all, of

the criticism. An overall impression of the critiques
is that they are generally positive, though less
enthusiastically so than critiques on New Yorker Novellen.

Several mention Becher's ties to Expressionism and the authors of the 1920s, but there is little
agreement as to which authors served as models. Wolfgang Schwerbrock mentions Döblin, Hülsenbeck, and Joyce
in his lengthy Frankfurter Allgemeine Zeitung article,
while Gerd Semmer in Geist und Zeit lists Dos Passos,
Döblin, and Hemingway.[17] Because of his relative
obscurity, Becher is always compared to more famous
authors and yet there seems to be little agreement
among these comparisons.

The characteristics of Becher's prose are
again singled out.

> Äußerlich fallen der eigenwillige Satzbau,
> die kaum schön zu nennende, abrupt in Stak-
> kato-Fetzen übergehende Sprache auf, die
> gelegentlich an szenische Beschreibungen
> erinnert, wie sie im Theaterstück vorkommen.
> Der Dramatiker ist da spürbar, der mit zwei,
> drei Worten eine Situation, einen Gedanken,
> eine Erinnerung beleuchtet. (Schwerbrock)

After calling Kurz nach vier one of the most exciting
books to emerge from post-war Germany, one critic finds
that its "tightly-packed, clipped telescopic prose

would be a labour of love" for any translator (Hilde
Spiel, "Kurz nach vier," International PEN, Summer,
1957).

Another source of discussion in the early
critiques is the structure of the novel, a two-level
story line imbedding the past of the hero into the
present of his trip to Rome by means of Proustian
flashbacks.

> Es ist die Methode der frühen zwanziger
> Jahre, die die Wirklichkeit in ihre tat-
> sächliche Diskontinuität zerlegt--wie es
> technische Apparate tun, z.B. der Film--
> um sie zu neuer Montage bereitzustellen.
> (Semmer)

The attitudes toward the use of this narrative device range from positive (in the case of the Hilde
Spiel critique) to sceptically reserved, as the
following quote from Schwerbrock demonstrates:

> Das Ganze ist aus einem Guß, vielleicht
> ein wenig gewaltsam zusammengeschweißt;
> der Abgrund zwischen der Gegenwart und der
> Vergangenheit wirkt freilich nicht ganz
> überbrückt, und so bleibt die Liebesge-
> schichte, die das Ganze zusammenhält, merk-
> würdig konstruiert.

The 1975 Benziger edition of Kurz nach vier
received similar critical treatment. Again, aside
from plot summaries, there is almost no critical dis-

cussion of content. There is more concentration on the biography of Ulrich Becher and the reception history of his works. As was the case with New Yorker Novellen, awareness of such facts seems to predispose a critic favorably to all aspects of Becher's work. Proof of this thesis must be undertaken in the following chapters.

The later edition of New Yorker Novellen met with increased opposition to its language; this does not seem to be the case with Kurz nach vier. There are indeed more negative critiques calling his language "floskelhaft und unerträglich milieugebunden" (p.w.s., "Ulrich Becher: Kurz nach 4," Imprint, January 1976), his structure "kein Seelenroman aus dem effekt-überladenen Abenteurerbuch" (Werner Wien, "Literarische Umschau," Radio Bremen. 22 January 1976), and calling Becher himself "traumatisch fixiert auf ein Zeit Nationalsozialistischer Unterdrückung" (Gertrude Pfannenstiel, "Bücherschwemme," Österreichischer Rundfunk, 20 November 1975). However, negative critiques represent less than 15% of all critiques (7 out of 47), and they do not appear to originate with one country over another. There are, however, no negative critiques from Switzerland, the home of Ben-

250

ziger and chosen country of residence of Ulrich Becher.

Almost 20% of the critiques appear to be copies of publisher advertising blurbs appearing word-for-word in several different sources. In the remaining original critiques there are few new points of discussion not already treated by earlier critiques. However, one major divergence is the tendency in later critiques to view Becher´s style as bordering on that of popular fiction.

> Ein kräftig, kolorisierter Reißer mit Sentiment, der so tut, als wäre er ein bißchen mehr. (Schr., "Ulrich Becher: Kurz nach 4," Berliner Morgenpost, 30 March 1976.)

> Becher schreibt flott, amüsant und geistreich. Wenn es für Nachkriegsleser in Deutschland noch eine Synthese zwischen Arno Schmidt und Johannes Mario Simmel möglich wäre, Ulrich Becher könnte sie bieten. (Manfred Rieger, "Eine Nacht in Piacenza," Kölner Stadtanzeiger, 28 February 1976.)

According to Rainer Fabian´s article in Die Welt, 11 October 1975, this effect is achieved through the combination of an elegant prose style with a subject matter familiar to all Europeans:

> Bechers Prosa wirkt zugleich konzentriert und beiläufig. Zum Beispiel in der Art, wie er im Fluß seiner Sprache das ganze Treibholz der europäischen Kulturgeschichte

> aufschwimmen läßt. Beiläufig entwirft Becher
> ein kulturgeschichtliches Bühnenbild durch
> das Leutnant Skizze seine Irrfahrt antritt.
> (Rainer Fabian, "Der private Krieg des
> Leutnant Skizze" Die Welt, 11 October 1975.)

The prose appeals to the more literary-minded reader, while the content, with its tender love story and adventuresome hero, speaks to the reader of popular fiction.

Kurz nach vier was received in much the same way as New Yorker Novellen, that is, critiques remain positive across the years. However, formal elements do not become the focus of negative comments to the same extent as with New Yorker Novellen. The reception of later prose works will reveal which is the more typical case.

In 1958 an enlarged edition of Becher´s earliest work, Männer machen Fehler, was published by Rowohlt. The critiques of this edition are very positive on both form and content, welcoming this collection as a rare opportunity to observe an author´s development over three decades. However, instead of pointing out differences between the early stories and the more recent additions, the critiques almost unanimously discuss the common ideological thread running through all the stories, Becher´s humanism.

Der Tenor in Ulrich Bechers Werk ist der
Mensch . . . so legt er damit ein Glaubens-
bekenntnis zum Menschen ab, zum Menschen,
der preisgegeben ist an eine Welt der Un-
menschlichkeit, der von abertausend durch
Menschen herbeigeführte Gefahren bedroht,
den Weg zu einer besseren Welt sucht.[18]

Die humane Grundidee, die dieses Buch wie
ein roter Faden durchzieht, die Aufrichtig-
keit, die Kunst der Menschendarstellung, die
fazinierenden Milieuschilderung und die
suggestive Sprache--all diese Attribute
eines großen Dichters beweisen Ulrich Bechers Platz als einen der ersten in der modernen deutschen Literatur.[19]

If the critics were not impressed with all

the stories in the collection, it was on the basis

of formal elements. Several mention Becher's roots

in 1920s Expressionism, traces of which are still

found in the style of the later works, although not

as much in the content. Becher's attempt to achieve

simultaneity through cinematic techniques is seen

as his major indebtedness to Expressionism.

So entsteht ein Nebeneinander und Über-
schneiden der Handlungsfäden, das der Dis-
kontinuität des realen Daseins durchaus
entspricht, und das ermöglicht, die Gesamt-
heit der Dinge und Verhältnisse unter neuem
Aspekt zu erkennen. Das ist Bechers Methode,
ist die bekannte Methode der zwanziger Jahre,
die er nur selten durchbricht--die er aber
meisterhaft beherrscht und konsequent weiter-
geführt hat. (Streblow)

This insistence on simultaneity lends Becher's prose

a breathless quality, which some critics find non-
artistic.

> Wer kritisch liest, fühlt sich versucht,
> dieses und jenes zu bessern, zu kürzen,
> um die Fabel prägnanter herauszubringen.
> Aber man merkt auch bald, wie unrecht es
> wäre, Geschliffenheit zu verlangen, wo hier
> alles Fülle und rückhaltlose Wahrnehmung
> ist. (anonymous, "Wechselnde Belichtung,"
> Frankfurter Rundschau, 7 March 1959.)

It is this apparent ease with which Becher's stories

unfold that causes some critics to assign the stories

with less psychological emphasis to the realm of

popular fiction.

> Das bebaute erzählerische Terrain erstreckt
> sich teils bis auf die Höhen großer Literatur,
> teils senkt es sich ins stille Tal der Kol-
> pertage. (Hanns-Hermann Kersten, "Becher,
> Ulrich: Männer machen Fehler," Buchanzeiger
> für öffentliche Büchereien, 12, No. 135, 3.)

> Sie [die Erzählungen] haben etwas Wildes,
> Ursprüngliches, Elementares. Ihr Autor
> . . . packt mit harten Fäusten zu und kümmert
> sich wenig um ästhetische Tüfteleien. Bech-
> ers Erzählungen haben einen weiten Handlungs-
> Spielraum, und ebenso unterschiedlich sind
> sie im Niveau. (Wolfgang Ebert, "Das Herz
> des Hais," Kölner Stadtanzeiger, 4 April
> 1959.)

The only stylistic difference one critic notes be-

tween the earlier and the later stories of this col-

lection is Becher's increasing reliance on dramatic

elements, for example swift change of scenery or interruptions by the author that read like stage directions (Wolfgang Schwerbrock, "Das Lachen der Gorgo," Frankfurter Allgemeine Zeitung, 6 December 1958).

The few East German critiques of the 1962 Aufbau edition of Männer devote themselves entirely to Becher´s content, which is seen as being closely related to the concerns of East German literature.

> Das alles sind mehr oder minder prägnant Variationen eines humanistischen Themas. Ulrich Becher verschafft mit seinen Erzählungen dem Ruf der Stillen nach einem besseren und reicheren menschlichen Leben Gehör. Es ist ein Ruf, der von uns verstanden wird. (Werner Liersch, "Ruf der Stillen," Neue deutsche Literatur, 10, No. 11, November 1962, 120-122.)

In 1957 the novella "Der schwarze Hut" had been castigated by East German critics as an example of Western formalism, thus it is interesting to note that only the humanistic content of Männer is mentioned.

The first reception of Das Herz des Hais must have been quite positive. Several later critiques mention the enthusiasm of the 1960 critics and Peter Härtling´s view that this story was a gift to the reader. The story was even serialized in the Frankfurter Allgemeine in 1958. Unfortunately, Rowohlt declined to release the critiques of this 1960 paperback edition. However, sales figures show that of the 42,000 copies printed, 40,000 sold.

Benziger Verlag has provided forty-eight critiques of their 1972 hardbound edition of Herz des Hais, of which 29% are negative. This is certainly an increase in negative response over New Yorker Novellen and Kurz nach vier. Formal considerations again appear to be the cause of the negative reactions.

Almost all of the critiques call Herz des Hais a love story, and there are certain formal expectations which accompany the concept. To the extent that Becher's novel fulfills these expectations in the critic's opinion, the evaluation is positive. If the critic chooses to see only the tragi-comic love triangle or the descriptions of characters and exotic landscapes and events, his attitude toward the book will be positive. The most frequent cause of criticism is Becher's tendency to build political and social commentary into his stories. Zeitkritik does not fit well with the concept of a love story.

256

However, most of the criticism of Becher's use of Zeitkritik is based on its outdated quality. The story written in the 1950s carries discussion of topics which were a matter of concern during the cold-war decade.

> Da wird in hochinteressanten Gesprächen
> . . . noch das ganze Sorgenmaterial der
> fünfziger Jahre ausgebreitet. Im ganzen
> also der sichere Weltuntergang, dem wir
> alle entgegengedeihen sollten . . . (Wer-
> ner Helwig, "Inselromanze wie gehabt,"
> Frankfurter Allgemeine Zeitung, 4 November
> 1972.)

Helwig's viewpoint received much attention; his critique appeared not only in the Frankfurter Allgemeine, but on an Österreichischer Rundfunk program, in the Berner Tagblatt and in Zeitlupe in Giessen.

In spite of the fact that most critiques which mention Becher's Zeitkritik are negative, there are some which contradict this trend. An example is one critic who dislikes the formalistic trend in German literature of the 1960s and 1970s:

> In einer Zeit, wo blutleerer Formalismus
> und ephemere Bindung an die Tagesaktualität
> die literarische Szene beherrschen, wirkt
> Bechers sprachlich grandios gestaltetes
> Bekenntnis zur Echtheit alles Lebendigen
> wie ein kleines Fanal. (G.W., "Magie des
> nackten Herzens," Domino, November 1972.)

The harshest criticism of Herz des Hais is
reserved for Becher's language and symbolism. Some
critics feel Becher's use of foreign words and references to mythology and legend are merely disturbing
to the reader (HS, "Herz des Hais," Abendzeitung
Zurich, 6 December 1972). Another feels that Becher
does not have enough talent to handle such a literary
juggling act, i.e., trying to balance literary merit
with entertainment.

> So also bemüht sich der Autor, seinem Thema
> Tiefsinn und Symbolik zu geben, in einer
> überzogen pathetischen Sprache, und er scheut
> sich nicht, die Ränder des Kitsches zu
> streifen. Ulrich Becher erzählt . . .
> eine nette Unterhaltungsgeschichte, die
> nicht gerade durch literarische Qualitäten
> besticht. Zwar fehlt es nicht an Anstren-
> gungen, aber sie scheitern . . . am allzu
> deutlichen Klischee. (Es) dürfte manchem
> [sic] Leser so etwas wie ein 'leises Grauen'
> gepackt haben, vor dieser geistreich-sein-
> sollenden und doch recht kitschig werdenden
> Sprache. (Hans Dieter Schmidt, "Das Herz
> des Hais," Main-Echo, 25 April 1973.)

There is counterbalancing praise of Becher's language
mostly from Swiss critics. One speaks of "unwech-
selbarer, wortmalender Ulrich Becher" (lis, "Ein
grosser Erzähler," Berner Tagblatt, 27 October 1972)
and another finds the most pleasure in Becher's "mit-
reissenden sprachlichen Fluß" (O.B., "Wilder Mann ge-

258

sucht," Der kleine Bund, 10 December 1972).

Once again many positive critiques show an awareness of the publishing history of this novel and of Ulrich Becher's reception in general. They either praise Benziger for taking a chance on a new edition (A. "Das Herz des Hais," Hamburger Abendblatt, 13 October 1972) or they criticize the publishing ' industry in general for making quality and entertainment mutually exclusive (anonymous, "Ehe im Becher," Sonntags-Journal, 27 August 1972). One calls Das Herz des Hais "ein Buch für Individualisten, Liebende, selbstbewusste Frauen und Bestsellerlisten-Verachter" (Paul Schorno, "Anders als früher--anders als üblich," Basler Volksblatt, 15 December 1972).

Between the first edition of Kurz nach vier (1959) and Becher's next new novel, Murmeljagd (1969), lay more than a decade of "silence" during which Becher published only newspaper essays or paperback versions of earlier works. As has been pointed out, it was this decade of the 1960s which brought about a fundamental change in the West German literary scene, establishing new forms for prose works and bestowing fame on a younger generation whose literary concerns were more formalistic.[20] In the previous chapter

it was speculated that Becher's long absence from
the literary scene during a period of immense change
accounts for the growing negativity of his reception,
especially in the area of formal elements. But do the
critiques themselves bear this out?

The fifty-five critiques available on Murmeljagd are overwhelmingly positive (89%), and because the novel was published by Rowohlt, they also
originate primarily in the FRG. In addition, Rowohlt's
prestige appears to be reflected in longer and more
original critiques; there are few critiques taken
primarily from advertising copy, as was the case with
Benziger editions of early novels.

Of these critiques 40% are aware of Becher's
long absence from publishing and even more speculate
on the causes of Becher's lack of success. As we
have determined in the case of previous novels, awareness of reception appears to be connected with the
positive tenor of the critique. Some of these specu-
lations about Becher's reception are especially interesting because they speak directly to the aesthetic
values implicit in West German literature of the late
1960s, i.e., they contain references to the "Erwartungshorizont" of critics. According to Hans Bender,

the causes of Becher's poor reception lie in his

age and in the prejudices of the industry:

> Wäre der Autor des Romans <u>Murmeljagd</u> im
> Twen-Alter, sein neuer Roman würde größeres
> Aufsehen erregen; er würde in unseren Lit-
> eraturblättern an auffälligerer Stelle
> rezensiert werden, und wahrscheinlich würde
> man ihm auch bald einen Preis zusprechen.
> Er ist Autor eines Verlages, der Weltlit-
> eratur vertritt, der sonst versteht, seine
> Bücher unter die Leute zu bringen. Ulrich
> Becher hat selbsterlebten Stoff mitzuteilen.
> Das wird in unseren Tagen von den Literatur-
> managern und Kritikern nicht sehr hoch ge-
> schätzt. Ausschnitte sollen's sein, Mon-
> tiertes, Collagiertes; die Programme sprechen
> gegen die realistische Schreibweise.[21]

For another critic Ulrich Becher's novel has little

in common with what is considered to be contemporary

prose and thus runs the risk of being indefinable for

the critics and book sellers (Dieter Lattmann, "Für

Sie gelesen--aus neuen Büchern," Bayrischer Rundfunk,

Munich, 28 July 1969). Sigurd Schimpf believes <u>Mur-</u>

<u>meljagd</u> is a provocation for the entire spectrum of

German writers, from formalistic experimentors to

formula novelists.

> Denn Becher hat, das ist eine Herausforderung
> für die einen, eine großräumige epische
> Architektur geschaffen, unangefochten von
> theoretischen Überlegungen, als habe es
> nie kritische Reflexionen der Form gegeben.
> Und er greift, das ist eine Herausforderung
> für die anderen, einen weitgehend gemiedenen

Or perhaps, proposes another critic, Becher is over-
looked because in the profit-motivated world of book
publishing only novelty and innovation count (Lothar
Streblow, "Murmeljagd" Deutsche Volkszeitung, Düssel-
dorf, 3 October 1969).

Becher receives high marks from most critics
for the content and characterization in Murmeljagd.
One Austrian critic calls it the most significant
epic accomplishment on the topic of fascism next to
Gerhard Fritsch's Fasching.[22] W.E. Süskind sees the
novel as the definitive portrayal of the neurosis which
was European history in the first half of the twentieth
century (W.E. Süskind, "Wildwest im Engadin," Süddeutsche Zeitung, 6/7 April 1969). Only one West
German critic finds the subject matter irrelevant to
contemporary readers (Lothar Romain, "Neue Bücher,"
Südwestfunk Baden-Baden, 10 May 1969). Almost all
of the critics mention Becher's unforgettable characters; especially popular is the episode on Giaxa's
last ride, in which Becher provides a fictional monu-
ment to his father-in-law, Roda Roda. Wolfgang Nagel

finds Becher's background in drama helped him draw
believable, carefully defined characters, excepting
the few Nazis, whose clichéd portrayal still can be
justified by the main character's antifascist views
(Wolfgang Nagel, "Ulrich Becher: Murmeljagd," Neue
Deutsche Hefte, 16, No. 3, 151-153). However, Georg
Zivier feels that Becher's characters need an actor
to help create a lifelike figure out of intellectual-
ized or symbolic theatrical roles (Georg Zivier,
"Der Frieden dieser Gebirgslandschaft," Tagesspiegel
Berlin, 14 September 1969).

By far the most discussion is generated by
consideration of the formal elements of the novel,
its structure, language, style and genre. It is again
in this area that negative evaluations appear. A
Spiegel critique calls Murmeljagd a voluminous, almost
"altmeisterlich-sorgfältig konstruierten Roman" (anonymous, "Roter Baron," Der Spiegel, 23, No. 17 (21
April 1969), 182-183). The word "masterful" is applied
to evaluations of structure in several critiques,
and one Austrian critic claims astonishment at the
"nahtlos, fast mathematisch präzise Komposition; die
denkbar perfekteste Geschichte" (P.). However, the
only negative Swiss critique, which is positive in

the area of content and characterization, finds Mur-

meljagd

> Ein anspruchsvolles Unterfangen, mit dem
> Becher kompositorisch nicht zu Rande kommt.
> Was als grossangelegter Roman konzipiert
> war, zersplittert sich, vom Autor schliess-
> lich kaum mehr cachiert, in eine nur mühsam
> durch die Gestalt des Helden zusammenge-
> haltene Geschichtenreihe . . . (Gustav
> Huonker, "Das Leben: ein Schauer- und
> Kriminalroman," Tages-Anzeiger Zurich,
> 16 June 1969.)

It is in the area of language that Murmel-

jagd garners the most negative comments. Although

some find Becher's use of foreign or technical ter-

minology and his coinages expressive and original,

most comments on his language tend towards the nega-

tive. Hans Bender kindly points out where Becher

could have trouble with some critics:

> Für Sprachpuristen gäbe es Verstöße gegen
> die Grammatik anzukreiden; und manche Leser
> könnten über die Strapaze stöhnen--das hat
> auch ein Literaturkritiker getan--, stöhnen
> über zu viele Wörter und Details. Aber
> diese Sprache Ulrich Bechers ist es doch
> an erster Stelle, die seinen Roman so
> lebendig, so glaubwürdig und so fesselnd
> macht. (Bender)

The critic Bender refers to is Martin Gregor-Dellin

in Die Zeit; his article, by virtue of its source,

is one of the more important critiques of Murmel-

jagd. Gregor-Dellin believes that Becher evaded
the danger of simply copying his Expressionist models
by incorporating exoticism into his language and content. This strategy worked until New Yorker Novellen,
because the exotic elements were integral to the
stories and helped to regenerate the language. However, Gregor-Dellin believes, only a few passages in
Murmeljagd retain the narrative freshness of the novellas, and the fault lies in Becher's attempt to recreate speech. His use of dialogue makes the novel
immobile because little happens to move the story forward:

> . . . und die Sprache fährt alsbald aus ins
> Forsche, Saloppe, Abstruse; sie kompensiert,
> gibt sich zunächst äußerst keck, weltläufig,
> rennt dann ins offene Messer der Schreib-
> weise, des Kursivgedruckten, der S-p-e-r-
> r-u-n-g-e-n und Lääängungen und überlädt
> sich an einem Namens- und Plauder-Exotismus,
> von dem sich das Buch in kaum einem Kapitel
> wirklich erholt. So überfrachtet Ulrich
> Becher den Roman mit Bildungsballast, Ge-
> wolltheiten, Überflüssigem, Nichts-als-
> Sonderbarem. Für mich ist das Plauderei-
> Literatur, auf welchem Niveau sie auch
> immer stehen möge.[23]

In essence, Gregor-Dellin objects to Becher's arti-
ficial use of language in Murmeljagd, which he calls a
tedious and tongue-twisting book. Becher's language
is synthetically produced and is therefore hard to

understand.

> Aufnahmeschwierigkeit, Unsprachlichkeit ent-
> steht da, wo Literatursprache quasi synthe-
> tisch erzeugt wird. Es sind synthetische
> Sätze, synthetische Vorgänge, synthetische
> Figuren, die an diesem Buch befremden und
> verwehren. Eine Literatur, die Exaktheit
> vorgibt. Eine Schreibweise, die Welthalt-
> igkeit wohl besitzt, aber überflüssigerweise
> auch noch vorzeigt. Ulrich Becher kann viel
> . . . er kann auch das, was er gar nicht
> können sollte. Verliebt in seinen Wort-
> schatz und in sein exotisches Erzählfieber
> verliert er den Boden unter den Füßen.
> (Gregor-Dellin)

Another important negative critique appeared

in the Frankfurter Allgemeine Zeitung; however, its

style is so gossipy and malicious that it is difficult

to consider this critic's pronouncements objectively.

Ulrich Becher suspects the name of the critic, Lothar
                                    24
Romain, to be a pseudonym.

> Da schreibt einer einen Roman mit soviel
> erzählerischem Ehrgeiz und lädt vor seinem
> Publikum eine geradezu unbescheidene Fülle
> von Bildungslast und wuchtig bis kapriziösen
> Sprachformen ab, als könne er unserer Zeit
> noch mit Methoden eines Jean Paul beikommen.
> Becher hat zuviel geschrieben, aber zuwenig
> Wichtiges. Das versteckt er durch Über-
> fülle an Zitaten und Bonmots sowie hinter
> einem barocken Sprachaufwand. (Lothar Ro-
> main, "Akrobatik ohne Abgrund," Frankfurter
> Allgemeine Zeitung, 21 June 1969.)

Romain states that Becher uses his language and style

to portray the uncertainty and neuroticism of emigration, but that Becher's style becomes an end in
itself, a compulsion from which Becher can no longer
free himself.

Thus, _Murmeljagd_ received devastating criticism from two of the culturally trend-setting newspapers
in West Germany, _Die Zeit_ and the _Frankfurter Allgemeine Zeitung_. In spite of the fact that negative
critiques represent only 11% of the total critiques
on _Murmeljagd_, the prominence of these two negative
critiques probably more than compensated for the 89%
of the articles in less prominent papers that were
positive.

Critics also seemed uncertain as to the
genre of _Murmeljagd_. Two Austrians proudly claimed
the book for their own literature, comparing the
style to Doderer's.[25] However, for one West German
critic, the novel's Austrian characteristics are no
recommendation. He accuses Becher of marrying into
the Austrian literary tradition and of consciously
copying "typisch österreichische Fabulierkunst" from
the likes of Joseph Roth (Jost Nolte, "Vom Wahnwitz
einer Epoche" _Welt der Literatur_, 24 April 1969).
The _National Zeitung_ in Basle claims Becher mixed

various genres according to the mixture of material

in the novel:

> Je nach dem Vorherrschen der verschiedenen
> Ingredienzien tendiert der Roman bald zum
> Kriminalthriller, bald zum historisch-
> politischen Sachbuch, bald zur Charakter-
> und Schicksaltragikomödie, und unversehens
> erweist er sich zum Schluss, überblickt man
> alles, als noch etwas anders: in der Ge-
> schichte Treblas und Xanes hat Becher einen
> der schönsten und zartesten Liebesromane
> geschrieben. (anonymous, "Saftstrotzende
> Erzählkunst," National Zeitung, Basle,
> 16 July 1969.)

Yet another compares Murmeljagd to the

"fabulierfreudigen Schubladenroman des vergangenen

Jahrhunderts" (E.H., "Ulrich Becher: Murmeljagd

Neue Züricher Zeitung, 13 November 1969). Several

critiques mention the name of Grass in connection

with Becher´s work, and one even calls Murmeljagd

the Simplicissimus of emigration (r., "Ort der Hand-

lung: Engadin," Luzerner Tagblatt, 30 May 1969).

Because Becher follows the rules inherent in no

genre completely, and mixes a highly literary style

with sensational subject matter, the critics find

his work difficult to define. Perhaps the best

solution was offered by Georg Zivier:

> Will man das Werk der Unterhaltungsliteratur
> angliedern, dann im allerbesten Sinne. Will
> man es hochliterarisch werten, dann als Exem-

plar des unterhaltsamen Genres dieser an-
spruchsvollen Spezies, also eine Selten-
heit in Deutschland. (Georg Zivier, untitled, Radio Bremen, 10 July 1969.)

This is a familiar problem by now. Ulrich Becher´s
works seem to be uncategorizable. This fact alone
tends to make literary critics uncomfortable. Why
it does not lead them to conclude that they are dealing with an innovator of literary style and form is
a question we have yet to answer. Perhaps the answer
lies in a combination of factors. He certainly did
not fit the post-modernist norm applied by most critics,
but rather employed a narrative and expressionistic
style of writing. In addition, it may have been
the mere fact of his exile that prevented critics
from viewing his works as innovative.

Although Das Profil, Becher´s grotesque
tribute to George Grosz published in paperback by
Rowohlt in 1973, received a smaller percentage of
positive reviews than Murmeljagd (76% compared to
89%), it was received positively by more influential
newspaper critics. Also important is the fact that
the positive evaluations are not limited to characterization or content, but include formal elements as
well.

The positive critique in the Frankfurter

Allgemeine concentrates on the stylistic and psycho-

logical method Becher employs in constructing the

novel:

> Diese Methode . . . könnte man grob mit der
> Formel Dialoge plus erweiterte szenische
> Anmerkungen umreißen. Dieser Zwang (zur
> Kommunikation) beherrscht Ulrich Bechers
> Roman. Er führt sozusagen von der zunächst
> als Hauptsache erscheinenden Zeichnung der
> besonderen Umstände und Charaktere der
> beiden Protagonisten in einem Verfahren
> ständiger Abschweifungen zu den Nebensäch-
> lichkeiten, die sich schließlich als Haupt-
> sache herausstellten: Eine Fülle in un-
> systematischer Sprunghaftigkeit angeschnit-
> tener Gedanken und geistesgeschichtlicher
> Themenkomplexe. Diese Passagen . . .
> in der Diktion oft Arno Schmidts Radio-
> essays vergleichbar--, halte ich für die
> eigentlichen Zentralpunkte des Romans.
> (Helmut Mader, "Turbulente Gedanken,"
> Frankfurter Allgemeine Zeitung, 6 October
> 1973.)

This critic is thus praising Becher for the inclusion

of cultural gossip in dialogue-form, the very char-

acteristic of Becher´s prose style singled out for

sharpest criticism in the case of Murmeljagd. Another

important critique agrees with the above evaluation

of Becher´s use of dialogue:

> Die langen Gespräche . . . füllen fast ein
> Drittel des Textes mit farbiger, welthaltiger,
> kulturkritischer und politisch brisanter Kon-
> versation, die wunderlicherweise niemals

langweilig wird. Im Gegenteil: solche
Gespräche versetzen den Leser in eine Art
trockenen Rausch. Die innere und die
äußere Story der ganzen Erzählung ist so
spannend wie der beste Detektivroman. Aber
was unter der brillanten Oberfläche moussiert,
macht doch noch einen tieferen Reiz aus.
Dann entladen sich Gedanken und Reflexe,
die das Lebensabenteuer des Autors, ja, auch
seine Leidensgeschichte, mannhaft und rührend
Wort werden lassen. (K.H. Kramberg, "Alles
relativ, auch Weltgeschichte," Süddeutsche
Zeitung, 30/31 May1973.)

Here is also a new understanding and acceptance for

the exile's tales of woe not at all apparent in the

critiques of Murmeljagd. A third influential article

appeared in Die Welt des Buches in which Rainer Fabian,

one of the best known contemporary literary critics,

concentrates on Becher's use of language:

Das alles wird von Ulrich Becher hinge-
sprochen, so atemlos und so torkelnd, daß
das Lesen dieses Buches zum Saufen wird.
Man kann sich vollaufen lassen mit Sprache.
Prosa on the rocks. Wir sind gewiß, die
beste Satire dieses Jahres gelesen zu haben.
Ulrich Becher ist ein deutscher Tom Wolfe.
(Rainer Fabian, "Neptun im Schmetterlingsstil," Welt des Buches, 24 May 1973.)

I have quoted these three articles at length

because they demonstrate an interesting phenomenon.

In precisely the same area in which Becher's so-called

masterpiece Murmeljagd received devastatingly nega-

tive evaluations from influential sources, in the

area of style and language, _Profil_ receives a positive evaluation and, in at least one case, from the
same source (_Frankfurter Allgemeine_). Perhaps it is
the content of the dialogue in _Profil_ which appeals
more to these literary critics since it includes
commentary on the arts as well as on politics. Perhaps it is simply the fact that _Profil_ is one-fourth
the length of _Murmeljagd_. This new appreciation of
Becher's style may be, however, an indication of a
basic change in attitude on the part of critics, i.e.
an indication of the waning of formalism or the effects
of the relatively new interest in exile literature.

The only negative critiques of _Profil_ did
come in the area of style and language; however, even
here the criticism was mild. One Swiss critic warns
that the discriminating reader might be disturbed
by Becher's concessions to popular taste as well as
his frequent use of gags and idiosyncracies in style,
content, and printing (Gustav Hounker, "Ist es ein
Report, ein Alptraum oder ein Satyrspiel?" _Tages-An-
zeiger_, Zurich, August 21, 1973). An Austrian critic
finds fault in Becher's somewhat overheated style and
dialogues which require great cultural and political
knowledge on the reader's part (Claudio Isani, "Treff-

272

punkt Bücherbar," Österreichischer Rundfunk, 7 August 1973). The most negative critique only refers to the style as a weakness in an otherwise absorbing, witty, and ironic book (dh, "Becher, Ulrich: Das Profil," Das neue Buch 18, 1973, p. 761).

The remainder of the critiques are positive in all areas. One major topic of discussion was the appropriateness of first edition fiction appearing in paperback. About half the critics which mention this topic are positive.

> Wenn ein renommierter Autor wie Ulrich Becher seinen jüngsten Roman gleich als Taschenbuch erscheinen lässt, so macht er damit seinen Lesern ein Geschenk. Ein derartiges Geschenk zeugt von Selbstbewusstsein. (Valentin Herzog, "Die lange Nacht: phantastisch und prophetisch," National Zeitung, Basle, 2 June 1973.)

If not a sign of Becher's self-confidence, paperback publication is at least suitable for the genre of books Becher writes: detective novels should be easy to carry around on vacation (R.H., "Erzähler, der erfinden kann," Neue Hannoversche Presse, 29 June 1973). However, others find it a mistake not to have published such a good novel first in hardback, for various reasons:

Romane gleich bei ihrem ersten Erscheinen
schon als Taschenbuch vorzulegen, würde
zwar Kurt Tucholskys alter Forderung an
die Verleger "Macht unsere Bücher billiger!"
entsprechen, ist jedoch nicht üblich, und
zwar aus zwei Gründen, die--Tucholsky zum
Trotz--mit dem Wohlergehen der Autoren zu
tun haben. Erstens) Der einzelne Titel
geht innerhalb der Massenproduktion einer
Reihe unter, sofern er nicht vorher bereits
bekanntgeworden ist; und zweitens) Taschen-
bücher mit ihrem niedrigen Preis bringen
den Autoren unangemessen niedrige Tantiemen
ein. Überdies . . . von einem gänzlich un-
bekannten Titel kann auch ein Taschenbuchverlag nur eine relativ kleine Auflage
riskieren. Heinrich-Maria Ledig-Rowohlt
hat Becher keinen guten Dienst getan, als
er dieser reifen Frucht schriftstellerischer
Mühewaltung einen Platz in Reih und Glied
der rororo-Bände anwies. (Günter Grack,
"Taschenbuch der Woche," Tagesspiegel, Berlin, 5 August 1973.)

As with other Becher novels that have been
well received, many critics are aware of Becher's
reception history. The explanations for Becher's
lack of success are familiar ones. Either his vital,
entertaining style makes him suspicious to the arbit-
ers of good taste (Hans Schwab-Felisch, "Vorgestellt-
vorgelesen," Westdeutscher Rundfunk, 12 July 1973),
or his outsider position, caused partly by his refusal to follow literary trends, is to blame for the
shoddy treatment he has received from his own publisher as well as from the critics (Günter Grack,
"Der Büchermarkt," Deutschlandfunk, 4 August 1973).

The publication of Becher's last major
novel, Williams Ex-Casino, by Benziger in 1974 brought
few changes in reception even though it represents the
first of Becher's novels to be published originally
by Benziger. The critiques were again heavily positive (83%). However, in contrast to previous Benziger publications, West German critiques dominate,
although there is still evidence of reliance on the
Benziger book jacket text among the small newspapers.
Like Profil, this novel garnered its share of important
reviews from influential West German publications, perhaps indicating an upswing in Becher's critical reception. All of these important critiques are positive,
and yet the Benziger hardbound edition of 3,600 sold
only 2,691 copies. The Rowohlt paperback edition one
year later sold 14,000 of 15,000 copies,[25] another
indication of the power of Rowohlt's reputation.

The Frankfurter Allgemeine critique by
Sibylle Wirsing ("Mord am Nachmittag," Frankfurter
Allgemeine Zeitung, 23 March 1974) concentrates on
the content of the novel, emphasizing the story of
the middle-aged artist Kandrian who, absorbed in
self-reflections, fails to prevent a crime just as
he has failed in every undertaking throughout his

life. Underlying this critique is the assumption that
Ex-Casino belongs to the popular fiction genre, thus
the absence of any attempt on Wirsing's part to analyze style. Her final judgment is that Ex-Casino
is not world-class popular fiction on a level with
Anglo-Saxon or French bestsellers, but by German
standards it is quite acceptable. However, this
is the only critique to view Becher's novel so simply.

In striking contrast to this positive critique is the vehemently negative article that appeared in the usually friendly Frankfurter Rundschau, on
whom Becher had counted to counteract earlier negative Frankfurter Allgemeine critiques. In a reversal
of roles, Volker Hage ("Beteiligt: die Unbeteiligten,"
Frankfurter Rundschau, 14 June 1974) emphasizes neither
Becher's political engagement nor his plea for political involvement but his style. Earlier Rundschau
critiques tended to overlook stylistic features of
Becher's novels in favor of what they saw as Becher's
pro-humanitarian, pro-leftist views. But Hage even
goes so far as to quote the Martin Gregor-Dellin
evaluation of Murmeljagd in Die Zeit, which more than
any other critique caused the negative reception of
Becher's "masterpiece." Thus for Hage, Becher's syn-

thetic language with its reliance on foreign words, puns, associative inserts, typographical and orthographical oddities, is inappropriate for the subject matter of the book. The characters and the events remain unbelievable; the book's theme is inadequately handled because the author is too concerned with playing games with language.

Klaus Podak in the Stuttgarter Zeitung ("Distanz in Nizza," Stuttgarter Zeitung, 12 January 1974) sees "urbanity" as the main characteristic of Becher's prose, because it is Becher's urbane attitude toward the world and its problems that creates the distance necessary for an objective appraisal of humanity. The problems of contemporary German literature--Podak mentions "gesellschaftliche Vermittlung, Kritik des Spätkapitalismus, Zweifel am Erzählen"--seem inapplicable by the end of the book. Instead, the reader peruses the gamut of world problems carried along by Becher's entertaining prose and absorbing in the process some of Becher's pleasure in language and coincidence.

For Rainer Fabian the "worldliness" of Ex-Casino comes from Becher's imitation of Hemingwayesque content: motifs like the hard-drinking man of action who burns out in the end.[27] However, according to Fabian, Becher´s style is original in German literature.

> Ulrich Becher ist einer der wenigen lebenden
> Autoren, die eine solch verspiegelte Prosa
> schreiben können. Sie wirkt weltmännisch
> und polyglott . . . Doch ihr wesentlichstes
> Charakteristikum ist, daß sie sich in einem
> Atemzug liest. Ulrich Becher . . . erzählt
> hemmunglos und flußartig. (Fabian, "Lebens-
> Poker")

There is no attempt in the critique to devalue this type of prose by assigning it to the realm of popular fiction á la Simmel.

However, Dieter Bachmann ("Das unaufhaltsame Verhängnis," Die Zeit, 21 March 1974) does view Ex-Casino as "Unterhaltungsliteratur," although the best of the genre. Unlike Simmel, Becher uses the political intrigue of the novel not just as a setting for James Bond-type adventure: ". . . hier ist Politik eine Kraft, die in die Schicksale hineinreicht und sie verändert." Of course, Becher´s style and use of language is completely foreign to popular fiction, and according to Bachmann here lies the source of Becher´s poor reception. Because he cannot be pinned down to one style, one genre, he stands "zwischen den Fronten," under fire from both camps, not quite popular fiction, but not yet high literature.

Another important critique discusses reception as well, but finds fault with the German literary scene instead of with Becher. Harry Neumann in reviewing Ex-Casino states:

> Zwei Eigentümlichkeiten der deutschen Literaturszene machen es weltläufigen Autoren wie Ulrich Becher schwer, sich wirklich durchzusetzen: einmal die fatale Tabula-Rasa-Gesinnung mancher deutscher Prosaisten und Lyriker, die alles verachten zu dürfen meinen, was gestern oder gar vorgestern war und die immer mal wieder ganz von vorn anzufangen glauben--zum anderen die offenbar unausrottbare Überzeugung des deutschen Bildungsbürgertums, ein literarisch anspruchvolles Werk müsse auch schwer lesbar sein.
> (Harry Neumann, "Einer, der erzählen kann," Deutsche Welle, May 1974.)

For Neumann, Becher is to be respected for his talent for fusing earlier styles (Expressionism) to produce a new, very modern and completely original style of his own. However, this is a different interpretation of "innovation," than that accepted as the primary criterion of quality by German literary critics. Again, almost without exception, critiques which mention Becher's reception history are positive.

The German critiques already mentioned discuss the major critical aspects of Ex-Casino. The Swiss critiques have little to add, because many

Swiss newspapers, due to their small circulation,
rely on book jacket blurbs. Of the three important
articles in Swiss papers, only one is negative.[28]
This article finds fault with Becher's imitation
of Hemingway, implying that Becher would be well
advised to leave this genre to the master:

> Becher schaut Hemingway über die Schulter,
> aber kann nicht recht lesen, was der da
> schreibt. Hemingway lauwarm serviert, ist
> ein Getränk, das man dem Kellner zurück-
> gibt . . . (NZZ)

Valentin Herzog sees in Ex-Casino Becher's
most blatantly autobiographical novel, and claims
that Becher admitted as much to him in a personal
interview. For Herzog the main characteristic of
Becher's style is the seemingly convoluted plot.

> Was auf den ersten Blick als Zickzack-
> Weg zwischen Schauplätzen, Zeiten, Per-
> sonen erscheint, erweist sich als Kunst-
> griff eines höchst bewusst arbeitenden
> Erzählers, Vorgänge, Beobachtungen, Motive
> behutsam aus ihrem zufälligen zeitlichen
> Kontext zu lösen und sie so in einen not-
> wenigen neuen Zusammenhang hineinzukom-
> ponieren, daß die wahre Bedeutung der ein-
> zelnen Handlungselemente ganz von selbst
> aufscheint. (Valtentin Herzog, "Ein Moby
> Dick in Basel," National-Zeitung Basle,
> 13 December 1973.)

The main cause of Becher's poor reception, according
to Herzog, lies in his fate as an exile and later

280

as an "Einzelgänger" in the literary world, at home
nowhere, accepted totally neither by East nor West.

In the preceding discussion, traditional
approaches to literary criticism have been employed,
always considering questions of reception, to develop
the major themes involved in the reception of Ulrich
Becher's work. The first chapters treated the primary
works chronologically along with Becher's biography
to highlight historically and psychologically motivated
explanations for Becher's reception. In this chapter
secondary works of literary criticism were then investigated, quotes from them being chosen to illustrate
and document the major elements of Becher's reception
as seen by the researcher. While the evidence collected by these traditional approaches may provide
reasonable proof of the researcher's views, they represent only the starting point for an empirical approach like reception aesthetics. Reception aesthetics calls for additional analysis of the material,
because it aims not only at identifying changing critical opinions, but also at measuring those opinions
against literary norms to determine the author's
place in the literary continuum. Thus, the themes
or patterns detected in the foregoing sections must

be translated into theses that can be tested empiri-
cally in the next chapter.

A brief summary of the themes that have
emerged is in order. For clarity these themes are
divided into two groups, internal and external themes.
Internal themes are those that developed from opinions
expressed about the content or formal elements (style,
structure, language) of the primary works. External
themes, logically, derive from opinions expressed
about the situation in which the works appeared
(critic's prominence, publishing criteria, political
scene, etc.). Of course, in any attempt at organization, there are themes that overlap.

The following are the internal themes developed in this chapter:

1) Becher's change from drama to prose produced a change in his reception. The fact
that this change coincided with a major
shift in German literary prose, with which
Becher was and is out of step, leads one to
believe that his plays have probably received
the more positive evaluation.

2) A variety of elements lead one to believe that there was a broader change in
Becher's reception around 1960. Not only

the increased emphasis on formal experimentation, but also the shift from plays to prose
and Becher's long absence from the literary
scene all account for a difference in how
critics viewed his works before and after
1960. In the case of Bockerer and Feuerwasser a change can be seen for individual works.
Generally, however, one must take the works
as a group in order to determine how critics
changed their response to Becher.

3) Austrian critics appear to be more negative than any other group concerning Becher's
style and language. This is perhaps due to
the personal animosity of critics like Torberg or to a generally more conservative
aesthetic stance among Austrian critics.

4) Swiss critics appear more positive on
formal elements than any other group, due
perhaps to Benziger Verlag's location in
Switzerland or Becher's choice of Basle as
his residence.

5) The acceptance of Becher's plays in East
Germany from 1954 to 1956 was due to his perceived political affinity. The content of

his plays fit in well with mid-1950s East
German views and for a time even the formal
elements of his works were accepted.

6) A related thesis is that all leftist
publications will be generally positive to
Becher, perhaps even more positive than the
GDR critiques, because they are not bound by
the constraints of GDR cultural policy.

7) After the 1957 return to a more repressive cultural policy, East German critics
reject Becher's works on the basis of formal elements, which is viewed as revisionism.
This is evident in the rejection of their
1957 edition of Der schwarze Hut, and in the
diminution of critiques or publications after
this date.

8) Critics are unable to categorize Becher's
prose works, calling them either literary
popular fiction or entertaining literature.
Because of this "zwischen-den-Stühlen" phenomenon, discussion of Becher's works is uncomfortable for critics, and thus avoided,
or the works are rejected for even partially
belonging to the realm of popular fiction.

Other themes, arising in circumstances outside the works themselves, appear to influence the
opinions expressed in newspaper criticism. The following external themes were brought out in this chapter:

1) The critic who is aware of Becher's
exile and poor reception history is predis-
posed toward his works. This phenomenon
became evident as early as the publication
of New Yorker Novellen and carries through
all Becher's prose works.

2) Critiques of Becher's works published
by Rowohlt are longer, more frequent, more
serious, and more prominent than critiques
of his works published by Benziger due to
the prominence of Rowohlt in the German publishing scene. Correspondingly critiques of
Benziger works are frequently copied from
short advertising blurbs distributed with a
copy of the book to the newspapers.

3) The prominence of the newspaper or critic
can override the frequency of articles in
lesser papers by obscure critics. In the
case of Murmeljagd, two extremely negative

critiques in <u>Die Zeit</u> and the <u>Frankfurter</u>
<u>Allgemeine Zeitung</u> offset the majority of
positive critiques in other sources.

There are other external factors, not specifically discussed in this chapter, which may correlate with the opinions expressed in the critiques.
Such factors as the circulation of the newspaper,
the amount of space devoted to an article, the country
of the newspaper, or even the type of article are
categories frequently used in content analysis. The
following chapter will discuss the methods of content
analysis and set up categories aimed at determining
the statistical validity of the explanations of recurrent themes discussed in this chapter.

FOOTNOTES

[1]Jauß, <u>Literaturgeschichte als Provokation</u>
(Frankfurt on Main: Suhrkamp, 1974), p. 169.

[2]Felix Vodicka, "Die Konkretisation des
literarischen Werks" in <u>Rezeptionsästhetik Theorie
und Praxis</u> ed. Rainer Warning (Munich: Wilhelm Fink
Verlag, 1975), p. 93. Further references to this
article will be given parenthetically in the text.

[3]Peter Glotz, <u>Buchkritik in deutschen Zei-
tungen</u> (Hamburg: Verlag für Buchmarkt-Forschung,
1968). Further references to this work will be given
parenthetically in the text.

[4]Jost Hermand, <u>Literatur nach 1945 I:
Politische und regionale Aspekte</u> (Wiesbaden: Akademische Verlagsgesellschaft Athenaion, 1979), p.
245.

[5]J.Z., "<u>Der Bockerer</u>," <u>Frankfurter Rundschau</u>,
15 November 1948. Further references to this article
will be given parenthetically as J.Z. Bibliographical
information for critiques which are cited only once
will be given parenthetically in the text, unless the
information is unusually long. The researcher fre-

quently had access only to photocopies of the critiques which only rarely included complete bibliographical information, such as page numbers. Bibliographical information is given to the extent known to the researcher. Photocopies of all cited critiques and radio criticism without exception are in the possession of the researcher.

[6]Gerhard Stadelmaier, "Womit sie leicht fertig werden," Stuttgarter Zeitung, 12 October 1978.

[7]Josef von Golitschek, "Widerstandskampf auf weanerisch," Mannheimer Morgen, 10 October 1978. Further references to this article will be given parenthetically as Golitschek.

[8]Dieter Schnabel, "Menschlichkeit Kontra Weltanschauung," Darmstädter Echo, 20 October 1978.

[9]Kurt Osterwald, "Luftsprünge am Rande des Grabes," Die Rheinpfalz, 10 October 1978. Further references to this article will be given parenthetically as Osterwald.

[10]Ethel Schwirten, "Verbannte in der Agonie," Frankfurter Rundschau, 14 April 1952. Further references to this article will be given parenthetically as Schwirten.

[11]Günter Kaltofen, "Samba von Ulrich Becher,"

288

Theater der Zeit, 10, No. 2 (Feb. 1955), 43-46. Further references to this article will be given parenthetically as Kaltofen.

[12]Herbert Ihering, "Episches und dramatisches Theater," Sonntag, 11, No. 3 (15 Jan. 1956), 11. Further references to this article will be given parenthetically as Ihering.

[13]Friedrich Heer, "Tragödie der Zwischenwelt," Die Furche, March 1954. Further references to this article will be given parenthetically as Heer.

[14]Effi Horn, "Falsche Töne," Münchner Merkur, 26 July 1978; herms, "Trostlos," Nürnberger Zeitung, 26 July 1978; Vivian Naefe, "Das Nacht-Milieu im Niemandsland," Abendzeitung (Munich), 26 July 1978; Richard Dölle, "Kritisch-ferngesen," Recklinghäuser Zeitung, 26 July 1978.

[15]Karl Heinz Kramberg, "Erzählte Gesichter," Süddeutsche Zeitung, 8 December 1974; anonymous, "Neue Bücher," Hessischer Rundfunk, 13 November 1974. Further references to the Kramberg article will be given parenthetically as Kramberg.

[16]hjt, "Das Lachen bleibt im Halse stecken," Deister- und Weserzeitung (Hameln), 13 Feb. 1975; R.H., "Ulrich Becher hat Atem zum Erzählen," Neue

Hannoversche Zeitung, 3 Jan. 1975.

[17]Wolfgang Schwerbrock, "Amoklauf eines
´Ostmärkers´," Frankfurter Allgemeine Zeitung, 2 March
1957; Gerd Semmer, "Ulrich Becher: Kurz nach 4,"
Geist und Zeit, 1957, No. 3, 154-156. Further references to these articles will be given parenthetically
as Schwerbrock and Semmer respectively.

[18]Lothar Streblow, "Ulrich Becher: Männer
machen Fehler," Geist und Zeit, 1959, No. 3, 124-129.
Further references to this article are given parenthetically as Streblow.

[19]Die Tat, Frankfurt am Main, no date. Xerox
on file.

[20]Hermand, Literatur nach 1945, p. 247-251.

[21]Hans Bender, "Bücher im Gespräch," Deutschlandfunk (Cologne), 14 September 1969. Further references to this review are given parenthetically as
Bender.

[22]P., "Ulrich Bechers Murmeljagd," Tagebuch
(Vienna), May/June 1969. Further references to this
article will be given parenthetically as P.

[23]Martin Gregor-Dellin, "Jeder Satz exotisch," Die Zeit, 29 August 1969. Further references
to this article will be given parenthetically as

Gregor-Dellin.

[24]Becher reveals his suspicions in a letter
to Karl Gerold, editor of the Frankfurter Rundschau dated
24 June 1969, in which he requests Gerold to print an
opposing article. I checked this point with Hans J.
Fröhlich, literary critic with the Frankfurter Allgemeine
Zeitung. Fröhlich reports that Lothar Romain is not a
pseudonym. "Es gibt diesen Lothar Romain, er ist ein
jüngerer Mann von ca. 40 Jahren, und folglich sind Rache-
akte oder dergl. ausgeschlossen." Hans J. Fröhlich,
Letter to Nancy Zeller, 15 July 1981.

[25]h.h.h., "Der große österreichische Roman,"
Die Zukunft (Vienna), April 1969; Gönther Poidinger,
"Das Grauen im Idyll," Arbeiter Zeitung (Vienna),
13 April 1969.

[26]Edition and sales figures were provided
in letters from Rowohlt (Personal letter of 21 Feb.
1969) and Benziger (letter of 21 December 1978).

[27]Rainer Fabian, "Lebens-Poker an der Theke,"
Welt des Buches, no date on xerox file copy. Further
references to this article will be given parenthetically
as Fabian, "Lebens-Poker."

[28]anonymous, "Fragen Sie mich nicht, wie ich
das meine," Neue Zürcher Zeitung, 14 June 1974. Further
references to this article given parenthetically as NZZ.

CHAPTER V:

Computer Study Design

The choice of reception aesthetics as an
approach to Ulrich Becher carries with it certain
practical limitations. Proper use of reception aesthetics requires that information from diverse areas,
in addition to that gleaned from the primary and
secondary literature, be evaluated and correlated.
Evaluation of the author's reception has to consider
publishing criteria, historical-social-political
events, literary trends, the author's place in the
literary canon, as well as the critical stance of the
researcher. All but the last of these have been
covered in the previous three chapters. This study
attempts to take one further step. Rather than permit the researcher's stance to influence the evaluation of the author's reception with some explicit
acknowledgment of bias, an attempt is made here to
minimize that bias through the use of statistical
techniques.

In view of the sheer volume of other information to be processed before conclusions could be

drawn, an inordinate share of research time could not
be spent on the compilation and statistical evaluation
of secondary material. Such practical considerations
have limited the use of reception aesthetics in recent years, especially in the case of better known
authors, whose bibliographies include tens of thousands of entries. Just the compilation of the secondary material presents such a formidable task that
many researchers are forced to stop short of analysis. The goal here is not only to collect secondary
texts, but also to analyze them using the objective
tool of statistics and then to correlate the results
of this analysis with other factors in Becher's
creative process. Multi-faceted correlation of
diverse areas is the principle underlying reception
aesthetics.

However, for the typical literary scholar,
statistical analysis by hand is prohibitive, both
in terms of the time spent learning the theory and
formulas, as well as the time spent in actual statistical manipulations, especially those involving multiple variables. The obvious answer to the problem of
statistical sophistication and the time it requires
is the use of the computer.

Use of the statistical capabilities of the computer in the analysis of non-numerical material required a methodology designed to transform linguistic content into a language of numbers the computer could understand. That methodology is content analysis, developed in the early part of the twentieth century by students of journalism and sociologists concerned with the growing importance of popular newspapers. However, it was the emergence of radio in the 1930s and the concurrent interest in the propaganda potential of the mass media that increased the use of content analysis. During World War II government intelligence agencies employed the technique to forecast Nazi political goals and to identify suspect organizations and individuals. In spite of its origins in the explication of newspaper articles, content analysis has studied almost every kind of verbal communications, such as music, gestures, maps, and art. Many concepts and assumptions underlying content analysis have always been a part of literary criticism, the major difference being the requirement for quantification of the material in content analysis. The reason for quantification is the same as that in all scientific inquiry, to reduce the influence of

294

the researcher's subjective viewpoint in the results.

The four steps of content analysis are the same as the four steps of any scientific research study. The first step is to formulate the research problem. Second, one must develop a study design with variables that provide information to answer the research problem. Within each variable one must set up categories or degrees of measurement to record individual pieces of information systematically. The final step is to perform statistical operations on the variables. Interpretation of the statistical findings should lead to the solving of the research problem.

That problem, in the terminology of reception aesthetics, was to determine the "concretization" (Konkretisation) of Becher's works. Concretization is defined by H. R. Jauß as the publically and socially recognized interpretation.[1] In addition, if this concretization has changed over time, the causes of the change must be discovered. The groundwork for the formulation of the research problem has been laid in the previous three chapters. Chapter II focused on the biographical, social, historical, political and artistic influences on Becher's works. Chap-

ter III discussed each work chronologically to highlight the shifts of emphasis over time and included
information on Becher's publishing history as a preliminary indication of his reception. Chapter IV
attacked the problem of reception more directly.
First, it provided a general view of the critical
establishment that is mainly responsible for an author's concretization. Second, it showed specifically
with regard to each work how that establishment re-
acted to Becher. If one could assume that every researcher were completely unbiased, and was capable
of sifting through the mass of information with objective selectivity, then at the end of Chapter IV
final conclusions about Becher's reception could be
drawn. Because that is not the case, all that exists
at the end of Chapter IV is a set of one researcher's
impressions about Becher's reception. Instead of
taking the normal route of reception aesthetics, namely,
somehow accounting for the critical stance of the researcher, the attempt here is to minimize that stance
as an influence on the final conclusions. As a result, the impressions left at the end of Chapter IV
will become a set of rigorously stated hypotheses,
which, taken together, are the final statement of the

296

research problem.

Once the general framework for a statement of the problem is established, a study design can be developed around those variables that help determine both the concretization of Becher's works and the factors influencing that concretization. In other words, the critic's opinions on such aspects as style and content are recorded in addition to any information that can explain the critic's motivation.

The first set of variables for recording the critics' opinions is simply an attempt to describe the content of the secondary material in such a way that trends can be discerned.[2] The following variables were chosen:

a) the attitude toward the work expressed in the article's title;

b) the opinion of the formal elements (style, structure, language);

c) the opinion of the content (ideas, characters, plot);

d) the opinion of Ulrich Becher (the man, the artist, the exile);

e) the opinion of the production or the publication;

297

f)   awareness of Becher's reception history;

g)   comparisons with other artists;

h)   the overall opinion of the work.

The first variable, the attitude expressed
in the title, is one of the most widely-used variables
in content analysis. Some analysts have even argued
that analysis of the titles alone could produce results as valid as detailed analysis of the entire
text.[3] However, these arguments are based on work with
front page newspaper articles, the titles of which are
designed to catch the reader's eye. Many book reviews lack titles completely, listing only bibliographical information. Therefore, it was decided to use
this variable in conjunction with variables describing the text as a cross-check on the validity of title-
only analysis of book reviews.

One option for describing the opinions expressed in the articles would simply have been to record the entire article as favorable, unfavorable or
neutral. However, such a gross measure provides no
indication of the complexity of the critical process
because it reduces a series of arguments to a single
opinion, thereby eliminating the explanations for the
opinions. In order to record purely literary judg-

298

ments the divisions of form and content, standard in
literary criticism, were chosen as variables. These
divisions were still broad enough that the majority
of critiques would address both issues in some way.
Under the variable "formal elements" were to be recorded judgments about style, structure, and language,
while opinions on plot, characters, setting and ideas
were subsumed under the "content" variable.

In addition to the above literary variables,
preliminary reading of critiques performed in the previous chapter indicated that non-literary factors
often contributed to the formation of the critics'
opinions. Some of these non-literary factors were
expressed within the text of the critiques and can thus
be called "internal contributing variables," as distinct from the "external contributing variables,"
to be discussed later. The internal contributing
variables were opinions of Ulrich Becher, opinions
on the productions of plays, awareness of Becher's
reception history, and the literary tradition critics
placed Becher in by comparing him with other artists.
If information recorded under these variables correlated with the literary variables, at least a partial explanation of the critics' opinions would be

possible.

Finally, as a check on the more specific variables, an overall opinion variable was included. If the measurement on the other variables was correct, the overall variable should show a high, though not perfect, correlation with each of them. Used in this way, the overall variable becomes a check on the validity of the other more specific measures.

The general investigation of the nature of German book criticism suggested other non-literary factors which could contribute to critics' opinions. Because these are not expressed within the text, they are referred to here as "external contributing variables." These variables included:

a) the political leanings of the sources;
b) the circulation of the source;
c) the country of the source.

In addition, content analysis suggests that the importance accorded the subject matter is indicated by the space and treatment it receives. Thus, the variables "length of article" and "type of article" were added as further external contributing variables.

All the above variables represent the ele-

ments of Becher's reception that are to be measured.
Within each variable several categories must be developed and these categories are the measurements of
the particular variable in question. Therefore, it
is important to discuss measurement in general before
discussing how and why the individual categories were
chosen.

Measurement is not limited to the hard
sciences. Whenever one assigns a value to an observed phenomenon, i.e., if one labels a phenomenon
as a particular subspecies of a more general category,
one measures it. Works categorized by literary period,
for example baroque or classical, are being measured.
Assigning an item to a category is, by definition,
giving that item a value, i.e., is a measurement of
the item. This type of measurement is, to be sure,
rather crude and is in fact the lowest level of meas
urement. Since it measures by name only, this type
of measurement is called "nominal" measurement. If
one can impose an order on these nominal categories,
the measurement of data is on a higher level, that
of "ordinal" measurement. For example, classifying
one work as more baroque than another is placing
an order on the categories and is, thus, an example

of ordinal measurement.

The hard sciences employ even higher levels of measurement, i.e., interval and ratio measurement. These permit statements about the degree of difference between values and about the ratios of one value to another, respectively.[4]

It is neither necessary nor at this time possible to utilize the higher levels of measurement employed by the physical sciences. Nominal and ordinal measures are already implicitly used in literary criticism; merely making their use explicit simplifies the analysis and improves its quality by reducing the influence of the researcher's subjectivity by making possible the use of statistical operations designed for the measurements.

To return to the project design, the next step in the process of content analysis is to establish categories, which are the measurements, to classify the data on each variable. The importance of this step cannot be overemphasized.[5] Not only must the categories be specific enough to be meaningful for the particular problem at hand, but they must also be general enough to relate to the broader discussion in the field. In addition, to insure statistical reliability, i.e., to insure the independence of the data from the measurement instrument, categories should be so clearly and explicitly defined that the same data results, regardless of when or by whom the analysis is undertaken.

This requirement highlights one of the basic assumptions of content analysis, namely that there is a common universe of discourse among the communicators and their audience, i.e., a manifest content, which is the valid unit of study for content analysis. This means that content analysis deals better with relatively denotative materials, such as news items, than with relatively connotative materials, such as a Rilke poem. Because content analysis makes the assumption of "manifest content," it obviates the necessity of dealing with the meta-psychology of semiotics.[6]

One way of increasing the reliability of the categories is to perform a pre-test, a trial analysis of a small sample of material not intended to yield statistically valid data but rather to serve as a check on the manifest content. Using the variables and categories developed by the researcher, other analysts assign values to the sample. If these values coincide with those of the primary researcher then he can have confidence that his categories are explicit enough to provide reliable data. If not, he can use the pre-test as a diagnostic device to redesign the categories. Such a pre-test was performed at the beginning of this project. Fifteen critiques were selected at random, one about each Becher work and analyzed by several native speakers of German using the variables and categories developed by the researcher. The results of this pre-test substantiated the primary researcher's recording of the content of the critique. This being done, final analysis could proceed.

Categories must be appropriate for the variables. Thus, directional categories are required for the literary variables because in their case opinions on form and content are expressed, i.e., they involve ordinal measurement. The establishment of directional categories dealing with opinions is extremely difficult given the complexities and ambiguities of language. One problem is to determine how many gradations of opinion can feasibly be measured. An infinite number of gradations of opinion from outright praise to censure of Becher's form or content is possible. Generalizations cannot be

304

made upon that basis. However, a 3-point scale using the categories positive, neutral, and negative did not provide enough information. The second problem was to determine at what point it was no longer possible to design directional categories distinct enough for other researchers. For the purposes of this study, that point seemed to have been reached with a 5-point scale using the categories praise, positive, neutral, negative, censure. With a 5-point scale it was still possible to give clear examples defining each category. But a 7-point scale, which distinguishes within the positive and negative categories between strongly positive and mildly positive or strongly and mildly negative, would have cost more time than it was worth in terms of the additional information gained. Only when norms or lists of symbols in German literary criticism have been established will it be feasible to go into as much detail as the 7-point scale requires.[7]

Each category on the 5-point scale was defined with several quotes from the critiques which demonstrated the distinctions between categories. Table I illustrates these distinctions. The researcher consulted a similar table for each directional cate-

TABLE I

SAMPLE STATEMENTS DEFINING CATEGORIES
FOR LITERARY VARIABLES

Category	Statements
PRAISE-Formal	Das Ergebnis . . .ergibt einen hohen literarischen Reiz. Der extravagante Versuch . . . läßt die große poetische Begabung des Erzählers Ulrich Becher erkennen. Es wird auch hier "erzählt", aber lyrisch, bildunersättlich, mit einer Freude an wunderlichen phantastischen Wortbildungen . . .
PRAISE-Content	Es gibt eben Stücke, die sind zu gut . . . So, und nun möchten wir das Stück nach allen Kanten empfehlen und versichern, daß es ein Dutzend andere auswiegt an Gedankentiefe und an Schönheiten aller Art . . .
POSITIVE-Formal	. . . in gekonnter Aufbereitung vorgestellt . . . in gelungen Schnitten geboten . . . Der Autor, Ulrich Becher, noch der gradlinig erzählenden, schilderungsfreudigen Schreibgeneration angehörend, die Anfang unseres Jahrhunderts hervortrat . . .
POSITIVE-Content	Sein letzter, neuer Roman heißt "Murmeljagd," ist bei Rowohlt erschienen-ein dickes, aber auf alle Fälle ein bemerkenswertes Buch.
NEUTRAL-Content	Becher hat in das Buch hineingestopft, was er in Jahren und Jahrzehnten an realen Erfahrungen und Einzelheiten bemerkt und gesammelt hat.
NEGATIVE-Formal	. . . ich hielt Ulrich Becher den handgreiflichen Einwand vor, das

	dieses Stück in zwei Stücke zer- fällt, in sechs Bilder eines Volks- stücks und zwei Bilder, die es . . . mehr zur Ballade machen. (Diese Kontroverse) zeichnet ein Mißverständnis ab, das dem allge- meinen Kategorien-Zusammenbruch dieser Zeit stammt. Das Drama von heute befindet sich in der Sackgasse der Experimente.
NEGATIVE-Content	Die Zirkus-Sentimentalität dieses Vier-Personenen-Stücks verbreitet den Geruch von Zuckmayers Knie- Stück.
CENSURE-Formal and Content	Da schreibt einer einen Roman mit soviel erzählerischem Ehrgeiz und lädt vor seinem Publikum eine ge- radezu unbescheidene Fülle von Bildungslast und wuchtig bis ka- priziösen Sprachformen ab, als könne er unserer Zeit noch mit den Methoden eines Jean Pauls bei- kommen. Er hat zuviel geschrieben, aber zuwenig wichtiges.

---

gory during the process of rating the individual critiques. Statements that depend on irony or implication
to convey opinions could not be taken out of context
and retain their meaning. In such cases, the researcher had to rely on the tenor of the text. It was clear
that irony in an article acted like a negative sign;
no matter what words were used, the opposite was intended.

In general the following procedure was used

in rating directional categories. The entire critique was scanned quickly to identify the sections dealing with each variable. Within each section, individual sentences were rated on the 5-point scale and the ratings were then simply added together and averaged. Not all sentences were equally interesting. Only those containing general pronouncements on the variable in question were rated; statements acting as qualifiers were not taken into consideration. In this way very short and very long articles could be equated, because no matter how few or how many pronouncements an article contained on a particular variable, it still received only one rating on the 5-point scale.

In addition to the literary variables of form and content, some of the internal contributing variables used directional categories and were rated on the same 5-point scale. The variables involved were opinion of Ulrich Becher and opinion of the production. Two other internal contributing variables were rated on a 3-point scale, namely, attitude expressed in title and the overall opinion, because the entire critique was being categorized by these variables and not individual statements.

TABLE II

VARIABLES AND CATEGORIES

Variable	Categories
Publisher of Critique	000=Unknown; 001-197=Consecutively numbered publications in which the critiques appeared; e.g., 001=Frankfurter Rundschau, 033=Nürnberger Zeitung.
Date of Critique	Six-digit number (day-month-year)
Country of Publisher	0=Unknown; 1=FRG; 2=GDR; 3=Switzerland; 4=Austria; 5=France; 6=Holland; 7=USA; 8=USSR; 9= Pre-war Germany.
Becher's Work Discussed	01-23 Each work received a 2-digit code; e.g., 01=Männer machen Fehler; 13=Feuerwasser.
Length of Critique	1=less than 250 words; 2=250-499 words; 3=500-749 words; 4=750-999 words; 5-1000¹ words.
Political Stance of Newspaper	0=Unknown; 1=Neutral; 2=Left-Communist; 3=Left-Socialist; 4=Liberal/Democrat; 5=Conservative; 6=Right.
Circulation of Newspaper	0=Unknown; 1=over 5 million; 2= 1-5 million; 3=500 thousand-1 million; 4=200-500 thousand; 5=100-200 thousand; 6=50-100 thousand; 7=under 50 thousand.
Type of Article	Two-digit number; first number listed is primary; e.g., 01=Objective report/content summary; 02=Evaluation/aesthetics; 12=Both 01 and 02 with 01 being primary.
Reception Mentioned	1=Yes; 2=No.

| Comparison with other Artists | Two-digit code assigned consecutively as each new named occurred; e.g., 08=Andersch; 19=Horvath. |

However, two internal contributing variables, namely, "awareness of reception" and "comparison with other artists," as well as all but one external contributing variable required only nominal measurements. Table II lists all these variables with their nominal categories.

The categories for the variable "length of critique" are the only ordinal categories in this group, included here with the other external contributing variables. Most of the other categories were simply names in the form of numbers assigned consecutively. However, the values for "political stance" and "circulation of newspaper" can be considered ordinal measurements. They were adopted from the <u>Fischer Weltalmanach 1972 Kulturstatistik</u> and from Stamm's <u>Leitfaden für Presse und Werbung</u>, which provided the most thorough and readily available sources of information on German-language newspapers.[8]

After the variables and categories have been devised and each critique evaluated according to the

310

categories, then the final step, namely, analysis,
can be completed. Before discussing the analysis,
it is important to recall the role of this step in
the overall scheme. The previous chapter ended with
several themes which will shortly be turned into formal hypotheses. Each theme as stated thus far can be
divided into two parts: a statement about Becher's
reception which can be tested and a statement of the
reasons for believing the first part to be true. The
latter derives from the examination of Becher's personal history and works as well as from his publishing history and a first impression of the critiques.
There is no way to test these reasons for validity,
but they can be corroborated by the results of the
tests on Becher's reception. Because the study design uses the critiques as the final arbiter of Becher's concretization and the influences on the concretization, the results of the statistical analysis
will differentiate between those aspects of his concretization about which one can be relatively certain and those which remain inconclusive to some
degree.

Thus, it is clear that, before the theses
from the previous chapter can be tested, they must

be turned into formal hypotheses. A formal hypothesis specifies the exact variables that are to be tested. In contrast, the theses from the previous chapter often included the combined effects of several variables. The task now is to try to separate the effects of one variable from those of another that may have similar effects.

This statement of formal hypotheses will begin with the internal theses listed at the end of the previous chapter.

1) The change in Becher's reception at the end of the 1950s appears to be connected with his change from drama to prose. The relationship becomes somewhat confused because some plays received new productions in the 1970s, even though they were written much earlier. Therefore, it seems reasonable to believe that there will be a difference in the reception of his plays and his prose works, but the direction of that difference is unclear.

Hypothesis I: Opinions of formal elements and content, as well as the overall opinions will show a statistically significant difference between plays and prose works.

2) The more direct way of testing a change
in Becher´s reception around 1960 is to compare critiques written before 1960 to those
written later. Because it has been postu-
lated that this change was due to an increasing emphasis on style and formal experimentation, one could expect the difference in
reception to show up primarily in the opinions of formal elements. The change in
reception is most likely not due to any
significant change in Becher´s style but
rather to a change in the kind of literature being produced, i.e., a change in the
norms. Thus, even in the case of works that
were produced in both periods one might expect a negative change in the opinions of
formal elements. The uncertainty of the
previous hypothesis is not justified in
this case because the focus is strictly on
formal elements, while the previous hypotheses examined all types of literary judgments.

Hypothesis II: Opinions of formal elements

will be positive more frequently in critiques published before 1960 than in critiques published after that date.

3) Austrian critics appear to be more negative towards Becher's style regardless of genre than critics of other countries.

Hypothesis III: Opinions of formal elements published in Austrian newspapers will be more negative than corresponding opinions in publications of other countries.

4) Country also appears to be a factor in Swiss critiques.

Hypothesis IV: Opinions of formal elements published in Swiss newspapers will be more positive than corresponding opinions in publications of other countries.

5) The initially positive reception of Becher's works in the GDR changed in the late 1950s due to the changes in GDR cultural policy.

Hypothesis V: East German opinions of pre-1957 works will be more positive than corresponding opinions of post-1957 works, if indeed there are enough GDR critiques after this year to make a valid comparison.

6) Positive reception of Becher's plays in the GDR appears to be based on perceived political affinities.

Hypothesis VI: East German opinions of content will be more positive than corresponding opinions from other countries.

The following hypotheses were developed from the external theses of the previous chapter.

1) One external factor that appears to influence the opinions of Becher's prose is the critic's awareness of Becher's reception history.

Hypothesis VII: Critiques which mention Becher's reception have a more positve overall rating, as well as more positive ratings under the literary variables, than do critiques which do not mention reception.

2) Publisher also effects reception. Works published by Rowohlt--together with Suhrkamp and Hanser--,one of the triad of respected West German publishers of serious literature, received more critical attention than works

published by Benziger.

Hypothesis VIII: Rowohlt publications received more critiques than Benziger publications. Critiques of Rowohlt publications
appear in newspapers with larger circula-
tions than do Benziger publications. Critiques of Rowohlt publications are longer
than critiques of Benziger publications.
Critiques of Rowohlt publications are more
likely evaluative while critiques of Benziger works are more likely to be reports
or content summaries.

3) There are two hypotheses concerning the
political leanings of the newspapers in
which the book criticism is published.
Hypothesis IX: Critiques appearing in leftist publications will be more positive in
their opinions of form and content than will
critiques in other journals. This follows
from the earlier discussion of Becher´s
favorable reception in the GDR. The second
and perhaps more telling hypothesis is:
Hypothesis X: Critiques in leftist publications will be more positive in their

opinions of form and content even when type of article is controlled for.

In addition to those hypotheses that can be drawn directly from the impressions of the critiques, there are several others which emerge from impressions of the various parts of this study, even from the methodology of content analysis alone. In some cases testing of these hypotheses will also permit special applications of the statistical techniques that are to be employed in the next chapter. Thus, it is useful to consider the following hypotheses:

> 1) The strength of aesthetic norms in influencing critics' opinions, as indicated by Glotz's survey, might lead one to believe that opinions of formal elements would have an impact on opinions of content. Hypothesis XI: There will be a significant, positive correlation between opinions of formal elements and opinions of content.
> 2) If, as hypothesized above, knowledge of Becher's reception positively influences the opinions of his works, it is not unlikely that opinions of Becher also influence opin-

ions of his works.

Hypothesis XII: There will be a significant correlation between opinions of Becher and opinions of his works.

The concerns of content analysis provide the basis for the following hypotheses. An important feature of these hypotheses is that they do not necessarily relate to Becher or to the content of the critiques; they would be reasonable hypotheses in any study using the same variables. They tend therefore to confirm or falsify the methodology of content analysis itself.

1) A frequent focus of content analysis studies is the space allotted to the article. It is hypothesized that the longer the article, the more important the subject matter. In the case of book critiques, this should translate into positive reception.

Hypothesis XIII: Length of the critique will correlate significantly with positive opinions of form and content.

2) Because short critiques are either notices of a book's publication or publisher's

blurbs used as filler in small papers, they tend not to be negative.

Hypothesis XIV: There will be a significant negative correlation between short critiques and negative opinions.

3) The Glotz study indicates that because of critics' concern with aesthetic quality, only those works which are considered significant are reviewed at all. It follows that among reviewed works those that fit the aesthetic norm best are given more serious consideration. The variable which measures the seriousness of treatment is type of article.

Hypothesis XV: Evaluative articles may be expected to be more positive on form and content than articles which are reports.

4) By their nature, evaluative articles may be expected to be longer. This relationship, together with the previous hypothesis, lead one to suspect that the statistics to be developed from these hypotheses will lead to confusing results. More specifically, if longer articles are

more positive, and if the evaluative articles
are also positive, then it will be impossible to distinguish the effects of length
from those of type of article, unless controls are introduced.

Hypothesis XVI: Longer articles will be
more positive in their opinions of form and
content, even when the effects of type of
article are controlled for.

6) Some content analysts use only headlines
in their studies, believing that the essence
of the opinion is contained in the headline.
To test this in regard to book critiques,
the following hypothesis is proposed:

Hypothesis XVII: The opinion expressed in
the title will correlate with the opinions
of form and content.

7) One of the principal findings of Glotz's
survey was that only a few large newspapers
are responsible for the real book criticism
in Germany. Thus, one would expect:

Hypothesis XVIII: Papers with low circulation publish only short critiques.

Before analyzing the data on the above hypotheses, it is important to note the limitations of statistical methodology in literary study. While the advantages of statistical computer analysis will become clear in the next chapter, it cannot do certain things. In the case of this study, there were two themes mentioned at the end of Chapter IV which cannot be tested with the current design. The first is the thesis that discussion of Becher's work is uncomfortable for critics and is often avoided because his works fit into no literary mold completely. This implies two things. First, the critics did not provide clear categorizations and thus no data are available on this thesis. Second, Becher probably would have received more critiques if his works could be categorized, but that is clearly not a testable hypothesis. It is impossible to analyze critiques that do not exist.

The second thesis is that a few critiques by prominent newspapers or critics can override the effect of a greater number of critiques by lesser known newspapers or critics. To test this hypothesis, data would have to be available at the interval level of measurement. Specifically, one would have to be able to measure the difference in the amounts of influence of two different newspapers. While this measurement is theoretically not impossible, as Glotz reports, data from market analyses of the newspaper industry in Germany are scientifically unsound and in any case not available outside the industry.[9]

Finally, a few variables included in the study design failed to yield enough data to be worthy of analysis. In the case of "opinion of production" Chapter IV showed that with some plays later productions were judged differently than earlier productions, and this almost certainly had an impact on Becher's reception. However, opinions about productions were not expressed often enough to yield sufficient data for analysis. The variable did serve one function, however; it assisted the researcher in separating the critic's opinions of Becher's works from the opinions on the way the work was presented, thus contributing to the validity of the study.

The problem with the variable "comparison with other artists" relates to the thesis mentioned above concerning critics' inability to categorize Becher's works. This variable was intended to serve as a measure of such categorization. However, it became clear even during the coding of the data that

there was so little agreement among the critics that
a new value for the variable had to be created with
each critic that compared Becher to another artist.
That is to say, Becher was compared to no one artist
or group of artists consistently. To some extent
this fact alone may confirm the thesis that critics
found his works uncategorizable.

FOOTNOTES

[1]Attributed to Jauß by Manfred S. Fischer, "Eigene Sprach-Welt: Komparatisten-Kongress in Innsbruck," Die Zeit, 34, No. 36 (7 September 1979), 17.

[2]This is essentially a question of validity. In a research sense validity may be defined as the degree to which the study measures what it wants to measure. See Claire Selltiz et al., Research Methods in Social Relations (New York: Holt, Rinehart and Winston, 1959), pp. 154-163, and Bernard Berelson, Content Analysis in Communication Research (Glencoe, Illinois: The Free Press, 1952), pp. 169-171).

[3]Ole R. Holsti, Content Analysis for the Social Sciences and Humanities (Reading, Massachusetts: Addison-Wesley, 1969), p.

[4]Selltiz, pp. 186-195.

[5]Berelson, p. 147.

[6]Berelson, p. 19.

[7]Selltiz, pp. 345-356.

[8]Gustav Fochler-Hauke, Der Fischer Weltalmanach 1972 (Frankfurt on Main: Fischer Taschenbuch Verlag, 1971), pp. 211-217, and W. Stamm ed.,

Leitfaden durch Presse und Werbung (Essen: Stamm

Verlag, 1976).

[9]Peter Glotz, Buchkritik in deutschen Zei-

tungen (Hamburg: Verlag für Buchmarkt-Forschung,

1968), p. 101.

CHAPTER VI:

Results

In order to clarify for the reader the
following test results, it is necessary to provide
a brief explanation of the various statistical operations performed on the data. These statistics were
included in the SPSS, a computer software package
designed for the social sciences. The subprogram
of SPSS used here was "CROSSTABS" with its related
statistics, chi-square, Cramer's V, Tau b, Tau C,
partial gamma, and zero-order gamma.[1]

Crosstabs is a type of contingency analysis
that investigates the relationships among two or
more variables. This operation takes the form of
a table of joint frequency distributions which can
be analyzed by statistical tests for significance
and strength of association. Take, for example,
a crosstab aimed at discovering if there is a relationship between religion and political affiliation.
The test of the hypothesized relationship would result in the following 2 x 2 table:

	Republican	Democrat
Catholic		
Protestant		

This basic 2 x 2 table can be extended by the addition
of other variables as controls as well as by the addition of categories within the variables. For example,
a 3 x 3 table would result from the addition of "Jewish" as a category under the variable "religion" and
of "Independent" under the variable "political affiliation." If the variable of "race" were added as a
control, the result would be a 3 x 3 table "religion
by politics" for each category under the variable
"race."

With the addition of variables and categories, tables become less self-evident and it is
desirable to summarize their results with one or more
statistical measures. Chi-square tests the statistical
significance of a distribution, i.e., the probability
that the same distribution would occur by chance in

another data sample. Taking the previous example,
suppose that a sample of 1000 persons was chosen
and that in this sample 500 were Democrats and 500
Republicans, while 300 were Catholic and 700 Pro-
testant. With this information alone, one would expect, assuming no relationship between religion and
politics, that the following table would be produced:

	Republican	Democrat
Catholic	150	150
Protestant	350	350

These are the expected values. If, however, the sample
shows a different distribution, this does not imply
by itself a relationship between the two variables.
Suppose, for instance, the table on the following page
were produced. The only way that one could tell whether
this distribution is likely to have occurred by chance
is by a statistical test. Chi-square measures the

328

difference between the expected values in each cell
of the table and the values actually observed. With
appropriate adjustments for the number of categories
involved, chi-square will reveal the likelihood that
the observed distribution occurred by chance. In
this study, as in most, a relationship will be considered to exist if the probability of the observed
distribution occurring by chance is less than 5%,
i.e., if 95 out of 100 samples of the same size would
produce essentially the same results.

	Republican	Democrat
Catholic	140	160
Protestant	360	340

Chi-square alone only determines that a relationship between variables exists. It does not
measure the strength of the relationship or the
direction. Cramer's V measures the strength of
association between variables with nominal categories
which produce tables larger than 2 x 2. Its range is

from 0 to 1, which means that the closer to 1 the value of Cramer's V, the higher the degree of association. This statistic does not reveal whether the association is positive or negative, because such a question cannot be answered with nominal data.

Tau b and c measure both degree of association and direction for variables with ordinal categories. Tau b is best suited to square tables, i.e., tables in which the number of rows equals the number of columns, while Tau c is used for rectangular tables. Tau b and c have a range of -1 to +1. When Tau b and c have values near -1, a strong negative correlation is indicated. Zero indicates a lack of correlation, while a statistic near +1 indicates a strong positive relationship.

Zero-order and partial gamma are appropriate for three dimensional tables, i.e., for cases in which a control variable is used. The zero-order gamma describes the relationship between the two primary variables when no control is considered. Partial gamma describes the same relationship after the effect of the control variable has been taken into account. Therefore, comparison of the two gammas provides a measure of the independent effect of the control vari-

330

able. Gammas range from -1 to +1, and thus they
are capable of indicating direction as well as
strength.

Although the SPSS subprogram CROSSTABS
produces other statistics, these are the only ones that
will be used in this study. No hypothesis will be
tested with all statistics because each statistic
has a different use. However, in all cases, chi-
square will be employed to determine the statistical
significance of the relationship.

> Hypothesis I: Opinions of formal elements
> and content, as well as the overall opinions
> will show a statistically significant dif-
> ference between plays and prose works.

To test this hypothesis, critiques were
divided into two groups, those on plays and those
on prose, and were cross-tabulated with the variables
"opinion of formal elements," "opinion of content,"
and "overall opinion." Tables 1-3 show the results
of these operations.

Table 1 shows a chi-square significance

Number Row Pct. Col. Pct.	TABLE 1 TYPE OF WORK BY FORMAL				
	Praise	Positive	Neutral	Negative	Censure
Plays	4 6.5 5.4	36 58.1 19.4	7 11.3 50.0	12 19.4 21.8	3 4.8 25.0	62 18.2
Prose	70 25.1 94.6	150 53.8 80.6	7 2.5 50.0	43 15.4 78.2	9 3.2 75.0	279 81.8
	74 21.7	186 54.5	14 4.1	55 16.1	12 3.5

Significance < .01   Cramer's V = .23408

level of less than 1%, meaning there is less than 1
chance in 100 that the distribution shown here occurred
by chance. This statistic indicates there is defi-
nitely some differences in the reception of Becher's
prose as compared to his plays on the basis of style.
The chi-square statistic by itself will not tell
which received more favorable reception from critics.
To determine that, one must examine the numbers and
percentages in the table.

Of all critiques 18.2% dealt with plays,
while 81.8% dealt with prose. If the distribution
were random among the categories (i.e., "praise,"
"positive," "neutral," "negative," and "censure"),

one would expect that approximately 18.2% of all critiques in any category would be critiques on plays (column percentage). A glance at the table reveals that this is not the case. The most striking feature of the table are that there are far more neutral critiques (50%) and fewer praise critiques (5.4%) on plays than would be expected. Of course, on a table comparing only two types of works, the converse would be true for critiques on prose. While the percentage of critiques on plays in the category "censure" is higher than 18.2%, the count (3) is so small that the presence or absence of even one critique would bring the percentage into line with the expected value. This means that the percentages under the negative category actually contribute more to the statistical significance than those under "censure," despite the fact that the former differ less from the expected values.

The most interesting aspect of this table is the positive category. Here, in contrast to the praise category, plays hold a slightly larger than expected share (19.4%) of the positive critiques. What this means is that there is no simple answer as to whether prose or plays were better received on

the basis of formal elements. If there were a
straight-forward answer to the question, there would
be a clear directional tendency that one or the other
type of work received more negative and less positive
response. For instance, if it were to show that
plays were consistently less well received on the
basis of form than were prose works, there would be
a descending order of the percentages across the
categories on plays, beginning with "censure" down
to "praise" and the neutral percentage would be approximately 18.2%. The converse would then hold for
prose works.

        Because there is no such clear directional
tendency, a more qualified answer must be given to
the question as to which genre the critics preferred
on the basis of formal elements. The paucity of critiques praising Becher's drama style indicates that
Becher was not considered a great dramatist, although
a significant number of critics liked his plays. In
contrast, Becher's prose works garnered a much larger
share of the praise for formal elements. The distribution of critiques in the neutral category indicates that critics were more likely to be neutral
about the formal aspects of Becher's plays, while his
prose was either liked or disliked.

334

                                  TABLE 2

                        TYPE OF WORK BY CONTENT

Number / Row Pct. / Col. Pct.	Praise	Positive	Neutral	Negative	Censure	
Plays	9 10.5 18.4	41 47.7 10.2	7 8.1 18.9	21 24.2 39.6	8 9.3 61.5	86 21.4
Prose	40 12.7 81.6	209 66.1 83.6	30 9.5 81.1	32 10.1 60.4	5 1.6 38.5	316 78.6
	49 12.2	250 62.2	37 9.2	53 13.2	13 3.2	

               Significance < .01   Cramer's V = .25935

A somewhat different picture is revealed
when the subject under discussion is content, as Table
2 makes clear. The chi-square significance level of
this table is also 1%. There is obviously a difference in the reception of the content of Becher's plays
and prose and examination of the row percentages show
there is a directional tendency for more positive
reception of the content of prose work.

12.2% of all critiques praise Becher's content. Of the critiques on plays only 10.5% are praise,
while 12.7% of prose critiques praise Becher's content.
The difference in the reception of plays and prose
becomes even clearer in the "positive" and "negative"

categories with plays being received far less positively and far more negatively than prose. Since
the prose critiques outnumber play critiques by
almost four to one, it is significant that there
are actually more "censure" critiques on plays than
on prose.[2]

The function of the "overall" variable was
to provide a validity check on the other variables,
and in this case at least, it helps to determine the
relative importance of formal elements and content
in Becher's reception. Table 3 confirms the more
positive reception of prose works in general; and
in conjunction with Table 2, it is clear that the
basis for this positive reception is favorable evaluation of the content of Becher's prose.

TABLE 3

TYPE OF WORK BY OVERALL

	Positive	Neutral	Censure	
Plays	51	7	32	90
	56.7	7.8	35.6	21.8
	16.3	25.0	45.1	
Prose	262	21	39	322
	81.4	6.5	12.1	78.2
	83.7	75.0	54.9	

```
313        28        71
76.0       6.8       17.2

Significance  <  .01      Cramer´s V = .26183
```

Certainly these three tables have provided confirmation of the hypothesis that prose and plays were received differently. Since the direction of this preference was not clear after the discussion of earlier chapters, it is now imperative to speculate on its causes.

Formal elements are less important in opinions of Becher´s plays than in opinions of prose. The reader will recall that, if formal consideration entered the picture at all, only the appropriateness of the form of the play to its content was discussed. As Table 1 shows, an inordinately high percentage of critiques are neutral on formal considerations, indicating that Becher´s plays fell well within the formal "Erwartungshorizont" of critics. This is not surprising if one examines the tenor of the postwar German theater with its emphasis on the reestablishment of links with the realistic classics abandoned during the Nazi era. Becher´s plays fit the mold. His detailed descriptions of setting have been

noted, as well as his three-act-plus-epilogue structure with limited scene changes and use of public
places as motivation. Not even Becher's penchant
for imitating conversation seems unusual in a play.

It is precisely Becher's imitation of spoken language, however, which created the most controversy among critics of his prose works. This is reflected in the fact that the prose was judged more
positively and less neutrally than expected. Becher's
use of language was outside the critic's horizon of
expectation for prose and thus had to receive some
commentary, as it turns out, more positive than negative.

However, the real difference in the evaluation of plays versus prose is content. What is puz-
zling is that this is so even though, as Chapter III
points out, Becher's themes remained unchanged over
the years. The explanation may lie in Becher's prox-
imity to exile. More of Becher's plays, being closer
in time to his exile experience, employed distinctly
exotic settings and situations few Europeans could
identify with or understand. The theme of the humanist
response to fascism was obscured by the Brazilian
milieu of _Samba_ and _Makumba_ and the New York under-

world in _Feuerwasser_. In contrast, most of Becher's
prose works bring the fight against fascism back to
European soil. In addition, prose allows more freedom in the developing of arguments than the realistic theater, which must rely on well-motivated dialogue
and cannot take advantage of silent thought processes.
As a result, the content of Becher's prose works becomes more believable, more understandable, and more
relevant to the European audience, and therefore is
more positively received. This positive reception
of content carried over into the overall positive reception of Becher's prose as compared with his plays.

> Hypothesis II: Opinions of formal elements
> will be positive more frequently in critiques
> published before 1960 than in critiques pub-
> lished after that date.

TABLE 4

YEAR BY FORMAL

	Praise	Positive	Neutral	Negative	Censure	
Pre-1960	6 11.5 8.2	35 67.3 17.9	1 1.9 7.1	10 19.2 17.5	0 0.0 0.0	52 14.8
Post-1960	67 22.4 91.8	160 53.5 82.1	13 4.3 92.9	47 15.7 82.5	12 4.0 100.0	299 85.2

```
    73      195       14       57       12
   20.8     55.6      4.0     16.2      3.4

   Significance > .05      Cramer's V = .142031
```

Table 4 shows that there is no significant difference in the reception of the formal elements of Becher's works before and after 1960. Examination of the percentages in the table confirm this impression, but they also show some interesting facts. Critiques written before 1960 were generally either positive or negative, with few critics taking extreme positions and also few neutral opinions. The post-1960 critiques show much greater variability, with proportionately more critics giving either praise or censure verdicts, but also more neutral verdicts. Thus, the increased attention to the formal side of aesthetics was also characterized by a decided lack of unanimity among the critics as to just what "proper" style was.

> Hypothesis III: Opinions of formal elements published in Austrian newspapers will be more negative than corresponding opinions in publications other countries.

TABLE 5

COUNTRY BY FORMAL

	Praise	Positive	Neutral	Negative	Censure	
Austria	3 10.3 4.2	14 48.3 7.4	2 6.9 13.3	8 27.6 14.8	2 6.9 16.7	29 8.5
Others	69 22.0 95.8	176 56.1 92.6	13 4.1 86.7	46 14.6 85.2	10 3.2 83.3	314 91.5
	72 21.0	190 55.4	15 4.4	54 15.7	12 3.5	

Significance > .05   Cramer's V = .1358902

To test the hypothesis, critiques on formal
elements in Austrian newspapers were crosstabulated
to critiques on formal elements from all other countries in an attempt to determine if Austrian critiques
were more negative. Table 5 shows that the relationship is not statistically significant. Interestingly
enough, however, the percentages shown in the table
indicate a very clear direction, with Austrian critics
providing Becher with fewer positive opinions and more
negative opinions than critics of other countries.
While the differences are not large enough to confirm
the hypothesis, one should also note that Austrian
critics provided Becher with very few critiques, lend-

341

ing some support to the notion of a tacit boycott.

Hypothesis IV: Opinions of formal elements
published in Swiss newspapers will be more
positive than corresponding opinions in
publications of other countries.

TABLE 6

COUNTRY BY FORMAL

	Praise	Positive	Neutral	Negative	Censure	
Switz-erland	19 33.9 26.4	27 48.2 14.2	3 5.4 20.0	6 10.7 11.1	1 1.8 8.3	56 16.3
Others	53 18.5 73.6	163 56.8 85.8	12 4.2 80.0	48 16.7 88.9	11 3.8 91.7	287 83.7
	72 21.0	190 55.4	15 4.4	54 15.7	12 3.5	

Significance > .05   Cramer's V = .1502602

This hypothesis was tested in the same manner as was the previous one, and again the statistics
are not significant. In this case, however, there is
not a clear direction to the results, making the analysis somewhat more difficult. While Swiss critiques
show fewer negative and censure opinions as a group

342

than do other critiques, they also show fewer positive critiques than had been hypothesized. The only
category which would tend to confirm the hypothesis
is that of praise, where Swiss critics show up in
clearly disproportionate numbers. This was not enough,
however, to make a statistically significant difference.
One point that should be noted is that there were almost twice as many Swiss critiques as there were Austrian critiques (see Table 5). Thus, even if Becher
is not receiving a significantly better reception in
his adopted country than in other places, he may at
least be receiving more notice, and for an author
who has struggled to become known, that may be important.

Hypothesis V: East German opinions of formal elements in pre-1957 works will be more
positive than corresponding opinions in
post-1957 works.

This hypothesis calls for a comparison of
pre-1957 GDR critiques with post-1957 GDR critiques
to determine if the change to strict socialist realism caused a more negative evaluation of Becher's
works. However, because of a lack of data (of a

total of 15 GDR critiques only 4 were post-1957),
this comparison would result in meaningless statistics. Yet, maybe even more significant than statistics is the fact that critiques from the GDR,
which had provided Becher's most noteworthy reception in the immediate post-war era, almost completely
stopped after 1957. The very absence of reception
thus would indicate the strength of the GDR's negative evaluation of Becher's works after that date.

Hypothesis VI: East German opinions of content will be more positive than corresponding opinions from other countries.

TABLE 7

COUNTRY BY CONTENT

	Praise	Positive	Neutral	Negative	Censure	
GDR	5 33.3 8.9	9 60.0 3.6	0 0.0 0.0	1 6.7 1.9	0 0.0 0.0	15 3.7
Others	51 12.9 91.1	242 61.3 96.4	38 9.6 100.0	51 12.9 98.1	13 3.3 100.0	395 96.3
	56 13.6	251 61.2	38 9.3	52 12.7	13 3.2	

Significance > .05   Cramer's V = .1288701

Table 7 crosstabulates opinions on content
in GDR critiques against the corresponding opinions
from other countries. While the table's results are
not significant (and the frequencies in each cell are
so small that significant results might be suspect
in any case), the frequencies shown in the table provide a clear enough picture. Of fifteen GDR critiques,
only one did not fall into the positive or praise
categories. It is thus clear that Becher's problem
in the GDR is lack of reception, not negative reception.

Hypothesis VII: Critiques which mention
Becher's reception have a more positive
overall rating, as well as more positive
ratings under the literary variables, than
do critiques which do not mention reception.

TABLE 8

RECEPTION BY FORMAL

	Praise	Positive	Neutral	Negative	Censure	
Yes	32 22.9 42.7	73 52.1 37.1	8 5.7 53.3	24 17.1 40.7	3 2.1 25.0	140 39.1
No	43 19.7 57.3	124 56.9 62.9	7 3.2 46.7	35 16.1 59.3	9 4.1 75.0	218 60.9

75	197	15	59	12
20.9	55.0	4.2	16.5	3.4

Significance > .05   Cramer's V = .09284

TABLE 9

RECEPTION BY CONTENT

	Praise	Positive	Neutral	Negative	Censure	
Yes	27 17.8 50.9	97 63.8 37.2	10 6.6 25.0	15 9.9 28.3	3 2.0 23.1	152 36.2
No	26 9.7 49.1	164 61.2 62.8	30 11.2 75.0	38 14.2 71.7	10 3.7 76.9	268 63.8
	53 12.6	261 62.1	40 9.5	53 12.6	13 3.1	

Significance < .05   Cramer's V = .15172

TABLE 10

RECEPTION BY OVERALL

	Positive	Neutral	Negative	
Yes	123 79.4 37.2	11 7.1 34.4	21 13.5 29.6	155 35.7
No	208 74.6 62.8	21 7.5 65.6	50 17.9 70.4	279 64.3
	331 76.3	32 7.4	71 16.4	

Significance > .05   Cramer's V = .05861

346

To test the hypothesis that critics' awareness of reception influences opinions of Becher's
works, the critiques were divided into two groups,
those which mention reception and those which do not.
These groups were then crosstabulated with the evaluative variables "opinions of formals elements," "opinion of content," and "overall opinion."

Table 8 indicates that awareness of reception played no role in critics' opinions of formal
elements. However, reception does correlate with
opinions of content according to Table 9, at a significance level of .05, although the Cramer's V statistic indicates that the correlation is not very
strong. As expected, critiques which mention reception have more positive and praise evaluations and
fewer negative and censure evaluations than do critiques which do not mention reception.

That this should be so is not too difficult
to explain. Critics who mention Becher's hard luck
tale of exile and post-war publishing are most likely
interested in exile literature and therefore favorable to the exile-connected themes of Becher's works.
Or these critics simply liked his works and researched
his life to learn more about him. At any rate, they

347

used other criteria entirely when judging the formal elements of Becher's works. These formal judgments outweighed the content judgments in the overall opinion, as is clear from the weak correlation of Table 9 as well as from the results of Table 10, which shows a lack of significance on the overall level.

> Hypothesis VIII: Rowohlt publications received more critiques than Benziger publications. Critiques of Rowohlt publications appear in newspapers with larger circulations than do Benziger publications. Critiques of Rowohlt publications are longer than critiques of Benziger publications. Critiques of Rowohlt publications are more likely evaluative while critiques of Benziger works are more likely to be reports or content summaries.

To test the hypothesis that works published by Rowohlt received more critical attention than those published by Benziger, several factors were considered. A frequency distribution indicated that works published by Rowohlt received 114 critiques, while Benziger publications received 198 critiques. Thus, the first factor

TABLE 11

PUBLISHER BY CIRCULATION

	500T-1Mil	200-500T	100-200T	50-100T	50T	
Rowohlt	3 2.7 60.0	15 13.6 38.5	24 21.8 44.4	8 7.3 36.4	60 54.5 33.9	110 37.0
Ben- ziger	2 1.1 40.0	24 12.8 61.5	30 16.0 55.6	14 7.5 63.6	117 62.6 66.1	187 63.0
	5 1.7	39 13.1	54 18.2	22 7.4	177 59.6	

Significance > .05   Cramer´s V = .1036154

TABLE 12

PUBLISHER BY LENGTH

	250	250-499	500-749	750-999	1000+	
Rowohlt	37 32.5 22.8	23 20.2 42.6	19 16.7 43.2	16 14.0 61.5	19 16.7 73.1	114 36.5
Ben- ziger	125 63.1 77.2	31 15.7 57.4	25 12.6 56.8	10 5.1 38.5	7 3.5 26.9	198 63.5
	162 51.9	54 17.3	44 14.1	26 8.3	26 8.3	

Significance < .01   Cramer´s V = .3434187

---

in the hypothesis was not substantiated, i.e., Rowohlt

publications did not receive more critiques than Benziger publications.

Table 11 indicates that there is no association between the publisher and the circulation of the paper in which the critique appeared. In contrast, Table 12 shows a moderate relationship between publisher and length. Critiques of Rowohlt publications are clearly longer than critiques of Benziger publications, substantiating the claim that just because a work is published by a well-known publisher, it automatically receives more serious attention than works by lesser houses.

TABLE 13

PUBLISHER BY TYPE OF ARTICLE

	Report	Evaluation	
Rowohlt	22 25.6 25.6	64 74.4 42.1	86 36.1
Benziger	64 42.1 74.4	88 57.9 57.9	152 63.9
	86 36.1	152 63.9	

Significance < .01   Cramer's V = .1769708

Table 13 provides further substantiation.

350

The table shows a weak association between publisher and type of critique.[3] Rowohlt publications received more evaluative critiques, while Benziger works received reports or content summaries.

Taken together, these results would appear to substantiate Becher's claim that Rowohlt was not making an effort to publicize his works. Rowohlt appears to have relied mostly on its own reputation for quality, which in fact did provide Becher's works with substantive literary criticism, i.e., longer evaluative articles. Benziger, on the other hand, actually provided more publicity for Becher's works and over a shorter period of time. In addition, Benziger's reports appeared in papers with essentially the same circulation as the papers in which Rowohlt critiques appeared. Although it does seem clear that the hypothesis is confirmed, it does not follow that Becher erred in switching to Benziger. If he receives more notices in the same size papers and notices that speak to more than Glotz's 5% of readers interested in literature per se, then the result may be that Becher is ultimately better received by the general public, because he switched to Benziger. Given the nature of German book critic-

ism according to Glotz, many authors may have to make
a choice between wide reception and serious reception.

Hypothesis IX: Critiques appearing in leftist publications will be more positive in
their opinions of form and content than
will critiques in other journals.

TABLE 14

POLITICAL STANCE BY FORMAL

	Praise	Positive	Neutral	Negative	Censure	
Neutral	40 22.2 54.1	98 54.4 52.1	6 3.3 46.2	32 17.8 56.1	4 2.2 33.3	180 52.3
Commun- ist	2 11.8 2.7	10 58.8 5.3	2 11.8 15.4	3 17.6 5.3	0 0.0 0.0	17 4.9
Social- ist	9 23.7 12.2	20 52.6 10.6	3 7.9 23.1	4 10.5 7.0	2 5.3 16.7	38 11.0
Liberal	10 22.7 13.5	25 56.8 13.3	1 2.3 7.7	4 9.1 7.0	4 9.1 33.3	44 12.8
Conser- vative	13 20.0 17.6	35 53.8 18.6	1 1.5 7.7	14 21.5 24.6	2 3.1 16.7	65 18.9
	74 21.5	188 54.7	13 3.8	57 16.6	12 3.5	

Significance > .05   Cramer's V = .10822

TABLE 15

POLITICAL STANCE BY CONTENT

	Praise	Positive	Neutral	Negative	Censure	
Neutral	24 10.6 56.2	147 65.0 59.3	21 9.3 55.3	26 11.5 59.1	8 3.5 61.5	226 55.9
Commun- ist	5 27.8 9.6	12 66.7 4.8	0 0.0 0.0	1 5.6 1.9	0 0.0 0.0	18 4.5
Social- ist	10 23.3 19.2	16 37.2 6.5	7 16.3 18.4	9 20.9 17.0	1 2.3 7.7	43 10.6
Liberal	3 6.3 5.8	31 64.6 12.5	9 18.8 23.7	3 6.3 5.7	2 4.2 15.4	48 11.9
Conser- vative	10 14.5 19.2	42 60.9 16.9	1 1.4 2.6	14 20.3 26.4	2 2.9 15.4	69 17.1
	52 12.9	248 61.4	38 9.4	53 13.1	13 3.2	

Significance < .01   Cramer's V = .14856

Tables 14-16 show the results of the cross-tabulation of the political stance of newspapers by the evaluative variables. These crosstabs were run in order to test the hypothesis that leftist newspapers would be more positive towards Becher's works

TABLE 16

POLITICAL STANCE BY OVERALL

	Positive	Neutral	Negative	
Neutral	175 75.4 55.4	18 7.8 58.1	39 16.8 54.9	232 55.5
Communist	16 88.9 5.1	0 0.0 0.0	2 11.1 2.8	18 4.3
Socialist	29 63.0 9.2	7 15.2 22.6	10 21.7 14.1	46 11.0
Liberal	40 80.0 12.7	4 8.0 12.9	6 12.0 8.5	50 12.0
Conserva- tive	56 77.8 17.7	2 2.8 6.5	14 19.4 19.7	72 17.2
	316 75.6	31 7.4	71 17.0	

Significance > .05   Cramer´s V = .11356

than papers with other political orientations.   Only
one of the three tables shows a significance level of
at least .05.   Table 14 indicates that political leanings were not significant in opinions of formal elements.   In contrast Table 15 does show a significant

correlation between politics and opinion of content, although the Cramer's V statistic of .14856 indicates the correlation is not very strong, i.e., there is not much impact on reception from the politics of the journal.

The actual percentages in the categories depict the lack of a clear direction. One significant number is the total number of newspapers which consider themselves neutral politically, i.e., 226 of the 404 involved. This means that less than half of the critiques contribute to testing the hypothesis. In addition, this large group of supposedly neutral papers undoubtedly contains many not-so-neutral papers, such as the entire output of the Springer Verlag. Such papers were classified as neutral by the standardized sources mentioned earlier, which in turn relied solely on self-reporting by the newspapers for their information. In general, a newspaper claims lack of bias as long as it is not specifically connected to a recognized political or religious group. Because of this, much of the influence from political leanings, if it exists at all, is hidden by the lack of scientifically acquired data.

Turning to the data that were produced by

Table 15, it is interesting that the communist critiques, though small in number, are overwhelmingly
positive, supporting the hypothesis. However, socialist critiques provide no clear indication of direction. Liberal critiques do show a slight tendency to
be more neutral and less negative in their opinions
of content, while conservative critiques are strikingly non-neutral and more negative than would be
expected by chance alone.

Once again the overall opinion table (Table
16) does not confirm the hypothesis, another indication of the weak correlation of Table 15 and of the
lack of correlation on formal elements.

> Hypothesis X: Critiques in leftist publica-
> tions will be more positive in their opinions
> of form and content even when type of article
> is controlled for.

As with the previous hypotheses on GDR critiques, the numbers of critiques involved here was
too small to test. Overall, of course, the same total
number of critiques were involved as were used in the
previous three tables. However, the control for the
type of article would have doubled the number of cells

and thus increased the chances of spuriously significant findings. Given the results of the previous tests without controls, however, there is really nothing lost. If a relationship is not significant without a control variable, it will not be significant when one is added.

Hypothesis XI: There will be a significant, positive correlation between opinions of formal elements and opinions of content.

TABLE 17[4]

FORMAL BY CONTENT

	Positive	Neutral	Negative	
Positive	238	17	14	269
	88.5	6.3	5.2	76.0
	85.6	60.7	29.2	
Neutral	7	8	0	15
	46.7	53.3	0.0	4.2
	2.5	28.6	0.0	
Negative	33	3	34	70
	47.1	4.3	48.6	19.8
	11.9	10.7	70.8	
	278	28	48	
	78.5	7.9	13.6	

Significance < .01   Cramer's V = .43831

Opinions of formal elements were cross-tabulated with opinions of content to discover if there was a correlation between them. Table 17 shows the results of this crosstabulation, significant at the 1% level. Tau b indicates that the correlation is a strong, positive correlation meaning that opinions on style will be similar to opinions of content. Taken in connection with Glotz's pronouncements on the primacy of stylistic norms in the critical process, Table 17 is most plausibly interpreted as confirmation of Glotz. While neither chi-square nor Tau b nor any other statistic reveals a causal connection, Glotz's research gives us reason to see the stylistic judgment as cause and the content judgment as effect, while there exists no such corroborative evidence for the reverse.

Hypothesis XII: There will be a significant correlation between opinions of Becher and opinions of his works.

To test whether critics' opinions of Becher correlate with their opinions of his work, these measures were crosstabulated. All three tables (Tables 18-20) are significant at the 1% level.

358

TABLE 18[5]

FORMAL BY OPINION OF BECHER

	Praise	Positive	Neutral	Negative	Censure	
Posi-tive	73 31.9 96.1	134 58.5 79.3	15 6.6 60.0	6 2.6 40.0	1 0.4 33.3	229 79.5
Neutral	2 28.6 2.6	3 42.9 1.8	2 28.6 8.0	0 0.0 0.0	0 0.0 0.0	7 2.4
Nega-tive	1 1.9 1.3	32 61.5 18.9	8 15.4 32.0	9 17.3 60.0	2 3.8 66.7	52 18.1
	76 26.4	169 58.7	25 8.7	15 5.2	3 1.0	

Significance < .01   Tau c = .212246

TABLE 19[5]

CONTENT BY OPINION OF BECHER

	Praise	Positive	Neutral	Negative	Censure	
Posi-tive	74 30.2 97.4	150 61.2 81.1	15 6.1 41.7	6 2.4 35.3	0 0.0 0.0	245 77.5
Neutral	1 4.0 1.3	14 56.0 7.6	10 40.0 27.8	0 0.0 0.0	0 0.0 0.0	25 7.9
Nega-tive	1 2.2 1.3	21 45.7 11.4	11 23.9 30.6	11 23.9 64.7	2 4.3 100.0	46 14.6

	76	185	36	17	2
	24.1	58.5	11.4	5.4	0.6

Significance < .01   Tau c = .28502

Table 18 shows a moderately positive correlation between critics' opinions of Becher and their opinions of formal elements (Tau c = .21246). The positive correlation between opinion of Becher and opinion of content is stronger but still moderate, as Table 19 indicates in its percentages and Tau c statistic of .285. Interestingly enough, the correlation is even stronger in the overall opinion (Table 20, Tau c = .31287). This means that the opinion of Becher has an effect on the critics' composite judgment which is to some degree independent of the critics' judgments on formal elements and content. The lower association of formal elements with opinions of Becher lends further credence to Glotz's belief that aesthetic norms play a larger role in formal judgments than in judgments of content.

Hypothesis XIII: Length of the critique will correlate significantly with positive opinions of form and content.

TABLE 20

OVERALL BY OPINION OF BECHER

	Praise	Positive	Neutral	Negative	Censure	
Posi-tive	76 29.0 98.7	167 63.7 87.4	14 5.3 35.0	5 1.9 29.4	0 0.0 0.0	262 79.9
Neutral	0.0 0.01 0.0	3 17.6 1.6	14 82.4 35.0	0.0 0.0 0.0	0 0.0 0.0	17 5.2
Nega-tive	1 2.0 1.3	21 42.9 11.0	12 24.5 30.0	12 24.5 70.6	3 6.1 100.0	49 14.9
	77 23.5	191 58.2	40 12.2	17 5.2	3 0.9	

Significance < .01   Tau c = .31287

TABLE 21

LENGTH BY FORMAL

	Praise	Positive	Neutral	Negative	Censure	
<250	27 17.2 36.0	93 59.2 47.2	8 5.1 53.3	25 15.9 42.2	4 2.5 33.3	157 43.9
250-499	13 18.1 17.3	37 51.4 18.8	4 5.6 26.7	16 22.2 27.1	2 2.8 16.7	72 20.1
500-749	16 28.1 21.3	30 52.6 15.2	0 0.0 0.0	10 17.5 16.9	1 1.8 8.3	57 15.9

750-1000	9 28.1 12.0	14 43.8 7.1	1 3.1 6.7	5 15.6 8.5	3 9.4 25.0	32 8.9
1000+	10 25.0 13.3	23 57.5 11.7	2 5.0 13.3	3 7.5 5.1	2 5.0 16.7	40 11.2
	75 20.9	197 55.0	15 4.2	59 16.5	12 3.4	

Significance > .05   Cramer's V = .10762

TABLE 22

LENGTH BY CONTENT

	Praise	Positive	Neutral	Negative	Censure	
<250	10 4.9 18.9	136 66.0 51.9	32 15.5 80.0	20 9.7 37.7	8 3.9 61.5	206 48.9
250-499	9 11.8 17.0	43 56.6 16.4	6 7.9 15.0	15 19.7 28.3	3 3.9 23.1	76 18.1
500-749	9 14.1 17.0	40 62.5 15.3	2 3.1 3.0	12 18.8 22.6	1 1.6 7.7	64 15.2
750-999	10 29.4 18.9	20 58.8 7.6	0 0.0 0.0	4 11.8 7.5	0 0.0 0.0	34 8.1
1000+	15 36.6 28.3	23 56.1 8.8	0 0.0 0.0	2 4.9 3.8	1 2.4 7.7	41 9.7
	53 12.6	262 62.2	40 9.5	53 12.6	13 3.1	

Significance < .01   Cramer's V = .19795

To test this hypothesis, length was crosstabulated with the opinion measures. Length does not
appear to correlate with the opinions of formal elements (Table 21). However, Table 22 indicates a
positive correlation significant at the 1% level
between length of critique and opinions on content.
The Cramer's V statistic indicates that this correlation is very weak. A glance at the table reveals
that disproportionately larger percentages of the longer
critiques judge Becher's content and themes as praise-
worthy while shorter critiques show a more neutral
attitude. One way of judging importance is by look-
ing at the extreme judgments; positive, neutral and
negative categories contain the bulk of opinions. If
the critic places sufficient importance on his opinion
of the work under consideration, he is more likely to
make a judgment that involves censure or praise. As
general evidence, one may note that the longer the
article, the less likely it is to contain neutral judgments.

Essentially the same pattern is found in the
overall opinion (Table 23). Once again the overall
opinion coincides with the opinion of content but not
with that of style.

TABLE 23

LENGTH BY OVERALL

	Positive	Neutral	Negative	
<250	158 72.8 47.6	26 12.0 81.3	33 15.2 46.5	217 49.9
250-499	56 70.9 16.9	4 5.1 12.5	19 24.1 26.8	79 18.2
500-749	53 82.8 16.0	1 1.6 3.1	10 15.6 14.1	64 14.7
750-999	28 82.4 8.4	1 2.9 3.1	5 14.7 7.0	34 7.8
1000+	37 90.2 11.1	0 0.0 0.0	4 9.8 5.6	41 9.4
	332 76.3	32 7.4	71 16.3	

Significance < .01   Cramer's V = .15214

Hypothesis XIV: There will be a significant negative correlation between short critiques and negative opinions.

Table 23 can also be used to test this hypothesis. The table indicates that although there is a

364

correlation, the hypothesis is not confirmed, because
the relationship lies in the opposite direction. Very
short critiques tend to be neutral, but the next shortest critiques tend to be more negative. This leads
to the conclusion that short critiques tend not to be
positive, precisely the opposite of the hypothesis. If
a work is not liked or the critic feels neutral about
the work, he may feel little need to waste words cri-
tiquing it. By implication, it also means that fewer
short critiques were publisher's blurbs than one would
have expected.

> Hypothesis XV: Evaluative articles may be
> expected to be more positive on form and
> content than articles which are reports.

To determine whether evaluative articles are
more positive in their opinions than reports, these
categories were crosstabulated with one another.
The hypothesis was not confirmed in the case of formal elements as shown by Table 24. Although the results are significant at the 1% level and the Cramer's
V statistic shows the association to be at least moderate, the direction is the opposite of what was hypothesized, while reports were more positive and neutral.

TABLE 24[5]

TYPE OF ARTICLE BY FORMAL

	Positive	Neutral	Negative	
Report	61 79.2 31.0	8 10.4 61.5	8 10.4 14.3	77 28.9
Evaluation	136 72.0 69.0	5 2.6 38.5	48 25.4 85.7	189 71.1
	197 74.1	13 4.9	56 21.1	

Significance < .01   Cramer's V = .22070

TABLE 25[5]

TYPE OF ARTICLE BY CONTENT

	Positive	Neutral	Negative	
Report	65 61.3 28.5	27 25.5 79.4	14 13.2 25.0	106 33.3
Evaluation	163 76.9 71.5	7 3.3 20.6	42 19.8 75.0	212 66.7
	228 71.7	34 10.7	56 17.6	

Significance < .01   Cramer's V = .33936

When one turns to opinions of content (Table

TABLE 26

TYPE OF ARTICLE BY OVERALL

	Positive	Neutral	Negative	
Report	79	22	13	114
	69.3	19.31	11.4	34.8
	32.8	88.0	21.0	
Evaluation	162	3	49	214
	75.7	1.4	22.9	65.2
	76.2	12.0	79.0	
	241	25	62	
	73.5	7.6	18.9	

Significance < .01   Cramer's V = .33526

25), again the relationship is significant and the
degree of relationship is somewhat stronger, as shown
by the Cramer's V value.   But as before, one finds
that a disproportionately large share of negative
critiques are evaluative articles and that a disproportionately large share of neutral judgments are
found in reports.   Unlike the results in the previous
table with formal judgments, however, a larger share
of positive articles are also evaluative.   In essence
all this table tells us is that evaluative articles
evaluate and report articles report.

Table 26 shows once again that the overall

judgment is more highly correlated with the content
judgement than with formal judgments, indicating
more influence from content than from formal elements.

Hypothesis XVI: Longer articles will be
more positive in their opinions of form
and content, even when the effects of type
of article are controlled for.

TABLE 27[6]

LENGTH BY FORMAL   (Reports)

	Praise	Positive	Neutral	Negative	Censure	
<500	6 10.3 50.0	41 70.7 83.7	6 10.3 75.0	5 8.6 62.5	0 0.0 0.0	58 75.3
500+	6 31.6 50.0	8 42.1 16.3	2 10.5 25.0	3 15.8 37.5	0 0.0 0.0	19 24.7
	12 15.6	49 63.6	8 10.4	8 10.4	0 0.0	

Significance > .05   Cramer's V = .29486

Although the basic premise, that long articles
are positive and evaluative articles are positive,
which served as a reason for testing if length of article
is associated with positive judgments even when type

368

TABLE 28[6]

LENGTH BY FORMAL   (Evaluations)

	Praise	Positive	Neutral	Negative	Censure	
<500	25 19.4 59.5	65 50.4 69.1	4 3.1 80.0	29 22.5 74.4	6 4.7 66.7	129 68.3
500+	17 28.3 40.5	29 48.3 30.9	1 1.7 20.0	10 16.7 25.6	3 5.0 33.3	60 31.7
	42 22.2	94 49.7	5 2.6	39 20.6	9 4.8	

Significance > .05   Cramer's V = .11528

TABLE 29[6]

LENGTH BY CONTENT   (Reports)

	Praise	Positive	Neutral	Negative	Censure	
<500	2 2.4 25.0	44 51.8 77.2	27 31.8 100.0	11 12.9 84.6	1 1.2 100.0	85 80.2
500+	6 28.6 75.0	13 61.9 2.8	0 0.0 0.0	2.2 9.5 15.4	0 0.0 0.0	21 19.8
	8 7.5	57 53.8	27 25.5	13 12.3	1 0.9	

Significance < .01   Cramer's V = .46315

TABLE 30[6]

LENGTH BY CONTENT   (Evaluations)

	Praise	Positive	Neutral	Negative	Censure	
<500	11	102	6	21	9	149
	7.4	68.5	4.0	14.1	6.0	70.3
	50.0	72.3	85.7	65.6	90.0	
500+	11	39	1	11	1	63
	17.5	61.9	1.6	17.5	1.6	29.7
	50.0	27.7	14.3	34.4	10.0	
	22	141	7	32	10	
	10.4	66.5	3.3	15.1	4.7	

Significance > .05   Cramer's V = .18948
Zero-order gamma = -.37544
Partial gamma = -.30461

TABLE 31[6]

LENGTH BY OVERALL   (Reports)

	Positive	Neutral	Negative	
<500	59	22	12	93
	63.4	23.7	12.9	81.6
	74.7	100.0	92.3	
500+	20	0	1	21
	95.2	0.0	4.8	18.4
	25.3	0.0	7.7	
	79	22	13	
	69.3	19.3	11.4	

Significance < .05   Cramer's V = .27246

TABLE 32[6]

LENGTH BY OVERALL   (Evaluations)

	Positive	Neutral	Negative	
500	113 74.8 69.8	2 1.3 66.7	36 23.8 73.5	151 70.6
500+	49 77.8 30.2	1 1.6 33.3	13 20.6 26.5	63 29.4
	162 75.7	3 1.4	49 22.9	

Significance > .05   Cramer's V = .03567
Zero-order gamma = -.26475
Partial gamma = -.20834

of article is controlled for, was proved wrong by
Tables 24-26, the results of the tests of this hypothesis are presented here in order to determine whether
the effects that did appear in the earlier tables continue to be seen when the control is introduced.

As expected from the results of Table 21,
Tables 27 and 28 show length is not associated with
the judgments made on formal elements when the type
of article is controlled for. Table 29 shows a significant strong correlation between longer reports
on content and positive judgments. However, length

makes no difference in the positive judgments of evaluative articles on content, as Table 30 indicates. Once again the results of tests on the overall judgments replicate those of content. There is a significant mild correlation between longer reports' overall opinions and positive judgments (Table 31), but no corresponding correlation between longer evaluative articles and positive judgments (Table 32).

When one looks at the composite statistics for Tables 29 and 30 and for Tables 31 and 32, one finds that controlling for the type of article has only a very small effect on the relationship between length and judgments. There is simply not much difference between the zero-order gamma, which measures the relationship between length and judgment without any control, and the partial order gamma, which measures the same relationship with the control for type. Therefore, one can confidently say that length is clearly associated with positive judgments independently of the effects of other variables.

Hypothesis XVII: The opinion expressed in the title will correlate with the opinions of form and content.

372

TABLE 33

TITLE BY FORMAL

	Praise	Positive	Neutral	Negative	Censure	
Posi- tive	42 32.8 58.3	69 53.9 34.7	5 3.9 33.3	9 7.0 15.5	3 2.3 25.0	128 36.0
Neutral	29 13.8 40.3	124 59.0 62.3	10 4.8 66.7	40 19.0 69.0	7 3.3 58.3	210 59.0
Nega- tive	1 5.6 1.4	6 33.3 3.0	0 0.0 0.0	9 50.0 15.5	2 11.1 16.7	18 5.0
	72 20.2	199 55.9	15 4.2	58 16.3	12 3.4	

Significance < .01   Tau c = .22745

Opinions on form, content and overall were
crosstabulated with opinions expressed in the title
of the article to determine if title-only analysis
could replace the more detailed content analysis.
All three crosstabs (Tables 33-35) are significant
at the 1% level and their Tau statistics indicate a
moderate positive correlation. In general, the hypothesis is confirmed. However, reliance on the title
along could lead to error in the case of short cri-

TABLE 34

TITLE BY CONTENT

	Praise	Positive	Neutral	Negative	Censure	
Posi-tive	31 22.1 62.0	93 66.4 36.2	9 6.4 22.0	7 5.0 13.5	0 0.0 0.0	140 33.9
Neutral	18 7.3 36.0	157 63.6 61.1	31 12.6 75.6	33 13.4 63.5	8 3.2 61.5	247 59.8
Nega-tive	1 3.8 2.0	7 26.9 2.7	1 3.8 2.4	12 46.2 23.1	5 19.2 38.5	26 6.3
	50 12.1	257 62.2	41 9.9	52 12.6	13 3.1	

Significance < .01   Tau c = .26811

TABLE 35

TITLE BY OVERALL

	Positive	Neutral	Negative	
Positive	131 91.0 39.7	7 4.9 21.2	6 4.2 10.5	144 34.3
Neutral	192 77.1 58.2	26 10.4 78.8	31 12.4 54.4	249 59.3
Negative	7 25.9 2.1	0 0.0 0.0	20 74.1 35.1	27 6.4

330	33	57
78.6	7.9	13.6

Significance < .01   Tau b = .29738

---

tiques that appear neutral from the title, because
all the title consists of is bibliographic information. It is clear from Tables 33-35 that the majority
of critiques with neutral titles actually contained
positive judgments, while critiques with positive or
negative titles contained positive or negative judgments, respectively. Thus, book critiques are different from other types of articles on which content analysis is usually performed, since titles or
headlines in the ordinary sense are often not used
in book criticism.

Hypothesis XVIII: Papers with low circulation publish only short critiques.

Table 36 shows the results of the cross-
tabulation of newspaper circulation by length of critique performed to substantiate the hypothesis that
short critiques appear in smaller papers. While
the relationship is significant, Tau b indicates it
is a weak correlation, and this makes interpretation

375

TABLE 36

CIRCULATION BY LENGTH

	<250	250-499	500-749	750-999	1000+	
<50T	111	31	28	10	25	205
	54.1	15.1	13.7	4.9	12.2	49.0
	53.4	40.8	44.4	31.2	64.2	
50-100T	12	13	7	6	6	44
	27.3	29.5	15.9	13.6	13.6	10.5
	5.8	17.1	11.1	18.8	15.4	
100-200T	47	24	13	15	6	105
	44.8	22.9	12.4	14.3	5.7	25.1
	22.6	31.6	20.6	46.9	15.4	
200-500T	36	5	14	1	2	58
	62.1	8.6	24.1	1.7	3.4	13.9
	17.3	6.6	22.2	3.1	5.1	
500T-1M	2	3	1	0	0	6
	33.3	50.0	16.7	0.0	0.0	1.4
	1.0	3.9	1.6	0.0	0.0	
	208	76	73	32	39	
	49.8	18.2	15.1	7.6	9.3	

Significance < .01   Tau b = -.00656

of the figures more complicated. The fact that most
critiques (284 out of 418), regardless of the size of
newspaper, are relatively short, makes analysis even
more difficult. The Tau b statistic is of some assis-
tance in this regard. The fact that it is negative

means that the hypothesis is not confirmed even though the relationship is significant. The most telling cells are those that show the numbers of critiques which are short, but appear in newspapers of 200-500 thousand circulation and those which are very long but appear in papers of under 50 thousand. While only 49.8% of all critiques are under 250 words in length, 62.1% of critiques in papers of 200-500 thousand circulation are under 250 words. Conversely, while only 9.3% of all critiques are more than 1000+ words in length, fully 12.2% of critiques in papers under 50,000 circulation are 1000+ words in length. Thus the relationship is inverse: the longer the critique, the more likely it is to have appeared in a paper of low circulation. Becher may be a special case, publishing as he does in Switzerland. There is a natural tendency for Swiss newspapers, which are generally small in circulation, to pay more than the usual attention to a native writer. A separate computer run to test whether these longer critiques which appear in small papers are Swiss was only slightly positive.[7] Thus using circulation as a measure of the importance of the paper is misleading, especially considering the reputation of Swiss papers as quality

sources of literary criticism. Nevertheless, it is
probably still true that the serious consideration of
Becher's work reaches a relatively small number of
people. Another confirmation of this tendency is the
lack of long critiques in large papers.

FOOTNOTES

[1]Norman H. Nie, Statistical Package for the Social Sciences Second Edition, (New York: McGraw-Hill, 1975), pp. 218-248.

[2]Detailed explanations have been given of the meaning of the percentages in these two tables. In the remainder of the tables the same percentages will be shown, but the explanation will be less detailed. It is assumed that the reader can, with the explanation that has been given, study the particulars of the various tables to supplement the information given in the narrative summaries.

[3]The Phi statistic shown in the table is essentially the same as the Cramer's V statistic usually used here, but Phi is appropriate for square tables, while Cramer's V is used for rectangular tables.

[4]The variables in this table were established with five categories each. The categories on either side of the neutral category have been collapsed in order to avoid having too many cells with very small frequency, which would increase the chances of spuri-

ously significant findings.

[5]The literary variables are shown with collapsed categories for the same reason as given in Note 4.

[6]The categories for length of critique were collapsed in these tables for the same reason as given in Note 4.

[7]The following crosstab of length by circulation controlling for the country of the critique, in this case Switzerland, while significant with a moderate correlation (Tau c = .32639), does indicate only a slight tendency for longer critiques to appear more often in Swiss papers than in papers of other countries.

TABLE 36[a]

LENGTH BY CIRCULATION   (Swiss)

	<250	250-499	500-749	750-999	1000+	
<50T	38 63.3 92.7	11 18.3 73.3	7 11.7 63.6	3 5.0 37.5	1 1.7 14.3	60 73.2
50- 100T	1 9.1 2.4	2 18.2 13.3	2 18.2 18.2	2 18.2 25.0	4 36.4 57.1	11 13.4
100- 200T	2 20.0 4.9	1 10.0 6.7	2 20.0 18.2	3 30.0 37.5	2 20.0 28.6	10 12.2

0	1	0	0	0	1
0	100.0	0	0	0	1.2
0	6.7	0	0	0	

41	15	11	8	7
50.0	18.3	13.4	9.8	8.5

Significance < .01   Tau c = .32639

CHAPTER VII:

Conclusion

The aims of this project were both specific
to Ulrich Becher and more general in their application to the methodology employed here. In relation
to Becher, two questions were to be answered, namely
1) What is the concretization of Becher's works and
2) How did it change over time? Methodologically,
the applicability of content analysis and reception
aesthetics was to be tested.

As was noted earlier, the statistics themselves cannot tell us what Becher's concretization
is; they can only confirm or falsify hypotheses that
are drawn from the rather lengthy discussion of his
works and the critiques dealing with those works.
To the extent that the hypotheses are confirmed, the
impression of what his concretization is finds substantiation. In this sense the statistics supply
much more direct evidence about how his concretization changed over time. The information gleaned from
the statistics provides, therefore, something of a
literary history of Ulrich Becher, and indeed a

literary history based on reception, not merely on a recitation of the dates and titles of his publications.

In response to the question of Becher's current concretization, the general view of Becher's works is that they lie somewhere between popular fiction and serious literature. The research of the last chapter has indicated that this is due in large part to the more negative reception of the formal elements of his works. Because formal innovation is a major prerequisite of serious literature, Becher's reliance on traditional narrative, while failing to respect the traditional triad of genres, disqualifies him from consideration by the tastemakers of German literature. This is evidenced by the fact that only 13% of all critiques appeared in the major newspapers Glotz lists. One element of Becher's style critics find objectionable is his mixing of genres, i.e., the inclusion of novelistic devices in his dramas and of dramatic devices in his prose as well as his mixing of media, i.e., the rendering of Grosz-like portraits. The dramas were criticized for lacking action, for merely being the recreation of a mood or milieu. On the other hand, his prose was criticized

for containing too much dialogue and naturalistic
imitation of spoken language.

Although not as negatively received as formal elements, Becher's content remained the same
through the years. Influenced strongly by his exile
in Brazil and New York and traumatized by his brush
with fascism, Becher presented his viewer or reader
with a host of bizarre situations to which most could
not relate. The content is in most cases so specifically "exile" that the receptive environment had to
be perfectly suited to exile themes before Becher's
works were well received. Thus, when the Nazi era
was a current event in the immediate post-war era
or in the late 1970s after a decade of exile studies
had led to a renewal of interest as evidenced by the
impact of Hitler books, films and the television
series Holocaust, Becher's works were received well.
However, during the decade of formal structural experimentation in the 1960s, Becher's plays were no
longer produced. In his later prose works, Becher
was able to adapt his political insights somewhat
to the current situation. For example, fascism became embodied in the atomic bomb in the 1950s Becher
novel Das Herz des Hais and in the CIA in Das Profil

384

written in the early 1970s. Perhaps this adaptability
explains why Becher's content was better received
than his style. In addition, as he moved further
away from his exile experience in time, Becher became less strident, resigning himself to the ineffectuality of the engaged artist. This, too, may have helped his later reception.

In summarizing Becher's concretization, one
might well use Jauß's terminology. In his style,
Becher certainly failed to follow the "bekannten
Normen oder der immanenten Poetik der Gattung."[1]
In fact, his style remained sufficiently constant
that as literary norms changed, he fell even further
out of step with those norms. In addition, an examination of his works and their "impliziten Beziehungen
zu bekannten Werken der literarhistorischen Umgebung"
reveals that both his style and his content dealt
with matters that had already been settled by others
who had gone before. Even when he adapted his images
to the concerns of the post-war years, he was at best
only addressing issues which were currently in vogue;
not providing new perspectives or insights. Finally,
when one examines the opposition "von Fiktion und
Wirklichkeit, poetischer und praktischer Funktion der

Sprache," the judgment on Becher is mixed. Some find
him to be a spell-binding story-teller; others think
he imitates naturalistic speech too closely; still
others find him bizarrely exotic, so far removed
from reality that he is simply incomprehensible.

The final judgment is, of course, not yet
in. Only when Becher is no longer read at all will
his work be complete. Change in his reception remains
a possibility until that time, just as it has changed
over the last thirty years. Even though Becher's
style and content were fixated by his exile trauma,
his concretization changed with the decades because
his relevance changed according to the current trends
in literature. In the immediate post-war period,
Becher's plays were hailed as promising models for
the rebuilding of the German theater. Most critics
agreed Becher had not yet found his own voice, but
that his plays held promise of greater works.

The change in Becher's early positive reception corresponded to a change in the concretization of
his works. Against the backdrop of the political and
cultural events of the late 1950s to the second half
of the 1970s it is evident why. The early years of
this period saw the height of bourgeois Adenauerism,

culminating in the economic crisis of 1965/1966
and the resultant revitalization of neofascist groups,
e.g. the NPD political party. The equivalent of the
Adenauer era in literature was the Gruppe 47, to which
Becher never belonged and which predominated until
1966. It was replaced in part by the formalism of
Junge Moderne writers such as Handke and Wondraschek.
For different reasons, neither Gruppe 47 nor Junge
Moderne had much interest in Becher´s brand of Vergangenheitsbewältigung. His plays were not produced
during these years, because they did not address the
concerns of the time, but rather were seen as the
nightmare reminiscences of an old man. In addition,
this period corresponded with Becher´s return to prose
and absence from the market.

However, the political and literary reaction
to the Adenauer era also began in the second half of
the 1960s with the student protest movement and the
APO, the extraparliamentary opposition to the coali-
tion of SPD and CDU. The other literary direction
concommitant with Junge Moderne was the literature of
committment, documentary literature, and the Brecht-
ianism of Enzensberger, Biermann and Fried. When
this radical interest in politics was superceded by

the new subjectivity and new sensibility of 1970s
literature, apparent in the diaries, biographies,
and feminist literature published in these years,
Becher's style was again alien to that representative
of the period. However, the political interest of
the late 1960s and early 1970s had led to a rediscovery of exile literature, which was made hoffähig
during the decade of the 1970s. Its reception received
a theoretical underpinning in the theories of the
Konstanzer Schule. Even topically, Becher became
relevant again with his tale of CIA machinations in
Das Profil (1973). Finally, after the general revival of interest in the Nazi period in the late
1970s, Becher is seen as an interesting and overlook-
ed older writer. His plays began to receive new
productions and Becher himself is being consulted
by beginning writers for his firsthand knowledge of
the period they find so compelling. First-time
novelist Georg Biron has dedicated his Der Dichter
und die Dirne to Ulrich Becher and has been influential in the renewal of critical interest in Becher
in Austria following the 1980 Vienna production of
Bockerer.[2] Thus the major causes for the changes in
Becher's concretization lie outside of Becher in the

changing social and political perspectives of the reading public. Instead of Becher's work having an impact on his times, as Jauß demands of great literature, the time had an effect on its reception.

To a certain extent Becher's own career decisions also influenced his reception. Becher's switch from plays to prose was the least significant factor. Although he had reestablished himself in the immediate post-war period as a dramatist, his audience was limited to those who happened to see each play. In contrast, one prose work reached a wider audience than all of his plays combined. This was enough to overcome the initial audience confusion connected with a playwright's turn to prose.

The single most important event in Becher's career remains his twelve-year absence from the market. Gradually during those years Becher's name slipped from the memory of all but the professional literary historian; when Becher finally returned, it was with nothing innovative in the view of the critics. In addition, Becher's return had the bad luck to coincide with the controversy surrounding Rowohlt's absence from the 1969 Frankfurt Book Fair. Given these negative factors, it is surprising that Murmel-

389

jagd was noticed at all.

It is not clear that Becher's change of publishers has had an undue negative influence on his reception. The previous chapter has shown that the major difference in critiques is in the type of article, i.e., Rowohlt books received more serious, evaluative articles, while Benziger books got wider exposure. This being the case, Becher's recent revival defies Glotz's findings that literary success is determined by reviews in a half dozen newspapers by not more than a dozen famous critics. It is clear that an author must also feel comfortable and confident in regard to his publisher. Becher's switch to Benziger is further evidence of his more resigned attitude; it is clear that at this late date he cannot expect fame, but at least he can work closely with people who respect him and who will see to it that he receives as much of their effort as they can give him. Becher is also still trying to speak to the four German-language countries; in this regard Benziger's base in neutral Switzerland is politically less objectionable to the GDR than is Rowohlt's in Hamburg.

In addition to determining Becher's changing concretization, this project was also designed to test two methodologies, content analysis and reception aesthetics in practical application. The underlying thought in testing some of the content analysis categories was to discover reliable shortcuts in the evaluating of individual critiques. Tables 21-35 indicate that neither the length of an article, nor the type of article, nor headline analysis alone is sufficient to categorize the article as positive, neutral, or negative. Length indicates only the importance placed on the work under discussion by the reviewer, and cannot be made a predictor of the importance or the circulation of a newspaper (Table 36). The country in which the critique appeared did correlate with the kind of judgment made, but not sufficiently to produce statistically significant results, indicating more uniformity than expected (Tables 5-7). The findings on the influence of the political affiliations of newspapers proved inconclusive due to the lack of scientifically obtained data. Aside from these specific findings, the methodology of content analysis provided a very useful framework for the systematic analysis of a large quantity of data. Future studies on the reception of other authors could use a refined version of the variables employed here

and arrive at different conclusions. Not until a
number of such studies have been performed can valid
conclusions on the nature of literary reception in
general be made. Content analysis remains a valuable
tool which must only be adapted and put to productive
use in literary analysis.

The main approach of this study was to provide a case study of the practical application of reception aesthetics on an exile author and to eliminate
as much subjectivity as possible in the evaluation of
the author's reception. Thus, this project included
analysis of all prescribed sources, then the additional
step was taken of checking the analysis of critiques
statistically with the use of the computer.

The reception hypotheses in this study received the strongest statistical confirmation of all
the hypotheses tested. The crosstabulation of formal
elements with content (Table 17) provided corroboration
for Glotz's thesis that formal considerations predominate in German book criticism. Further confirmation of this thesis was provided in Tables 18-20 which
examined the correlation between the opinion of Becher
and of his works. In a sense these tables were also
metamethodological, because they revealed that the

392

kinds of questions posed by reception aesthetics can provide insights into the nature of literary reception in general just through the analysis of a single author's reception.

Yet the computer analysis section of this project was, in addition to a confirmation of the methodology, also an extension of that methodology, in that it contributed to the analysis of this specific case study. For example, prior to computer analysis it was impossible to determine which Becher works were judged best by the critics, an important consideration in determining the concretization of an author's works. The analysis showed that the plays were better received and that there was less difference before and after 1960 than had been expected. The latter result may be attributed to the 1970s versions of Bockerer and New Yorker Novellen, both early works that have grown increasingly popular. If this trend continues, these two works may yet provide Ulrich Becher with a solid place in the literary canon.

Although limited in scope, this project has disclosed possibilities for more extensive use of the computer for performing content analysis as a last step in future applications of reception aes-

thetics. At present computers are incapable of performing the complex cybernetics involved in reading
and evaluating the content of critiques. The most
frequent form of computerized textual analysis done
today employs techniques that are limited to the
lexical level of analysis, i.e., the computer identifies individual words and makes frequency lists. It
remains for the investigator to draw conclusions
from the rearranged data.

The General Inquirer developed by Philip
J. Stone at Harvard, and other textual analysis pro-
grams hold more promise. These systems combine word
search capabilities with area-specified dictionaries,
to identify basic word groups (somewhat like a the-
saurus). The most recent version of General Inquirer
also includes in the dictionary surface syntactic
rules (inflectional endings, word class markers) to
help the computer guess the meaning of an ambiguous
word from context. Unfortunately, General Inquirer
still depends on a time-consuming, elaborate encoding
technique that assigns markers to each word as a text
is processed. A project at the Rochester Medical
Center headed by H.P. Iker represents a step beyond
General Inquirer, in that "the content categories

394

and content themes are generated by the data themselves and not imposed on the data by the use of predetermined encoding methods."[3] The software package WORDS developed by this project divides the input into segments, calculates frequencies of words in each segment, and uses factor-analysis to establish intercorrelations between words, thus identifying major content themes in the raw data automatically.

Another area of development that could make computerized content analysis achievable is in mechanical translation. This field has benefited greatly from advances in computer technology (magnetic tape, disc storage) and the development of computer languages, such as COMIT, SNOBOL, LISP, designed for working with non-numerical data. Most current machine translation projects aim a third generation systems, i.e., those which deal with deeper syntactic and semantic levels of language, as well as the lexical and surface syntactic levels. At the Linguistics Research Center of the University of Texas the current machine translation project uses technical German as a source language and English as a target language, although the goal is to develop the capability of translating any Western European language into any other such language, given a lexical and grammatical base. Translation is limited to technical writings, since the treatment of metaphors, etc., is not within the capability of the system.

All of these efforts demonstrate the potential for computer reading of natural language texts, which could eliminate the last traces of subjectivity in a project such as this. While not all literary criticism aims at the elimination of subjectivity, a method such as reception aesthetics, which attempts to discover a concretization, a barely measurable phenomenon, will find future capabilities of the computer to be of immense value, perhaps even indispensable.

FOOTNOTES

[1]Hans Robert Jauß, <u>Literaturgeschichte als
Provokation</u> (Frankfurt on Main: Suhrkamp, 1974), p.
177.

[2]Georg Biron, Personal Letter to Nancy Zeller,
16 October 1980.

[3]H.P. Iker, "Recognition and Analysis of
Content by Computer," in: <u>Computer Assisted Research
in the Humanities</u> Ed. Joseph Raben (New York: Pergamon, 1977), p. 8.

BIBLIOGRAPHY

I. Primary Literature

A. Books and translations

Brasilianischer Romanzero. Vienna: Wilhelm
    Frick Verlag and Zurich: Werner Classen
    Verlag, 1950. Enlarged edition with the
    same title: Reinbek bei Hamburg: Ro-
    wohlt Verlag, 1962.

Die Eroberer: Geschichten aus Europa. Zurich:
    Oprecht, 1936.

Franz Patenkindt: Romanze von eimen deutschen
    Patenkind des Francois Villon in fünfzehn
    Bänkelsängen. Munich: Universitas, 1980.

Das Herz des Hais. Reinbek bei Hamburg: Ro-
    wohlt Taschenbuchverlag, 1960. New edi-
    tion: Zurich, Cologne: Benziger Verlag,
    1972.

Kurz nach vier. Hamburg: Rowohlt, 1957. New
    edition: Zurich, Cologne: Benziger Ver-
    lag, 1975.
    L´Heur juste. trad. de l´allemand par
        Addy-Frederique. Paris: Editions
        du Seuil, 1960.

Männer machen Fehler: Vom Unzulänglichen der
    Wirklichkeit. Berlin: Ernst Rowohlt Ver-
    lag, 1931. Second enlarged edition with
    the subtitle: Geschichten der Windrose.
    Hamburg: Rowohlt Verlag, 1958. East
    German Edition: Berlin: Aufbau-Verlag,
    1962. Paperback edition: Reinbek bei
    Hamburg: Rowohlt Taschenbuchverlag,
    1970, 1974.

Murmeljagd. Hamburg: Rowohlt, 1969. Paper-
    back edition: Reinbek bei Hamburg: Ro-
    wohlt Taschenbuchverlag, 1974.
    La Chasse à la Marmotte. trad. de l´alle-

mand par Jacques Legrand. Paris:
Editions du Seuil, 1972.
Woodchuck Hunt. Trans. Henry A. Smith.
New York: Crown, 1977.

New Yorker Novellen: Ein Zyklus New Yorker
Novellen in vier Nächten (contains
"Nachtigall will zum Vater fliegen,"
"Der schwarze Hut," "Die Frau und der
Tod" und "Beim Apfelwein") Wien: A.
Sexl-Verlag and Munich: Willi Weismann
Verlag, 1950.
Die ganze Nacht. Reinbek bei Hamburg:
Rowohlt Taschenbuch Verlag, 1955.
New Yorker Novellen: Ein Zyklus in drei
Nächten. Berlin and Weimar: Auf-
bau-Verlag, 1969.
New Yorker Novellen. Zurich, Cologne:
Benziger Verlag, 1974.

Das Profil. Reinbek bei Hamburg: Rowohlt
Taschenbuch Verlag, 1973.

Reise zum blauen Tag. Verse. With a line
drawing by George Grosz. St. Gallen:
Verlag Buchdruckerei Volksstimme, 1946.

SIFF: Selektive Identifizierung von Freund
und Feind. Zurich, Cologne: Benziger
Verlag, 1978.

Williams Ex-Casino. Zurich, Cologne: Ben-
ziger Verlag, 1973.
Paperback edition: Reinbek bei Hamburg:
Rowohlt Taschenbuchverlag, 1975.
East German edition: Berlin, Weimar:
Aufbau Verlag, 1977.

B. Dramen

Biene, gib mir Honig. Munich: Theaterverlag
Thomas Sessler, 1972.

_____ and Preses, Peter. Der Bockerer. Dramatisches Possenspiel in drei Akten. Berlin: Aufbau Verlag, 1949.

Also in: Wiener Volksstücke. Munich,
    Vienna: Langen-Müller, 1971.
Premiere: Theater in der Scala. Vienna,
    1948.
Other productions: 1963 on Österreich-
    ischer Rundfunk, 1978 at National-
    theater Mannheim, 1980 Volkstheater
    Vienna, 1981 Schillertheater Berlin.

Feuerwasser in Spiele der Zeit. Hamburg: Ro-
    wohlt Verlag, 1957.
Premiere: Deutsches Theater Göttingen,
    1952.
Other productions: 1954 Volkstheater,
    Vienna, 1954 Deutsches Schauspiel-
    haus Hamburg, 1956/1957 Volksbühne
    Berlin (DDR), 1978 ZDF Television
    play.

Die Kleinen und die Grossen. Zauberposse aus
    der Atomzeit. in Spiele der Zeit. Ham-
    burg: Rowohlt Verlag, 1957.

Mademoiselle Löwenzorn: Fatale Komödie in drei
    Akten. In: Spiele der Zeit II. Berlin:
    Aufbau-Verlag, 1968.
Premier: Schlossparktheater Berlin 1954.
Mademoiselle Löwenzorn. Traducción de
    Mariano Santiago Luque. in Teatro
    aleman contemporaneo. Madrid:
    Aguilar, 1965.

Makumba. In: Spiele der Zeit II. Berlin:
    Aufbau-Verlag, 1968.
New edition of Der Herr kommt aus Bahia.
Premier: Deutsches Theater Göttingen
    1957/58.

Niemand: Ein neuzeitliches Mysterienspiel.
    In: Spiele der Zeit II. Berlin: Auf-
    bau-Verlag, 1968.
Premiere: Stadttheater Bern 1936.

_____ and Preses, Peter. Der Pfeifer von
    Wien. Munich: Thomas Sessler Theater-
    verlag, 1949.
Premiere: Volkstheater Vienna 1950.

<u>Samba</u>. In: <u>Spiele der Zeit</u>. Hamburg: Ro-
wohlt Verlag, 1957.
Premiere: Schlossparktheater Berlin 1952
Other productions: 1951 im Theater in
der Josefstadt Vienna.

C. Shorter publications

"Abendländisches Gelübde," <u>Das andere Deutsch-</u>
<u>land</u> (Buenos Aires), 8, No. 80-81 (25
April 1944), 12.

"Abseits vom Rodeo," <u>Poesie. Zeitschrift für</u>
<u>Literatur</u> (Basle), December 1975/January
1976, 36.

"Ahnung und Versprechen: Am 29. August 1939
an Max Hermann-Neisse," <u>Freies/Neues</u>
<u>Deutschland</u> (Mexico City), 4, No. 10
(Sept. 1945), 21.
Also in: <u>An den Wind geschrieben. Lyrik</u>
<u>der Freiheit, 1933-1945</u>. Collected,
selected, and introduced by Manfred
Schlösser with the collaboration of
Hans-Rolf Ropertz. Darmstadt: Agora,
1961, p. 37.

"Das arme Licht," <u>Aufbau</u> (NY) 11, No. 1 (5
January 1945), 20.

"Aus der Spielmacher-Schule geplaudert," <u>Spiele</u>
<u>der Zeit II</u>. Berlin: Aufbau-Verlag,
1968.

"Auszug vom Ulrich Bechers ´Schwarzen Hut,´"
in: <u>Interview mit Amerika</u>. Ed. Alfred
Gong. Munich: Nymphenburger Verlags-
anstalt, 1962, pp. 212-225.

"Drohlied der Erschlagenen," <u>Das andere Deutsch-</u>
<u>land</u> (Buenos Aires), 5, No. 56 (Nov. 1942),
21.

"Eine sehr baltische Geschichte," <u>Deutsche Er-</u>
<u>zähler der Gegenwart. Eine Anthologie</u>.
Edited and introduced by Willi Fehse.

Stuttgart: Philipp Reclam Jun. 1959,
1976, pp. 43-46.

"Einigt Euch um Gottes willen," <u>Europa</u>, No. 13
(28 March 1936), p.u.
Also in: <u>Mitteilungen der Deutsche Freiheitsbibliothek. Das Freie Deutsch-
land</u> (Paris), 1936, No. 12 (1 May
1936), 12-21.
Also in: <u>Deutsche Volkszeitung</u> (Prag-
Paris-Basel), 1, No. 4 (12 April
1936), 7.

"Ein ´innerer Emigrant´. Der Typ Frank Thiess,"
<u>Aufbau</u> (NY) 11, No. 47 (23 November 1945),
6.

"Es war einmal ein freier Kritiker," <u>Weltbühne</u>
25 (1971), p. 787-790.

"Gefallene Kameraden der Freiheit. Zum Ge-
denken an die ersten Bücherverbrennungen
in Europa," <u>Das andere Deutschland</u> (Buenos
Aires), 6, No. 66 (1 June 1943), 1-6.

"George Grosz´ Dreissigjähriger Krieg gegen
den Krieg," <u>Das andere Deutschland</u>
(Buenos Aires), 9, No. 133 (1 January
1947), 14-15.

<u>Der Grosse Grosz und eine grosse Zeit</u>. Rein-
bek bei Hamburg: Rowohlt Verlag, 1962.
In: <u>Schweizer Annalen</u> 3 (1946/1947),
pp. 641-655.

"Der Grosse Grosz und eine grosse Zeit," <u>Das
andere Deutschland</u> (Buenos Aires and
briefly in Montevideo due to prohibition),
8,
Part 1 in: No. 83 (June 1944), 21-23;
Part 2 in: No. 84 (July 1944), 16-19;
Part 3 in: No. 85 (Aug. 1944), 21-23;
Part 4 in: No. 86 (Sept 1944), 14-17.

"In der Alpenkatakombe," <u>Das andere Deutschland</u>
(Buenos Aires), 6,
Part 1 in: No. 62 (1 April 1943), 6-9;
Part 2 in: No. 63 (15 Apr. 1943), 3-7.

"Ihre Sache, Madame," Neunzehn deutsche Er-
    zählungen. Munich: Nymphenburger Ver-
    lagshandlung, 1963.

"Junge deutsche Dichter für Aufhörer," Welt-
    woche (Zurich), No. 1609 (11 September
    1964), 25 & 29.

"Krieg der Mirakel," Das andere Deutschland
    (Buenos Aires), 6, No. 69 (15 July
    1943), 5-7.

"Ein Leben lang Krieg gegen den Krieg. Zum
    Tod des Malers George Grosz," National-
    Zeitung (Basle), 117, No. 306 (7 July
    1959), 2-3.

"Märchen vom Räuber, der Schutzmann wurde.
    Moritat," Notbücherei deutscher Anti-
    faschisten, No. 1, Rio de Janeiro: 1941.

"Mahn-Sonette," Das andere Deutschland (Buenos
    Aires), 5, No. 54 (15 September 1942)
    14.

"Ein Nachwort zum Nürnberger Prozess," Das
    andere Deutschland (Buenos Aires), 8
    Part 1 in: No. 131 (1 Dec. 1946), 6-8;
    Part 2 in: No. 132 (15 Dec. 1946), 8-9.

"Ostersegen," Das andere Deutschland (Buenos
    Aires), 6, No. 63 (15 April 1943), 16.

"Roda Roda, der lächelnde Zentaur," Weltbühne
    15 (1972), p. 457-460.

"Der Rosenkavalier," Das andere Deutschland
    (Buenos Aires), 9, No. 152 (15 October
    1947), 12-14.

"Die Seine fliesst nicht mehr durch Paris.
    Porträt eines literarischen Kriegsver-
    brechers," Freies/Neues Deutschland
    (Mexico City), 3, No. 8 (July 1944),
    27-28.

"Die sieben stummen Fragen," Das andere Deutsch-
    land (Buenos Aires), 5, No. 57 (Dec. 1942),
    19-20.

"Stammgast im Liliputanercafe," Afterword to
 Ödön v. Horvath, Stücke. Ed. Traugott
 Krischke. Reinbek bei Hamburg: Rowohlt,
 1961.

"Das Theater--die Welt," Blätter des Deutschen
 Theaters in Göttingen, No. 129 (1957/
 1958).

"Väterchen," Freies/Neues Deutschland (Mexico
 City), 4, No. 12 (Nov./Dec. 1945), 55-
 57.

Verhör eines Passlosen," Das andere Deutschland (Montevideo), 1, Nos. 1-2 (15 Feb.
 1944), 25-26.

"Zehn Jahre," Das andere Deutschland (Buenos
 Aires), 6, No. 60 (March 1943), 20-21.

D. Unpublished writings (in possession of Nancy
    Zeller)

 Letter to Prof. H.-B. Moeller, Austin, Texas,
  19 October 1976.

 Letter to Prof. H.-B. Moeller, Austin, Texas,
  23 August 1976.

 Letter to Prof. H.-B. Moeller, Austin, Texas,
  24 March 1977.

 Letter to Prof. H.-B. Moeller, Austin, Texas,
  3 June 1978.

 Letter to Prof. H.-B. Moeller, Austin, Texas,
  17 September 1978.

II. Sekundärliteratur

A. Books and sections of books on Becher

 Alker, Ernst. Profile und Gestalten der
  deutschen Literatur nach 1914. Ed.

Eugen Thurnher. Stuttgart: Alfred
   Kröner Verlag, 1977, pp. 229-230.

Die deutsche Exilliteratur: 1933-1945. Ed.
   by Manfred Durzak. Stuttgart: Philipp
   Reclam jun., 1973, pp. 523-524.

Geschichte der deutschen Dichtung. Ed. by
   Fricke/Klotz. Hamburg and Lübeck: Matt-
   hiesen Verlag, p. 501.

Handbuch der deutschen Gegenwartsliteratur,
   I: A-K. Ed. by Hermann Kunisch. Munich:
   Nymphenburger Verlagshandlung, 1969, pp.
   92-93.

Internationale Bibliographie zur Geschichte der
   deutschen Literatur, Teil II, 2. Munich-
   Pullach and Berlin: Verlag Dokumentation,
   1972. p. 108.

Lexikon deutschsprachiger Schriftsteller, Bd.
   I. Albrecht, G. et al (ed.). Kronberg
   Ts.: Scriptor Verlag, 1974, p. 55-56.

Mittenzwei, Werner. "Deutsche Dramatik gegen
   die Atomkriegsgefahr," in Frieden und
   Sozialismus. Berlin: Aufbau Verlag,
   1961, pp. 201-260.

Riewoldt, Otto F. Von Zuckmayer bis Kroetz:
   Die Rezeption westdeutscher Theaterstücke
   durch Kritik und Wissenschaft in der DDR.
   Berlin: Erich Schmidt Verlag, 1978.

Sternfeld, Wilhelm and Tiedemann, Eva. Deutsche
   Exil-Literatur 1933-1945: Eine Bio-Bib-
   liographie. Heidelberg: Verlag Lambert-
   Schneider, 1970, p.39.

Wiesmann, Louis. Siebzehn Basler Autoren.
   Basle: Verlag Benno Schwabe, 1963.

B.   Articles in newspapers and journals

Bab, Julius. "Der Dramatiker Ulrich Becher,"
   Staats-Zeitung und Herold (New York),

15 March 1953.

Beck, Wolfgang. "Zeit auf den Brettern: Bemerkungen zu Thematik und Technik des Dramatikers Ulrich Becher," Theater der Zeit 12, Special addition to No. 3 (March 1957), pp. 8-32.

Breicha, Otto. "Am Graben, nachts um halb eines," Frankfurter Rundschau, 6 March 1971.

Feuchtwanger, Lion. "Ulrich Becher," Das Wort, No. 8 (August 1937), 90-92.

Hühnerfeld, Paul. "Auf der Suche nach dem alten Europa: Die Wege und Irrwege des Schriftstellers Ulrich Becher," Die Zeit, No. 21 (23 May 1957), 6.

Künzli, Arnold. "Ulrich Becher - Dichter havarierten Europäertums," National-Zeitung (Basle), No. 103 (3 March 1957), 1-2.

Kusche, Lothar. "Ein unmodischer Schrift-steller," Weltbühne, No. 8 (1970), 248-250.

Mann, Klaus. "Ulrich Becher," Das Neue Tage-buch 5 (1937), No. 30, 719.

Mueller-Stahl, Hagen. "Das Recht auf menschen-würdige Existenz," Theater der Zeit 11, No. 2 (Feb. 1956), 8-10.

Seiler, Alexander J. "Europa im Urwald - Ur-wald Europa: Der Schriftsteller Ulrich Becher," Die Weltwoche (Zurich) 29: No. 1417 (6 January 1961), 17.

C. Representative criticism of individual works

Der Bockerer

Butterweck, Hellmut. "Theater: Erhellendes Lachen," Die Furche (Vienna), 20 April 1980.

v. Golitschek, Josef. "Widerstandskampf auf
    weanerisch," Mannheimer Morgen, No. 232,
    10 October 1978.

Melchinger, Siegfried. "Der wahre Bockerer,"
    Stuttgarter Zeitung, No. 66, 19 March
    1963.

Schnabel, Dieter. "Menschlichkeit kontra Welt-
    anschauung," Darmstädter Echo, 20 October
    1978.

Schmitz, Helmut. "Ein gemütvoller Totentanz,"
    Frankfurter Rundschau, No. 230, 16 October
    1978.

Stadelmaier, Gerhard. "Womit sie leicht fertig
    werden," Stuttgarter Zeitung, 12 October
    1978.

            Die Eroberer

Weiskopf, F.C. "Neue deutsche Novellen," Das
    Wort, No. 4-5 (April-May 1937), 117-120.

            Feuerwasser

Andrießen, Carl. "Charlie Brown und seine
    Stammgäste," Weltbühne 11, No. 4 (25
    January 1956), 109-111.

Heer, Friedrich. "Tragödie der Zwischenwelt,"
    Die Furche (Vienna), 20 March 1954.

Ihering, Herbert. "Episches und dramatisches
    Theater," Sonntag (Ost-Berlin) 11, No.
    3 (15 January 1956), 11.

Johann, Ernst. "New Yorker Nachkrieg," Frank-
    furter Allgemeine Zeitung, 26 July 1978.

Linzer, Martin. "Feuerwasser, deutsch-ameri-
    kanische Chronik von Ulrich Becher in
    der Volksbühne Berlin," Theater der Zeit
    11, No. 2 (Feb. 1956), 49-51.

407

Seringhaus, Will. "Feuerwasser - Uraufführung, in Göttingen," Frankfurter Neue Presse, 2 December 1952.

Thieringer, Thomas. "Geschlagener Hund," Süddeutsche Zeitung, 26 July 1978.

Wanderscheck, Hermann. "Bechers Feuerwasser an der Volksbühne," Frankfurter Abendpost, 13 January 1956.

Ziermann, Horst. "Prima Husten," Die Welt, 26 July 1978.

Das Herz des Hais

Helwig, Werner. "Inselromanze wie gehabt," Frankfurter Allgemeine Zeitung, 4 November 1972.

Moschner, Manfred. "Die Bücherkiste - Ulrich Becher, Das Herz des Hais," Deutsche Welle (Cologne), 5 December 1972.

Wien, Werner. "Mehr als ein Dreiecksromänchen," Bremer Nachrichten, No. 302, 27 December 1972.

Kurz nach vier

Clausen, Erwin. "Ulrich Becher: Kurz nach vier," Neue Deutsche Hefte (1976), pp. 149-153.

Drewitz, Ingeborg. "Lesezeichen," Süddeutscher Rundfunk (Stuttgart), 28 January 1976.

Fabian, Rainer. "Der private Krieg des Leutnant Skizze," Die Welt, 11 October 1975.

Schwerbrock, Wolfgang. "Amoklauf eines Ostmärkers," Frankfurter Allgemeine Zeitung, No. 52 (2 March 1957), 47.

Semmer, Gerd. "Ulrich Becher: Kurz nach 4," Geist und Zeit (1957), No. 3, 154-156.

Mademoiselle Löwenzorn

Rühle, Jürgen. "Karneval der Heimatlosen,"
    Sonntag (Ost-Berlin) 9, No. 17 (25 April
    1954), 4.

Sander, H.D. "Mademoiselle Löwenzorn von Ul-
    rich Becher an den Städtischen Theatern
    Leipzig," Theater der Zeit 10, No. 8
    (August 1955), 51-54.

Wanderscheck, Hermann. "Bechers Mademoiselle
    Löwenzorn in Barlogs Schloßparktheater,"
    Frankfurter Abendpost 7, No. 60 (12 March
    1954), 10.

Männer machen Fehler

Liersch, Werner. "Ruf der Stillen," Neue
    Deutsche Literatur 10, No. 11 (November
    1962), 120-122.

Schwerbrock, Wolfgang. "Das Lachen der Gorgo,"
    Frankfurter Allgemeine Zeitung, 6 December
    1958.

Streblow, Lothar. "Ulrich Becher: Männer
    machen Fehler," Geist und Zeit (Düsseldorf)
    1959, No. 3, 124-129.

Murmeljagd

Bachmann, Dieter. "Gegenwart als Geisterbahn,"
    Die Weltwoche (Zurich), No. 34, 21 August
    1970.

Bender, Hans. "Gejagt wie ein Murmeltier,"
    Deutsche Welle (Cologne), 25 June 1969.

Clements, Robert J. "European Literary Scene,"
    Saturday Review 52, No. 31 (2 August
    1969), 23.

Gregor-Dellin, Martin. "Jeder Satz exotisch,"
    Die Zeit, 29 August 1969.

Nagel, Wolfgang. "Ulrich Becher: Murmel-
    jagd," Neue Deutsche Hefte 16, No. 3,
    151-153.

Nolte, Jost. "Vom Wahnwitz einer Epoche,"
    Die Welt der Literatur, No. 9, 24 April
    1969.

de Rambures, Jean-Louis. "Une farce sortie de
    derrière le miroir," L'Exprès, 20/26
    November 1972, p. 74.

Romain, Lothar. "Akrobatik ohne Abgrund,"
    Frankfurter Allgemeine Zeitung, 21 June
    1969.

"Roter Baron," Der Spiegel 23, No. 17 (21 April
    1969), 182-183.

Süskind, W.E. "Wildwest im Engadin," Süd-
    deutsche Zeitung, No. 82/83 (6/7 April
    1969).

Tank, Kurt Lothar. "Die groteske Murmeljagd
    des Herrn Ulrich Becher," Die Welt am
    Sonntag, No. 24 (15 June 1969).

New Yorker Novellen

Braun, Hans-Werner. "Von den Schwierigkeiten,
    das Wahre darzustellen," Bibliothekar
    (Leipzig) 11, No. 7 (July 1957), 708-715.

Herzog, Valentin. "Schicksalsnächte in New
    York und Basel," National Zeitung (Basle)
    20 November 1974.

Kramberg, K.H. "Erzählte Gesichter," Süd-
    deutscher Zeitung, 8 December 1974.

Kuhn, Christoph. "Das Ende von Hitler-Deutsch-
    land--in New York erlebt," Tages-Anzeiger
    (Zurich), 8 January 1975, p. 17.

Leutenegger, Béatrice. "Gegen den falschen
    Optimismus," Vaterland (Lucern), 11 Jan.
    1975.

Schwachhofer, René. "Im Dickicht der Einsamkeit," <u>Sonntag</u> (Ost-Berlin) 11, No. 18 (29 August 1956), 8.

Niemand

H., K. "Theater, Musik, Vorträge," <u>Berner Tagwacht</u>, 19 January 1936.

_____. "Neue Bücher: Ulrich Becher, <u>Niemand</u>," <u>Das andere Deutschland</u> (Buenos Aires), 10, No. 164 (1 April 1948), 15.

Das Profil

Fabian, Rainer. "Neptun im Schmetterlingsstil," <u>Die Welt des Buches</u>, 24 May 1973.

Herzog, Valentin. "Die lange Nacht: phantastisch und prophetisch," <u>National Zeitung</u>(Basle) 2 June 1973.

Kramberg, K.H. "Alles relativ, auch Weltgeschichte," <u>Süddeutsche Zeitung</u>, 30/31 May 1973.

Mader, Helmut. "Turbulente Gedanken," <u>FAZ Literaturblatt</u>, 6 October 1973.

Samba

Degenhardt, Jürgen. "Mit der Hand eines Dichters geschrieben," <u>Sonntag</u> (Ost-Berlin) 12, No. 29 (21 July 1957), 8.

Kaltofen, Günter. "Samba von Ulrich Becher im Meininger Theater," <u>Theater der Zeit</u> (Ost-Berlin) 10, No. 2 (Feb. 1955), 43-46.

Schwerbrock, Wolfgang. "Der Marodeur Ulrich Becher," <u>Frankfurter Allgemeine Zeitung</u>, 20 July 1957.

Williams Ex-Casino

Bachmann, Dieter. "Das unaufhaltsame Verhäng-
     nis," Die Weltwoche (Zurich), 20 Feb. 1974.

Bachmann, Dieter. "Krieg im Frieden," Die Zeit,
     21 March 1974.

Biergann, Armin. "Mit Hitsch am Kitsch vorbei,"
     Kölnische Rundschau, 15 March 1974.

Hage, Volker. "Im Weltbürgerkrieg unseres Jahr-
     hunderts," Frankfurter Hefte, No. 8 (1975),
     71-72.

Herzog, Valentin. "Ein Moby Dick in Basel,"
     National Zeitung (Basle), 15 December
     1973.

Kramberg, K.H. "Fabelhaft, Hitsch!", Süd-
     deutsche Zeitung, 5/6 January 1974.

Wirsing, Sibylle. "Mord am Nachmittag," FAZ
     Literaturblatt, 23 March 1974.

D.   General Secondary Literature

Benziger Verlag, Letter to Nancy Zeller, 21
     December 1978.

Berelson, Bernard, Content Analysis in Communi-
     cation Research, Glencoe, Illinois: The
     Free Press, 1952.

Biron, Georg. Letter to Nancy Zeller, 16
     October 1980.

"Blinder Moment," Der Spiegel 23, No. 38
     (15 September 1969), 206.

Boyer, Richard C. "Demons in the Suburbs,"
     The New Yorker 19, No. 41 (27 Nov. 1943),
     32-42; "The Saddest Man in all the World,"
     The New Yorker 19, No. 42 (4 December
     1943), 39-48; "The Yankee from Berlin,"
     The New Yorker 19, No. 43 (11 December
     1943), 37-43.

412

Cazden, Robert E. German Exile Literature
in America 1933-1950: A History of the
Free German Press and Book Trade. Chicago:
American Library Association, 1970.

Durzak, Manfred, "Rezeptionsästhetik als Literaturkritik," in Kritik der Literaturkritik. Ed. Olaf Schwencke. Stuttgart:
Kohlhammer Verlag, pp. 56-70.

Eckardt, Wolf von and Sander L. Gilman, Bertolt
Brecht's Berlin: A Scrapbook of the
Twenties. Garden City, N.Y.: Anchor
Press, 1975.

Eisenberg-Bach, Susan. "French and German
Writers in Exile in Brazil: Reception and
Translations," to be published in A Com-
parative View of European Exiles and
Latin America. Ed. H.-B. Moeller.

Fernandez Artucio, Hugo. The Nazi Underground
in South America. New York: Farrar &
Rinehart, 1942.

Fochler-Hauke, Gustav. Der Fischer Weltalmanach 1972, Frankfurt on Main: Fischer
Taschenbuch Verlag, 1971.

Franke, Konrad. Die Literatur der Deutschen
Demokratischen Republik. Munich: Kindler
Verlag, 1971.

Gay, Peter. Weimar Culture: The Outsider as
Insider. New York: Harper & Row, 1968.

Glotz, Peter. Buchkritik in deutschen Zeitungen. Hamburg: Verlag für Buchmarkt-
Forschung, 1968.

Grimm, Gunter. "Einführung in die Rezeptions-
forschung," in Literatur und Leser:
Theorien und Modelle zur Rezeption lit-
erarischer Werke. Ed. Gunter Grimm.
Stuttgart: Philipp Reclam, 1975.

Hellmann, Lillian. Scoundrel Time. Boston:
Little, Brown, 1976.

413

Hermand, Jost. Literatur nach 1945, I: Politische und regionale Aspekte. Wiesbaden: Akademische Verlagsgesellschaft Athenaion, 1979.

Holsti, Ole R. Content Analysis for the Social Sciences and Humanities. Reading, Mass.: Addison-Wesley, 1969.

Iker, H.P. "Recognition and Analysis of Content by Computer," in Computer-Assisted Research in the Humanities. Ed. Joseph Raben. New York: Pergamon, 1977.

Institut für Zeitgeschichte, Unpublished Interview with Willy Keller, 5 October 1971.

Jauß, Hans Robert. Kleine Apologie der ästhetischen Erfahrung. Constance: Universitätsverlag, 1972.

_____. Literaturegeschichte als Provokation der Literaturwissenschaft. Constance: Universitätsverlag, 1967 and 1969. Revised in Literaturgeschichte als Provokation. Frankfurt on Main: Suhrkamp, 1970, pp. 144-207.

_____. "Paradigmawechsel in der Literaturwissenschaft," Linguistische Berichte 3 (1969), 44-56.

_____. "Provokation des Lesers im modernen Roman," in Die nicht mehr schönen Künste: Grenzphänomene des Ästhetischen. Ed. Hans Robert Jauß. Munich: W. Fink Verlag, 1968.

_____. "Racines und Goethes Iphigenie. Mit einem Nachwort über die Partialität der rezeptionsästhetischen Methode," neue hefte für philosophie 4 (1973), 1-46.

Kesten, Hermann. Deutsche Literatur im Exil: Briefe europäischer Autoren 1933-1945. Munich: Verlag Kurt Desch, 1964.

Kossok, M. "Sonderauftrag Südamerika," in
    Lateinamerika zwischen Emanzipation und
    Imperialismus. Ed. W. Markow. Berlin:
    Akademie Verlag, 1961.

Kuhn, Thomas S. Die Struktur wissenschaft-
    licher Revolutionen. Frankfurt on Main:
    Suhrkamp, 1967.

Landestheater Tübingen, Letter to Nancy Zeller,
    3 December 1979.

Maas, Lieselotte. Handbuch der deutschen
    Exilpresse 1933-1945. Ed. Eberhard
    Lämmert. Munich: Carl Hanser Verlag,
    1976, 1978.

Mandelkow, Karl Robert. "Probleme der Wirkungs-
    geschichte ," in Jahrbuch für Internationale
    Germanistik 2 (1970), No. 1.

Matthias, L.L. Die Kehrseite der USA. Ham-
    burg: Rowohlt, 1964.

Nachlaß Prinz z. Löwenstein, No. 11/1, 13 March
    1941, Institut für Zeitgeschichte, Munich.

Nie, Norman H. Statistical Package for the
    Social Sciences Second Edition. New York:
    McGraw Hill, 1975.

Radkau, Joachim. Die deutsche Emigration in
    den USA. Dusseldorf: Bertelsmann, 1971.

Rowohlt Verlag, Letter to Nancy Zeller, 23
    February 1979.

Seelisch, Winfried. "Das andere Deutschland.
    Eine politische Vereinigung deutscher
    Emigranten in Südamerika." Unpublished
    thesis for the Otto-Suhr-Institut, Ber-
    lin, undated.

Selltiz, Claire et al. Research Methods in
    Social Relations New York: Holt, Rine-
    hart and Winston, 1959.

Die sogenannte Zwanziger Jahre. Ed. Reinhold
    Grimm and Jost Hermand. Bad Homburg:
    Gehlen, 1970.

Sontheimer, Kurt, "Weimar--ein deutsches
    Kaleidoskop," in: Die deutsche Literatur
    in der Weimarer Republik. Ed. Wolfgang
    Rothe. Stuttgart: Reclam, 1974.

Stamm Leitfaden durch Presse und Werbung.
    Essen: Stamm-Verlag, 1976.

Tendenzen der zwanziger Jahre: 15. Europäische
    Kunstausstellung Berlin 1977. Berlin:
    Dietrich Reimer Verlag, 1977.

Telejour, 24 July 1978. Allensbach: Teles-
    kopie Gesellschaft für Fernsehzuschauer-
    forschung, 1978.

Ulrich Becher file with letters from Dr. Felix
    Pinner, Helga v. Löwenstein, and Alexander
    Roda Roda, Deutsche Bibliothek, Frankfurt.

Vodicka, Felix. "Die Konkretisation des lit-
    erarischen Werks" in Rezeptionsästhetik:
    Theorie und Praxis. Ed. Rainer Warning.
    Munich: Wilhelm Fink Verlag, 1975.

Willett, John. Art and Politics in the Weimar
    Republic: The New Sobriety, 1917-1933.
    New York: Pantheon, 1978.

Zeller, Nancy. Interview with Mr. Heepe of Ro-
    wohlt Verlag, December 1978.

Die Zeit ohne Eigenschaften: Eine Bilanz der
    zwanziger Jahre. Ed. Leonhard Reinisch.
    Stuttgart: Kohlhammer, 1961.